Carmen Monica Oprea

Unveiled Secrets

Carmen Monica Oprea

Also By Carmen Monica Oprea

Forever Rose

Carmen Monica

Oprea

Unveiled Secrets

A Novel

CREATESPACE

Carmen Monica Oprea

The characters and events in this book are fictitious. Any similarity to real persons, living or dead, is coincidental and not intended by the author.

Copyright @ 2017 Carmen Monica Oprea

All rights are reserved. In accordance with the U.S. Copyright Act of 1976, the scanning, uploading, and electronic sharing of any part of this book without the permission of the publisher constitute unlawful piracy and theft of the author's intellectual property.

Thank you for your support of the author's rights.

ISBN: 978-1979964180

Cover design by Katie Mefford

Printed in the United States of America

To my son and my husband,

May our past, present, and future be a gift to each other. May our bond be formed by love, strength, and compassion, now and always.

With all my heart and love forever,

Mom / C.M.O.

Carmen Monica Oprea

One

The apartment still wore my mother's scent, a combination of lemon and clay. Her room remained intact—the same silk curtains hanging at the windows, books about sculpting lying open on the floor, and pictures on her desk, gathering slight traces of dust. I picked up a photo from the nightstand. In it, I was twenty-one, and my mother and I were in Egypt, visiting the pyramids. That was fourteen years ago. The woman I called Mother Gabriela, looked youthful with her hair in a ponytail and her skin tanned from the daily exposure to the Egyptian sun. After that trip, we had never seemed to get our schedules in sync. After several failed attempts, we decided that it would be best not to make plans together. That was the reason that trip to Egypt was ever so special.

Since her sudden death five months ago, I often came into her rooms to breathe in the fragrance lingering in the things she had touched. There was still unfinished work in Gabriela's studio. Her apron was on the back of a chair, and three unopened cans with clay lay on shelves, along with prints for orders she would never finish. Her funeral had been short and painful. Clair, her best friend, had helped me scatter her ashes across Black Lake during a freezing February afternoon. Clair had hugged me tightly and told me to come and visit her in Vigo Bay. I had promised her I would do so on my first vacation. But life—and Denis Fraga—happened in between.

The only thing I knew for sure was that Gabriela had adopted me when I was five. It made complete sense to think my parents were dead, because if they were dead, then I understood the reason behind my adoption. Gabriela didn't confirm or deny, and I dropped the issue after many unsuccessful attempts. Whenever I asked her about it, she said, "Leila, the answers you seek are in the locked box on my desk."

Now, for the first time in thirty-five years, I was on the verge of finding out the truth.

I closed the studio door. After I poured a glass of Porto, I sank into the old rocking chair by the window and stared into the night.

Carmen Monica Oprea

Gabriela's words resonated in my mind. I had to open the box. Five months since Gabriela's death was plenty of time. I rose from the rocking chair and grabbed the key from the crystal bowl I kept on the kitchen table before going to her bedroom. Everything was just the way she had left it. The bed still maintained her contour, right in the middle, where she loved to cuddle with a book about new molding or sculpting techniques. A corner of her blue scarf showed from under her pillow. I picked it up and inhaled its perfume—jasmine.

"Time heals broken hearts," Gabriela always said.

But months after her death, I still missed her, and my heart hadn't healed.

I unlocked the wooden box she kept on her desk and pulled out a diary with a burgundy silk cover with gold-splashed edges. The scent of aged paper wafted through the air. The writing was calligraphy, but the ink had faded. A few pages were missing in the back, and I discovered an envelope with a letter inside. I set the diary on my mother's writing desk and read the very first entry which was dated decades ago.

***

Spain, Madrid

May 11th, 1964

The evening was impressive, and my words were too scarce to describe it. I launched my first book at Agumar Hotel in Madrid. The hotel management suggested holding the book signing in the grand lobby, where people roamed back and forth. The brown floor shone as brightly as any polished glass. There were flowers, beautiful, the perfect shade of orange to compliment the woody hues and creams. A chandelier made rainbow colors dance across the elegant lobby where embroidered silk sofas surrounded a large cherry wood table. Twin doors leading into the hallway were pristine white with golden handles. Exquisite paintings hung on the creamy walls, and the sound of jazz drifted from the hotel's restaurant, where a live band performed every evening.

Swept away by autographs and chats, I didn't distinguish him in the far corner of the lobby until the crowds thinned out. Dark suit, light-purple shirt, and a tie hanging loosely—he looked out of place in the

Unveiled Secrets

setting, like he'd just arrived from a business meeting. He had my book in his hands and looked absorbed by the last page—the one about me. He lifted his gaze, and everything disappeared when his eyes locked on mine. I didn't want the moment to end. He took a few steps toward my table.

"May I have your autograph?" he asked, his voice almost a whisper.

"Of course," I said, "if you tell me your name."

"Anders Isidro."

My cheeks were on fire as I wrote.

'To Anders from a newborn star shining into this world of chaos. True happiness comes from the small pleasures life lays in front of you.

Myrna Clarisse Elmer'

Anders took the book and smiled when he read the dedication.

"A beautiful name for a beautiful woman," he said.

"Thank you for giving my book a chance," I said.

He smiled and turned toward the front doors.

I gathered my things and thanked the marketing manager for a grand evening before heading home. Gray clouds brought the rain, refreshing the air and chasing tardy pedestrians to the comfort of their homes or the street cafes still open at the late hour. Raindrops descended with a melodious plink sound, washing away the strays of dust from plants and people alike. I was soaked to the bone, but I was too happy to care. I didn't acknowledge the tap of the raindrops or the fact I could have used an umbrella? For me, it was perfect weather for a stroll.

Anders was fighting with the wind, trying to open his umbrella. I looked at the taxies cruising back and forth on the main street. The lights came on, shimmering in the puddles forming on the road. I waved my hand, hoping to attract the attention of one of the drivers. A hot meal and a warm cup of tea were all I could wish for at this late hour.

Carmen Monica Oprea

"Do you want to come out of this rain, Clarisse?" Anders asked, stopping next to me, and offering his arm and a place under his huge umbrella.

I looked at him, then up and down the street, and chuckled. "I should have carried one too," I admitted as I accepted his arm.

He smelled of rain and resin, a distinctive and refreshing smell. His arm tensed when I touched him.

We walked side by side, looking for a taxi. The shadow of another couple, right ahead, caught my attention. The man was embracing the girl's shoulders with one arm while wrestling his umbrella with the other. When the wind snatched the umbrella, the girl laughed, and they started to run through the stinging droplets fat with water.

"Are you in a hurry?" Anders asked.

"No. Why?"

"Would you care for a glass of wine? To celebrate your success."

I nodded.

We chose Raffaello's, a famous café in Madrid that happened to be not too far from the hotel. I had never been to the restaurant, and since the air had turned cold and the rain thick, I was happy he had made the suggestion. It was the perfect opportunity to find out more about him. Anders stooped to pass through the glass doors with the restaurant's monogram imprinted in silver on one side. I chased the rain away from my hair and clothes as Anders requested a table for two. Candles shone in crystal candle holders in the center of tables covered in burgundy tablecloths. Tucked away in booths far from windows, two couples giggled. What were they talking about? Weather? A romantic evening? Maybe about love.

As we waited for one of the waiters to bring a bottle of champagne, we followed the rhythmical movement of the raindrops washing the windows. I have never believed in love at first sight, but I felt charmed by Anders, by how I felt when he looked at me—as if I were the only woman in the restaurant.

Unveiled Secrets

"You're not from around here," I said.

"Good observation." Anders chuckled. "I live in Vigo Bay."

"Vigo Bay? You're far from home. What brought you to Madrid?"

"Business," he said. "My meeting lasted longer than I expected, and I'm stuck in town for the evening."

His dark hair brought out the lavender of his eyes, and his full lips curved into a mischievous smile at the corners. The absence of a wedding ring left me surprisingly happy. I blushed when he caught my gaze. Although I had just met him, I told him about my passion for writing, my addiction to poetry, and calla lilies. He said that his mother used to grow lilies in her gardens, and he lowered his gaze as he whispered her name. He had lost his parents in a car accident, four years ago, and since then, he'd been running around the world, burying himself in his work. I could relate to his loss because my parents had died in similar circumstances.

I took a sip from the tulip-shaped glass where bubbles of bright golden liquid tasted like green apples. "My grandmother raised me after my parents died and she encouraged me to write," I said, placing the glass back on the table.

"She would have been proud of you today. A toast to your success," Anders said, raising his glass.

"To new friends," I added, following his gesture.

"Would you like to dance?" Anders asked.

I accepted. Anders's arms were warm and comfortable. The sensation of flying flooded my senses and the entire world spun around me, then faded away. It was a perfect moment when the past, the present, and the future combined, and I realized that sometimes life offered unique circumstances to lift your spirit. I knew it was crazy to have these thoughts, but I didn't care one bit. Even the song seemed suitable for the moment. It talked of passionate embraces lovers gave to each other, and, although we weren't lovers, not even close friends, the song brought us closer to each other. The floor became ours, and we took advantage swirling and twirling, wrapped in the sounds of the Spanish guitars.

Carmen Monica Oprea

As soon as the song ended, I made a wrong move and twisted my ankle, the sharp pain spoiling the magic of our evening. Anders asked the waiter for ice while he lifted me and went to the nearest chair. I felt the steady beat of his heart through the silk of his shirt. Not sure if I should feel panic, concern, or frustration for an evening not going as planned, I remained quiet. Anders grabbed a towel and filled it with ice, wrapping it around my ankle.

"How unfortunate," I whispered. "I spoiled everything."

"Nothing got spoiled," he said, kissing my hand.

As I looked into Anders's eyes, I feared that I had left my guard down and exposed myself to feelings I wasn't ready to accept. Those magical moments scattered as soon as the song ended. I asked him to call me a taxi, and I was surprised when he picked me up, carried me to the car, and even traveled with me to my house. He helped me out of the car when we stopped in front of my home, on Via Rosa, on Madrid's outskirts.

"Does your ankle feel better? Shall I carry you inside?"

"I'll manage."

I pressed the back of my palm against his chest and waited next to the taxi. I didn't know what I was waiting for, but one thing was sure—I wasn't prepared to let go.

"Clarisse, may I see you again?" Anders asked.

"That would be lovely."

We exchanged phone numbers. He wrote down the address of my house, and I asked for his. Before entering the taxi, he said, "Thanks again for the book."

"I'll write to you," I said.

"I'll look forward to every one of your letters."

The burden of our separation left my mouth dry. After waving goodbye, Anders merged with the night. I didn't know when or how we would get together again, but I knew somehow that our story wasn't

Unveiled Secrets

complete. I had to trust that fate would set things the way they were meant to be.

Seasons had passed, and I spent them writing my next novel. Every week, I sent Anders a letter. Sometimes, he wrote back, but we mostly spoke on the phone. He traveled around the world and, although he promised he would stop in Madrid on his way back to Vigo Bay, an unexpected meeting with a client in Italy hindered his decision.

***

I lifted my gaze from the page and poured myself a second glass of Porto. It was almost one o'clock in the morning, and I knew I should grab a few hours of sleep before daybreak. I shook my head and let the diary fall into my lap as I tried to imagine who Myrna was and why Anders had captured her heart. Gabriela knew this woman, and I wondered why I had never seen her in our apartment and why, over the years, she didn't mention Myrna's name.

Why did my mother want me to read this old story? I couldn't deny that it was compelling: the settings were attractive, and the characters engaging. After I had taken another sip of wine, I turned another page in the diary.

***

December 24th, 1964

The big day had arrived. Wreaths hung on the bookstore's windows in preparation for the holidays, and light snow had dusted the streets last night. The marketing team had suggested calla lilies with a touch of red roses in the background instead of a Christmas tree. I was standing behind the table, signing a book when I saw him.

My Christmas gift had come in the form of a tall man with lavender eyes, almost-black hair, full lips, and a mischievous smile. He was holding a book in his hand. The spark in his eyes burned brighter as he approached the table, the long months of separation fading away. Over the past months, I had wondered if everything had been a figment of my imagination, and seeing him close now made my heart quiver. When Anders finally stopped in front of me, I was convinced he could spot my nervousness by the way I arranged and rearranged the book signs and the

Carmen Monica Oprea

rest of the books on the table. I finally stopped what I was doing and went to him, getting lost in his hug. His cologne reminded me of pine trees, the ones he had described in his letters. I had learned about his loneliness from his letters, about his passion for riding horses and reading mystery novels. He assured me that, since we met, he had thought about me, day and night.

Minutes passed before he asked, "Are you ready to leave?"

I nodded. The book signing was over, and after I thanked my agent, I wrapped a shawl around my shoulders and picked up my purse.

Anders grabbed his wool coat and offered me his arm. He had pointed to a limousine with a driver in a black suit, waiting in front of the bookstore. Millions of snowflakes covered the asphalt, some of them melting as soon as they touched the ground. The driver held the door open as he greeted us. We moved away from the crowds already celebrating Christmas Eve. It was warm and cozy inside the limousine. Afraid to break the magic, I stared at the houses and the streets vanishing from our sight. All along the boulevards, bundled pedestrians dashed about to purchase sweets and last-minute holiday gifts for their families and friends.

And only after Madrid was behind us, with all its glimmering decorations, joyful laughter, and carols, did we talk.

Anders spoke first. "I was never good at chatting. As a child, I was quiet, lost in a world filled with dreams. I never thought one day I would have to make hard decisions."

"Was being here with me tonight one of your tough ones?"

"The hardest," he said with a twinkle in his eye.

We both stared into the night as his hands cupped mine.

"My Christmas gift involves some travel. Don't worry! Danni is an experienced driver," Anders said.

Anders pressed his back into the cushion of his seat and closed his eyes. He startled me when he finally spoke again, his tone deep and sensual.

Unveiled Secrets

"With every letter that you wrote me, you got deeper and deeper into my heart. You brought light when I needed it. You gave me a reason to wake up in the morning and want to live. Before meeting you, I was only passing through life, living the same day over and over, talking to people I didn't know or care about. I'm so happy to spend Christmas with you."

My pulse raced. I felt a grin stretching across my face. My eyes opened wide as if absorbing the significance of his words. We talked for a while about art, poetry, and his business, without noticing the passing of Christmas Eve. Hours later, we entered Vigo Bay. The car turned onto a paved driveway secluded by pine trees glistening with snow. A redbrick house with a smoky chimney came into view. The limousine stopped in front of the entrance, and winter's frigid air slapped our faces as we got out. The wind scattered snowflakes around us, and the sun struggled to break through thick clouds without success. It was Christmas morning.

Anders opened the door and let me go inside first. A few logs burned in the fireplace, their scent wafting throughout the house along with the smell of cinnamon. The whole place was filled with the holiday spirit, from the garland hanging at the spiral stairway to the wreaths suspended above every window.

"Come!" Anders signaled me to follow. He closed the door, leaving the winter and my previous life outside. Danni went to his family and left us to deal with whatever Christmas Day had in store for us.

Anders led the way to the second floor and the guest room. Huge French windows opened onto a white garden. I spotted a statue in the center of a deserted, frozen fountain. Anders said that I would find all I needed if I looked in the closet. And there it was—a beautiful silver cocktail dress, a string of blue pearls, and bracelets. Unable to contain my happiness, I picked up the dress—it was silk—and waltzed in the space between the walls and the sofa until a knock on the door stopped me.

"Dinner is at six in the dining room," Anders said before he left the room.

I checked my watch. With three hours at my disposal until dinnertime, I had enough time to stretch out on the enormous bed. I fell asleep the moment my head reached the pillow. Darkness enveloped the

17

room when I opened my eyes. I stared at the clock. Dinner was just an hour away.

After I had taken a last look in the mirror, I closed the bedroom door and walked down the staircase into the living room, where carols were playing. The Christmas lights from a tree decorated in red and gold shone brightly, and the dinner table had been laid for two. A small box with my name on the top rested under the tree. When I opened the box, a diamond ring sparkled from the satin fabric of the gift box. I quickly put it on and was amazed that the ring fit perfectly as if a jeweler had taken my size. It wasn't the sophistication of the ring or the sparkle of the stone that touched my heart, but the words written on the card.

'I won't ask for your hand if my intentions will be just to break your heart. I won't look into your eyes and lie because I love you more than words can ever say. Will you stay by my side forever?

Eternally yours,

Anders'

My entire being screamed with excitement. If everything was just a dream, then I didn't want to wake up. I had imagined this moment, I had wished for it, and when faced with the beautiful reality, I cried softly.

"I never knew diamonds made pretty girls cry," Anders whispered into my ear, and his touch on my shoulders was gentle.

"Only when diamonds stand for love and marriage," I said, turning around to face him.

Anders took me into his arms and kissed me while we danced. Later, the hunger sweeping our bodies was finally satisfied, and the most valuable present we received for Christmas was the gift of love.

We married on the 31st of December and started the new year and a new chapter in our lives together. Our voyage through life had begun, and I was ready for it. In my excitement, I thought I could grow wings and fly.

Unveiled Secrets

Two

After closing the diary, I fell asleep in my mother's bed and dreamed of Denis. In my dream, a beautiful woman clenched his arm and looked right through me, as though warning me to stay away from him. I touched Denis's hand, to make him see me, but he turned away, staring instead at the woman who leaned on his arm. Then, I saw myself running away. I raced into the blue vastness of the sea, every new wave carrying me farther and farther away from shore. I woke up sweating profusely but quickly felt chilled to the bone. I grabbed the blanket and wrapped it around my body as I tried to go back to sleep but sleep never returned. I put my hands under my head and stared at the ceiling while my thoughts drifted to the moment when I had gone for my job interview and what had happened afterward.

***

One year ago

"Why should I hire you, Miss Isidro?" Denis asked.

"If you want the best for your business, then you need me," I said, hoping I didn't sound as desperate as I felt after losing my job as an office manager with Boyle Investments.

The offer letter came two weeks later, and from that time on, I studied and learned everything about hotel management.

***

I had worked at the hotel for a year and five months and traveled with Denis all over the world. But lately, he had decided to let me handle the hotel's operations in New York while he visited the other properties on his own. He had been traveling to Asia to assist in the opening of a new hotel from the Golden Leaves chain and had then spent other two months in Spain. I hadn't seen him since my mother's death. He had just returned from his trip and wasn't in high spirits. Rumor had it he had discovered the general manager in Madrid was skimming money from the restaurant employees' tips. The entire affair had been documented on videotape, and Denis had had to involve the authorities.

Carmen Monica Oprea

One evening, I went after Denis's return from Spain. I had to ask his opinion regarding the integration of our managers' expenses into the new program.

"Can I show you something?" I asked, stepping into his office.

He nodded and leaned back in his chair with his legs crossed, his fingers beating out a rhythm on each arm. Shades of gray touched his dark hair at the temples, and he wore the beginning of a beard.

I set the papers on his desk and looked him in the eye. "I checked them twice, and the reports do not match," I said, pointing at the differences marked in red on the two reports.

"Why not?" he asked.

"I don't know, but if we have to go through with the expenses' integration, we must have accurate information. Both reports should match to the last penny."

"Did you ask Drew why there are differences?"

Drew Hyatt was the hotel's chief financial officer. Denis had wanted the integration project finished two months ago, including analyzing the inconstancies and coming up with a plan to fix them. But the plan was still sitting in a folder on Drew's desk, waiting to be approved. When I'd asked him about the status of the project, he waved me out of his office and suggested I return another time. I'd thought I'd be able to clean everything up before Denis returned from overseas trips, but we'd been slammed with work and hadn't finished it.

I chewed on my nail and shook my head.

"Then, let's go," Denis said, his face clouding. He jumped from his chair so abruptly that he knocked the chair over but caught it just before it fell, muttering. Not good.

Still hugging my reports, I followed him toward Drew's office. My decision to come to Denis was a terrible idea, as it was wearing stilettos to work today.

"We can do it another time, Denis. No hurry," I said, out of breath, as I climbed the stairs to Drew's office.

20

Unveiled Secrets

When he reached the top of the stairs, Denis turned around and waited for me. "Now is as good a time as any," he snapped when I stopped next to him.

Drew's office was on the third floor, and when we stopped in front of his door, Denis's face was a combination of dark red and purple. He opened his mouth and then quickly closed it. I lowered my gaze and swept invisible lint off my dress. In truth, I wanted to turn around, to run back to the safety of my office, but that wasn't an option. Denis practically pushed me into Drew's office. Drew was working on the spreadsheet and judging by the creases on his forehead, the numbers weren't adding up.

Denis tossed the reports on Drew's desk. "Can you explain these credit card discrepancies?"

"Just keep in mind that this is a test report and not the final," I whispered.

"They still have to match," Denis said. "Why aren't these entries matching?"

Drew scratched his bald head and looked over the reports again, pointing at the first highlighted entry. His lips were a barely visible line as he compared my report to the one on his computer's screen.

Drew said, "The system doesn't seem to do what we expected. We need to call Concor's customer service and go over the settings again."

"Then I've wasted my money," Denis said, raising his voice even more.

"I need more time to make the reports agree, and I don't have that luxury," Drew said, his voice neutral.

Denis turned to me, pointing the finger at my face. "You're calling those guys again and straighten this out. Do you hear me?"

I nodded. Denis turned around and marched out of Drew's office. I stood staring at Drew, incapable of moving or saying a word. Denis' fury had sucked the air out of my lungs. I knew Denis didn't want to use the new system, but Drew had suggested it would make the tracking of the

21

Carmen Monica Oprea

expenses easier, especially for the managers traveling overseas for business. It was obvious that the fact the implementation hadn't gone as smoothly as we'd hoped angered Denis, along with the problems he had encountered in Madrid. Without saying a word to Drew, I gathered up the reports and sprinted down the hallway to my office, where I grabbed a bottle of water and promptly spilled half of it on the carpet. I wouldn't be able to call customer service until tomorrow, so I tried to work on other things but couldn't concentrate. Denis's words rang in my ears. Finally, at close to eight in the evening, I picked up my purse and shut down my computer. I stopped at Tessa's office on my way out.

"He breathes business, dreams business, and talks business," Tessa said after she had listened carefully and given me one of her emergency chocolates. She blew a lock of blond hair out of her eyes and straightened a few papers on her desk. There wasn't a trace of dust in her office, not a folder out of place, and I always wondered how she managed to keep everything so immaculate.

"Gee, thanks, Tess," I said with my mouth full of chocolate.

Tessa looked at me. "Your cheeks are on fire. Are you falling for him?" She paused. "You'd better stay away, or you'll end up hurt."

I felt my cheeks burning. What if Tessa was right? What if I saw Denis as something more than just my boss? He was constantly on my mind since we'd met. I had the feeling that he wasn't unaffected by me either by the way his eyes locked on mine when we met in the hallway and the way he came close to me when we looked at the sales reports together. The air felt more energized when we were in the same room together as if electricity flew through both of us. I had never felt this way before, and George, my former fiancé, had never raised such feelings in me.

"His words were mean and rude, and you're right that he's all business," I said, rocking on my heels while I finished eating the last bit of chocolate. "But it feels that every cell in my body is on full alert when I'm near him. Just hearing his voice makes me breathe a little faster."

Tessa narrowed her eyes. "He's not the once-upon-a-time type of guy. Should I worry about you?"

I laughed. "No, I'm a big girl."

22

Unveiled Secrets

"Leila, keep away from him. He'll break your heart if you let him," Tessa said, frowning. "I see the way he looks at you. Everyone in the hotel talks about it."

"Everyone?"

Tessa nodded. "Last week, the *Enquirer* interviewed him about his relationship with Liz Thurber, the actress."

I shook my head, eyes popping out of their sockets. "And?"

"He said they were just close friends."

"No way—"

"I don't want you to end up as just another entry in his black book," Tessa said, looking me in the eye. "And I have the feeling he is not immune to your charm."

Tessa was right. About everything.

"Romance belongs in fairy tales," I said, "and I'm too old for Cinderella stories."

"We need fairy tales, Leila. They give us hope."

Tessa looked out the window and blinked rapidly, and I pretended not to notice the slight tremor in her voice.

"Denis is no Prince Charming," I said, laughing more from nervousness than from the humor of the situation.

My thoughts circled back to the moment when my life had changed. Becca, my best friend, had walked to the front of the altar that late summer day, where I had stood with George. Before we could exchange vows, Becca looked into George's eyes and said, "I'm pregnant with your child."

Whispers rose, then quietness fell over my guests. My brain stopped functioning, and a shiver crossed my body. It took me what felt like at least five minutes to register what had just happened. George, the man I had loved for the past five years, lowered his gaze, and I knew that what Becca had said was indeed true. I smacked the bouquet of roses hard across his face, snatched the lace veil off my head, and left the church, dragging shattered dreams and a broken heart. That had been three years ago, and, since then, I had succeeded in keeping everyone at bay. Love was just another word in the dictionary, and I was determined to keep it that way.

Tessa patted my shoulder. "Heed my warning, little lady, and don't give in to his allure."

"Well, thanks for your concern," I said. "I'll see you in the morning."

Tessa blew me a kiss.

I walked from the hotel to my apartment because I didn't own a car. I didn't even have a driver's license, and Tessa always teased me that I would die an old maid who had never experienced the joy of riding in a car with the wind caressing my face.

The apartment was dimly light. I threw my shoes off as I entered the kitchen. After settling on a quick sandwich for dinner, I returned to my mother's room and climbed into the middle of her bed, devouring the food and sipping club soda. How I missed our conversations about the fate of the world! I thought of Denis, too. What could have happened to put Denis in such a terrible mood today? Even Drew had remained speechless when Denis had raised his voice and pointed that finger at my face. The same knot I felt earlier formed in my throat again. I pushed the plate aside and leaned against the pillows, opening the diary, and scanning the next page.

***

Spain, Vigo Bay

June 20th, 1970

The city and the beach have become nourishment for my soul. How can I describe this romantic city filled with art and history? Vigo's estuary, with its dark blue hue, is renowned for stunning sunsets and the fresh scent brought by the sea breeze. The large, almost-white sandy beach bordered by tall pine trees sweetens the air with an overpowering fragrance of resin. For anyone who appreciates art, the town is a mixture

Unveiled Secrets

of modern and Romanesque architecture, with statues erected in the gardens and squares. My favorite spot is the rose garden in Quinones de Leon, where beauty is eternal. You can walk endlessly on hidden paths while admiring the sunsets over the town. Anders comes with me when he isn't busy running around the world for business matters.

Every moment of the past five years seems like a beautiful dream. Anders has taken me to places I never imagined I would visit; other times I choose to remain in Vigo Bay and wait for his return. When he is gone, I miss him terribly, and a life without him is hard to imagine. He is my friend, my lover, a man I found by accident, and the one with whom I want to grow old. The little things he does every day, from the flowers he leaves on my pillow before he goes to work, to the walks in the gardens or the beach, everything is sweet and gentle. He says I am just like spring to him, and this makes me happy beyond reason.

***

I set the diary aside, hugged my pillow, and drifted off to sleep. It was seven in the morning when the thunder and the lightning woke me up. The rain was shredding through a pall of white mist, ripping it apart. With less than an hour to make it to the hotel, I hailed a taxi as soon as I reached the street.

"It's horrifying today," Sam, the front office manager, said when I entered the lobby.

"Awful," I said, shaking the rain from my umbrella and turning toward the elevator.

It was quiet inside my office, a pale light coming from the desk lamp. I turned on the computer and began typing. As I worked, from time to time I looked out the window at the park. Nobody was in sight, not even a dog. I finished the sales reports around noon, and it was still raining. Since there was no point in going out in the rain and hitting a local restaurant for lunch, I decided to stay in my office and read a novel.

I was deeply engrossed in the story when I heard Denis say, "You looked mesmerized. I don't remember ever seeing your face light up like this."

Carmen Monica Oprea

I jumped and felt my cheeks burning. Mother's advice rang in my ears: — *"Never mix business and pleasure, and never get involved with people where you work."*

Avoiding his insistent stare, I looked around the office.

"This book has that effect on me. I wonder if people even think or act with the same passion they had hundreds of years ago," I said.

"Maybe they do when they find the right person," Denis said.

"How would you know?"

Denis shrugged his shoulders.

"From experience, of course—"

"Ah, yes, and you have loads of it, from what I read in the *Enquirer*. I don't picture you as a romantic man, Mr. Fraga."

Denis touched his chin, his eyes dancing. "Romance belongs in books. Don't tell me you believe in it."

Jerk, I thought but bit my tongue. "Not at the moment," I said. If I had ever believed in romance, George had cured me with his infidelity. And, from his reputation, Denis wasn't too far behind George. Rumor had it that he changed women with the seasons.

"I hope I'll meet the lucky man in your life one day," he said.

I rolled my eyes. "Me, too," I said.

Denis clamped his lips shut, nodded, and then he continued. "Isn't it a lonely life? All work and no play?"

"What do you know about loneliness, Denis?"

A hint of sadness crossed his face. "More than you think."

I stopped breathing for a few seconds. Then, I buried the book in a drawer while I threw away the other half of the apple.

26

Unveiled Secrets

"Will you read to me sometime?" Denis asked. "I'd love to find out what you find so appealing in that book. Who knows? Perhaps, I'll discover how to attract the right woman."

My mouth fell open. "I'll bet you don't need to further your education. As you said, romance is not your forte."

I narrowed my eyes. This guy was a high risk since he didn't seem to care that we worked together or that our colleagues gathered in the corners and gossiped about who his next victim would be. I couldn't figure out Denis Fraga. No one could.

"I can lend you my copy of the book," I said.

"It won't serve the same purpose."

I looked Denis in the eye. "Be serious. Why don't you tell me what you want?"

"You'll run scared if I do," he said, looking boyish, with his tie loosened up and sleeves rolled above his elbows. He seemed relaxed, and that didn't happen too often. He acted as if nothing had happened the previous day. No apologies, either.

"Drew's birthday is coming up, the big fifty," he said. "We need to plan a party for him."

"A surprise party?"

Denis nodded. "On the top floor."

I opened the computer and checked the reservations for the ballroom on the top floor for the month. Only a miracle would allow us to throw Drew's party at the hotel. So, I prayed silently for one. No luck.

"His birthday is in two weeks, but the ballroom is booked," I said. "Maybe we can move it to the garden. What do you think?"

"Are we booked every weekend?"

"Yes," I said, examining the schedule. Just then the system updated. "Oh, wait, we have Friday's event moved to Saturday."

Carmen Monica Oprea

"Book it!"

"Done!" I said, marking the day in the system with my initials. "I'll get in touch with his wife."

"Good! Please do that! I'm leaving for Paris tonight, and I'll be back in ten days." Denis leaned toward me and whispered, "I'm sure you'll miss me."

"I'll count the minutes."

Denis rose from the chair and laughed. I trembled. His fragrance reminded me of cassia. I stood too and went to the black filing cabinet to pick up the folder with the budget for the month, my back turned toward him.

Denis Fraga had just become dangerous.

"I have to put out this flame," I whispered. My heart was beating fast, and the rush of blood through my veins told me to pay more attention. I had to keep Denis away from me— to protect my heart. I couldn't allow another man to walk all over me as George had done.

Weeks after the breakup, George and I had met and talked about the entire situation. He had finally said that my decision to never have children had scared him, and after he had drunk a few glasses of whiskey, he had run into Becca just as he had left the night bar. He offered to take her home, and Becca had invited him over to her apartment. The last thing he remembered was making love to her. It only happened that one night, but after what had happened during our wedding, he had decided to do the right thing with Becca. After George and I had parted ways, I found out from common friends that he and Becca had a healthy boy and that their marriage seemed to be doing okay. Although my heart hurt, I felt happy for George.

I sighed as I reached for the phone and buzzed Tessa.

"Leila, what's going on?" Tessa asked.

"I need you in my office ASAP. Code red. Denis wants to throw a surprise party for Drew, and we only have two weeks to put it together."

28

Unveiled Secrets

"Oh, dear Lord, that's just what we need. No wonder we're behind schedule if we have these pop-up events all the time. I'm on my way," Tessa said.

I could almost envision Tessa slamming down the phone and rushing to the elevator. This woman was always running as if she ate batteries. While waiting for her, I called Randolph, the food and beverage director, and afterward Kevin, the hotel chef, and asked them both to come to my office.

"What's the matter?" Kevin asked as soon as he opened the door.

Tessa was already sitting next to Randolph.

"All right, everyone," I said. "Drew turns fifty this month, and Denis wants to give him a surprise party. I need suggestions."

Kevin scratched his ear, his habit when he was concentrating. Randolph drew a sketch of the bar on a napkin, and Tessa leaned toward my desk and grabbed a marker.

Randolph chuckled before saying, "Do you remember the time the sprinklers turned on, and we were all soaked?"

"Drew told us to wrap ourselves in white sheets while we sat in the budget meeting, waiting for our clothes to dry," Tessa said.

"On top of that," Kevin added, "the lights went out because of that big thunderstorm. We scared the hell out of our guests when we meandered through the hallways."

While Kevin just smiled, Randolph chuckled and said, "The good part was the free publicity."

"I recall the event became the theme for the Halloween party that year," I said.

"We need something special for Drew but not ghosts," Tessa said. She rose from the chair and went to the whiteboard. She drew as she spoke. "Envision this. The tables are decorated with crisp, white tablecloths and golden-rimmed plates. We add wine glasses and assorted napkins trimmed with gold stripes. Red roses in clear vases will add a splash of color."

29

Carmen Monica Oprea

"Fabulous," Kevin chuckled.

"The band can play songs from Drew's high school and college days, and a slideshow showing pictures of the man and his family through time will run on the TV screens," I said.

"We should add a candle for each decade rather than cause a fire hazard with fifty candles," Randolph said.

Kevin's eyes twinkled as he jotted notes. He loved parties.

"This sounds like fun. I'll inform Denis about our plan," I said, concluding the meeting.

After everyone had left, I wrote down a plan for the party and called Denis but got his voice mail. I e-mailed him the details of the party instead, knowing it would be a few hours before I heard back from him.

Then, I called Concor's customer service and explained that the integration of the hotel's expenses with our accounting system wasn't successful. They promised to look at the settings and come back with a solution to avoid future credit card discrepancies when we posted the charges.

By the time I left the hotel, the rain had stopped, and a few rays passed through the mist.

Golden Leaves Hotel, or GLH to those of us who worked there, used the same architectural design all over the world, with the rooms built around central gardens. The waterfalls throughout the hotel and the gardens with narrow pathways were the perfect places for weddings, birthdays, and fashion shows. A turmoil of room service, waiters, housekeepers, and bellmen carrying luggage met me at the front desk where everyone seemed to want to check in and out at once.

"Need some help?" I asked Sam.

Sam nodded.

"Thank you, Leila," he whispered. "It's crazy!"

After we had cleared the crowd from the lobby, Sam, Irene—the assistant front desk manager—and I dropped into chairs behind the front

Unveiled Secrets

desk, exhausted. Irene was from Brazil, and she had once introduced me to one of her brothers. Not for my taste. She had laughed when I explained to her that my idea of having fun was going to the theater or the opera, not dirty dancing in nightclubs. Her brother hadn't called me again, and I hadn't inquired about him, though I wished him all the best.

"It's the same thing every time we have a wedding. We ought to hire more personnel," Irene said.

"We're on a budget, and Denis wants to keep expenses down," I said.

"Working our butts off is what he does," Irene said.

I chuckled. I occasionally suggested adding a few part-time employees, but Denis didn't want to hear about increasing personnel. We returned to work, and around four, we took another break and had a cup of fresh coffee. Those addictive Goo-Goo chocolates looked inviting in their case, and as always, I took one while Sam pretended not to notice as he enjoyed his cup of hot coffee. He seemed satisfied that we finally had our guests settled for the night.

"You deserve it, but don't make a habit of it," Sam said.

"I won't," I said, knowing too well that I would break my promise at the first chance I got. I bit the chocolate and closed my eyes, reveling in the taste.

The phone rang, and Irene answered. After hanging up, she looked at me. "Chef wants to go over some menu with you. I'll handle the station. Leave now, darling," she said, pushing me away.

"Duty calls," I said, finishing the second chocolate while I walked to the kitchen.

One of the reasons I was always stealing chocolates was that I lived on protein bars and hadn't had a decent meal since my mother had died. Cooking was as alien to me as driving. From time to time, Kevin sent me a hot dish and didn't charge me for it. Everyone I worked with at GLH was thoughtful, open, and kind.

Carmen Monica Oprea

The aroma of freshly baked rolls permeated the hallway outside the kitchen, and as soon as I stepped inside, I helped myself to one of them. An army of cooks busied themselves around stoves and counters. I found Kevin in his small office, at the back of the kitchen, making menus.

"What's up?" I asked, licking the last crumb of bread from my lips.

"I was thinking of Drew's party. I believe a combination of American and French dishes is appropriate since his wife is French," Kevin said.

I nodded. "What do you suggest?"

"It's still a work in progress, but I have some ideas." He showed me a list of possible dishes to serve at the party. We discussed the pros and cons of each and finally settled on several.

"I'll call Helen tonight to tell her of our plans," I said.

"Then, it's settled. I'll email the menu for the party to you in the morning, but right now I have to get back in the kitchen. We don't need three hundred hungry guests running around the hotel."

"Do you have enough cooks?"

Kevin nodded as he opened the storage room's door and went inside with two of his assistants.

I returned to my office to catch up on some unfinished paperwork regarding the budget for the quarterly meeting. I texted Denis about the menu, and when I looked out the window, twilight with shades of oranges and reds stretched over the sky.

My cell beeped once when I got a text message. Denis's answer was short. "Good plan! I like the idea of French cuisine combined with American dishes."

"I promised you a surprise," I texted back.

"I can't wait."

The clock on the wall showed eight, so I stopped for the day. I picked up my purse and umbrella and left the hotel, deciding to walk back

Unveiled Secrets

home. A few icy raindrops touched my face, and the crowds I typically met during the day had thinned out. The few like me who were willing to defy the cold rain walked rapidly on the sidewalks, some talking on their cell phones, others jogging. I was ready to unwind after another long day, but I still had a call to make.

I dropped my bag as soon as I entered the apartment and grabbed my phone. I dialed.

"Hi, Helen! It's Leila Isidro from GLH. Did I catch you at a bad time?"

"Not at all," Helen said in her rich, charming, French accent. "I remember you from last year's Christmas party. How can I help you, Cherie?"

As a fashion designer with her own business, Helen traveled to Paris a few times during the year for her shows, and she used our hotel for her fall presentations. It was my good fortune that she was still in town and not running around the world.

"We decided to have a surprise party for Drew at the hotel. We need your help to get in touch with his friends and relatives."

Helen giggled. "That is a fantastic idea. Drew will love it. *J'adore* this idea already."

"I'll send you an e-mail with the details later."

A dog barking interrupted our chat. Helen silenced the dog before returning to our conversation.

"When did you say this is happening?"

"We thought about Friday, July eighteenth at six, on the top floor ballroom. Your job is to make sure Drew thinks he's on his way to somebody else's party," I said.

"All right, *Cherie*, leave it to me. I have to go now. Keep in touch and let me know if I can help in any other way."

What a day! I opened the windows, and the air was crisp after the earlier shower. A mixture of jasmine and lilac combined with the fresh

Carmen Monica Oprea

aroma of rain. From my apartment on the tenth floor, the city seemed bathed in light. The sounds of the traffic faded as the night settled in. I wrapped my arms around myself as I thought of how my life had changed since my mother's death.

Unveiled Secrets

Three

Not a single cloud had shown in Friday morning's sky. I took the stairs to the second floor of the hotel, where my office was. Two messages from Denis popped on the screen. He was pleased that he had finished the job in Paris and that the preparations were going according to plan. It was the second e-mail that aroused me.

Dinner at eight at Balthazar. Wear lavender—it goes with your eyes,

Denis

I'd been so deep in thought about Denis I gasped when the phone rang. It turned out to be one of the sales staff reminding me we had a meeting in half an hour, which I suddenly remembered would be followed by one with key people from catering to go over preparations for all the weddings scheduled for the next month. I picked up the reports and hurried to the conference room just in time for the first meeting, still thinking of Denis's dinner invitation. I was the last one to sit down at the oval wooden table. Chef Kevin had brought a basket with recently baked croissants filled with raspberry jam. I grabbed one while I went over the statistics. Sales looked good. We had come in under the budget and despite losses in the first quarter— we'd had two weddings, and a fashion show cancel—we'd made up the profits in bookings. The meeting lasted only fifteen minutes, and then everyone left. I was alone in the conference room, finishing the last of the croissant and taking notes for my upcoming meeting with Denis.

My cell phone rang.

"Are you coming to the meeting?" Tessa asked. "We're running late."

"I am on my way," I said, picking up the folders from the table. Caught in preparations for the meeting with Denis, I forgot all about my next scheduled meeting.

Tessa's office was on the first floor. Chef Kevin was there too.

35

"Howdy," Kevin said after I closed the door. "It's not like you to be late."

"Sometimes, it just happens to be late." I approached Tessa's desk. "Are these the menus?"

Tessa nodded. I picked up the first one of the three event orders and studied it. If everything went according to plan, we were making around thirty thousand.

"It looks good. Listen, why don't you both decide what works best? You know better."

"Is everything okay?" Kevin asked.

"Everything is good. I am a little busy," I said, setting the paper back on the desk and turning toward the door. "I'll be in my office if you need me."

I returned to my office and finished the projects for the day, still thinking of Denis's invitation. I couldn't deny my attraction to him, but I also knew we were colleagues, and he had a reputation. I felt pulled toward him, and I needed a distraction. Anything would help. He was no different from George.

Last year, at the Christmas party, he had shown pictures he called golden personal moments in the history of the hotel. One of the pictures stood out from the dozens of them. He was sitting at a table next to a beautiful brunette. Denis said that when he had discovered the picture among the ones he had collected, he couldn't remember who the woman next to him was. He thought she had been one of the employees working in the hotel until he realized that he had dated the woman for over a year, and he couldn't remember her name. I remembered laughing as I studied his profile, feeling sorry for the woman he had dated. That's why my growing attraction to Denis was terrifying, as was our upcoming dinner. The fact he had suggested I would wear lavender, made it clear that he was becoming interested in me.

Friday evening came fast and, after a quick check in the mirror, I applied a drop of perfume, and, half an hour later, I was on my way toward Balthazar. I had decided to wear a lavender dress that day, just to see his reaction. Hues of purples and blues painted the evening sky. My heart throbbed in my chest, waves of excitement filled the pit of my stomach. I started to count to calm myself as my mother had taught me when I was only a child. Sometimes it worked, and sometimes it didn't. I tried it anyway.

Although Gabriela had been gone for a few months now, I couldn't bring myself to close her art gallery, so I kept it open weekends and a couple of nights a week. Tessa was helping me fill the last orders Gabriela had received. It was still hard being in a place where Gabriela spent most of her days—except when she was volunteering at the orphanage every third Saturday of the month. Tessa said that time would heal all the wounds, so I threw myself into my job and read the diary she had left for me when time permitted. I almost felt like Myrna and Anders were friends of mine.

Balthazar, located at 80 Spring Street between Broadway and Crosby Street, was famous for its French cuisine and its pastries. I glanced through the window. The restaurant was packed. Servers ran back and forth, carrying plates with steaming food or slices of decadent chocolate cake and other delicious-looking desserts. And there sat Denis, handsome and tanned, and my breath caught in my throat. He rested his hands on the table and checked his wristwatch every so often. Then, as if sensing my presence, he gazed toward the door just as I entered the restaurant.

"Denis Fraga, a reservation for eight o'clock," I told the hostess.

"Follow me," the hostess said, smiling and leading the way toward the table.

Denis was sipping from a glass of red wine when I stopped next to the table. I noticed there was a second one in my place setting.

"I knew lavender would look good on you," Denis said, rising from his chair and pulling mine out for me. As he pushed my chair in, he leaned toward me, whispering in my ear. "It's my favorite color."

"Since when?" I asked, looking at him as he walked back to the table and took his seat.

"For as long as I remember knowing you," Denis answered. His mouth curved into a big smile and his eyes twinkled. He wore blue jeans and purple shirt, and he smelled divine.

Carmen Monica Oprea

"Welcome back," I said, deciding to change the subject.

"Thanks."

"How was Paris?"

"Busy, chic, sunny," Denis said, his tone heavy with thought. He unbuttoned two buttons on his shirt and passed his hand through his hair. He had a gleam in his eyes, their intensity terrifying and thrilling me, and I felt goosebumps on my arms.

"Paris is a romantic city. One day, I'll go for a visit," I said.

"What would you like to see while you're there?"

"First, I'd visit the gardens. If I close my eyes, I can see myself sitting on one of the benches lining the pathways in front of the Louvre or perhaps Versailles, feeling the breeze ruffle the trees in the pale sunshine, watching children as they pull their toys along narrow paths, listening to birds singing as they rest on statues. And then, I envision myself drinking a cappuccino in one of those street cafes and sitting in one of the iron chairs that rock back and forth on the pavement."

Denis laughed. "You're talking as if you've been there already."

"Only in my dreams," I said. "I still have my honeymoon tickets for Paris."

"Are you getting married?" Denis asked, raising a brow.

"Not anymore," I said with a bitter laugh that caught in my throat.

"From the look on your face, I don't think is something you want to talk about."

I shook my head. The last light of the day had slipped away, and darkness had closed in. Denis nodded once and shifted in his chair.

"Red wine is my favorite," I said, clutching the glass tightly. I licked my lips but stopped when I spotted Denis slowing his breathing as he watched me.

"I wish I'd be that glass in your hand."

Unveiled Secrets

"What?"

Denis picked up the bottle of wine and filled both glasses. "I ordered for both of us. I hope you don't mind."

My throat was dry, my head light, and my tone a bit husky. I rested against the cushion of the chair to steady myself. "Not at all," I said, thinking that the wine on an empty stomach could have been the cause of my dizziness.

"So, what's new?" Denis asked.

I told him about the need of hiring more people to help with the front office and the weddings we booked. He listened while the waiters served frisee fux fardons first, a chicory salad with warm bacon shallot vinaigrette and a soft poached egg, followed by capers and roasted chicken with mashed potatoes for two. We kept the conversation light as we ate—the weather, the hotel, and the other places Denis had traveled.

We shared a crème Brule and profiterole with vanilla ice cream and chocolate sauce while we talked about the surprise party for Drew and Tessa's idea for the slideshow marking the critical moments in Drew's life. Denis signaled for the check. Then, he led the way out of the restaurant and took a deep breath before gathering enough courage to articulate the first words.

"Are you sure everything is all right? You're not acting like yourself. Is anything wrong with the opening of the new hotel?"

"One question at the time, please," Denis said. "First, everything is fine. I'm the same person who left a few days ago, though I am a bit wiser. Second, the commencement went according to plan. Mr. Haden decided to visit Spain next. And third, I have a surprise for you."

When the valet brought Denis's car to the front of the restaurant, Denis drove into the night, providing no clues to our destination or elaborating about what he'd meant by "surprise." Since my misfortune with George, I hadn't given the time of day to the few brave men who had tried to date me. My long work hours provided the best excuse to avoid getting involved with anyone, but I found others when I needed to, and I had succeeded in preventing any romantic entanglements—at least until now.

39

Carmen Monica Oprea

After a few minutes, he said, "I missed you, Leila. I can't explain it, but I came back early just to be with you. I counted the minutes before seeing you."

"Why?" I asked.

Denis remained silent. We drove for an hour, listening to soft music on the radio. New York remained behind us, and he stopped the car when we reached the beach. We took our shoes off, the sand slipping between our toes. It was a bright night with billions of stars around a moon that seemed to have emerged straight from the ocean. A gust of salty wind scattered my hair, licking my skin and cleansing my lungs. I had expected the area to be deserted this time of night, but I could see other people—mostly couples—scattered up and down the beach.

"Just like silk and dark as the night," Denis said, touching my hair.

My pulse raced. Emotions I'd tried to keep from surfacing chilled me to the bone. I didn't want to fall in love. I wasn't prepared to trust another man just yet. I had a lot on my plate at work, a diary to read, my mother's work to continue at the orphanage, a birthday party to prepare for, and Denis was about to ruin all of my plans. The waves crashed against the shore, just as my thoughts crashed against my skull. Ahead of us, a couple kissed and hugged. There was a smell of seaweed all around us.

"This is way too romantic for you," I said, looking back at Denis.

"I thought you'd like a walk under the moonlight," Denis said, smiling.

Denis embraced me, and then he kissed me, his lips still wearing the spicy taste of the wine. I didn't pull away but kissed him back, and all my sound judgment disappeared. I didn't have the power to fight the mixture of sensations taking control of my body. Although I felt trapped, I also felt that I had discovered the place destined for me—his heart. I knew I had to stop before it was too late before something happened that I'd regret, but I found it the hardest thing to do. As if reading my mind, Denis released me from his embrace, and we walked hand in hand along the shore.

"One day I'll reach your heart, Leila."

Unveiled Secrets

I smiled noncommittally at Denis as I bent to pick up a few shells thrown on the seashore by the Atlantic Ocean. The air had turned chilly, and the seawater felt cold on my toes. I rubbed my arms, and Denis put his arm around my shoulders. I shivered from more than the cold. A lonely seagull rested on a rock swelling straight from the ocean. We stopped and watched as a second one landed next to it, nuzzling the first bird's neck.

"They must be a couple," I whispered.

Denis laughed. His eyes twinkled, then they darkened, and for a split second, my heart ceased its beating. The look on his face as he gazed at the waves was closed and hard, and his eyes narrowed. His arm around my shoulders pulled me tighter.

Suddenly the hairs on the back of my neck stood up. "I have this strange feeling we're being followed," I said, turning around. There were other couples walking hand in hand along the winding shore. Some were kissing, their giggles disturbing the night, while others seemed to be arguing hotly. Nobody seemed to be paying any attention to us.

"You have a flair for the dramatic," Denis said.

"Drama has a role of its own in our lives. Without it, we wouldn't be able to survive a constant feeling of happiness. We need a little bit of drama in our lives, to appreciate what we have."

"And what do *we* have?" said a woman's voice immediately behind us.

We turned around in shock to come face to face with Liz Thurber, the actress Denis was rumored to have been seeing. She held a half-empty bottle of champagne. Her eyes were bloodshot, and tears slipped down her cheeks.

"Liz?" Denis asked. "What are you doing here? Are you alone? Are you hurt?"

Liz rolled her blue eyes and pursed her full red lips. She took a drink straight from the bottle and handed it to me. "Here, have some so that this handsome man can get lucky tonight."

Carmen Monica Oprea

I swallowed hard. "It's not what you think," I said. "And 'this handsome man' has better things to do than get lucky with me tonight."

Denis burst out laughing, his guffaws echoing in the night. But neither Liz nor I were finding the situation humorous.

"Doesn't the hotel have a rule that colleagues shouldn't fraternize with each other?" Liz asked.

"Rules are meant to be broken," Denis answered, looking straight at Liz. "Let me take you home. Leila can drive your car."

"What? I don't drive," I said, my eyes popping.

"Why?"

"It's complicated," I said.

Liz laughed. Denis scowled, thinking.

"All right, then. I'll send someone to pick up Liz's car in the morning."

Denis snatched the bottle of champagne and passed it to me. Then he lifted Liz and signaled me to follow him to the car. Liz laid her beautiful head on Denis's shoulder, her arms tight around his neck. Their bodies looked like they'd been designed for each other, her shape fitting perfectly to his, just like the two seagulls we'd been watching earlier. I'd thought I was safe from romance and heartbreak, but now I wondered if Tessa might have been right when she had advised me to keep away from Denis if I cared about my heart.

I walked next to him and picked up the sandals that Liz had thrown off her feet. They probably cost more than my salary for an entire month.

"Open the back door," Denis said as soon as we stopped next to his car.

I complied and entered the car, steadying Liz who had a hard time staying awake. She fell asleep as soon as we laid her down, and I got in the passenger's seat. When Denis drove us away, I thought of the beach behind us and the kiss we had shared, but that was dangerous. So instead,

42

Unveiled Secrets

I concentrated on the song on the radio to avoid the stinging I felt in my heart along with the shortness of breath. Denis kept his eyes on the road, but from time to time I saw him looking over at me.

"She's a close friend, Leila. Nothing serious," he said.

"I didn't ask," I said, looking out through the window at the sights of New York. "It's your choice to live your life as you please."

Denis fell quiet until he stopped in front of my building. Liz was fast asleep in the back. I opened the door and got out of the car. Denis did too.

"You know what I like most about you?" Denis asked, coming around and blocking my way toward the front door of the building.

"Why don't you enlighten me?"

"You always smile, you're always happy, and you laugh a lot. Please, don't change."

"I love to laugh," I said, warming up. "And I have no reason to change."

"That's good," he said.

Denis pushed a strand of rebellious hair from my eyes. I counted the beats of his heart as he put his arms around me and kissed me once more.

"I had a lovely evening," he whispered in my ear.

"I did too."

The warmth of his body penetrated through the silk of my dress. Every cell in my body was wide awake, and I stood there breathless, just gazing into his hazel eyes. I was shocked to find myself thinking about a relationship with this man.

"I have to take Liz home," Denis said.

He returned to the car and drove away.

Carmen Monica Oprea

As I showered and got ready for bed I couldn't stop thinking about him. Rumors about his love affairs had spread over the entire hotel, to say nothing about the tabloids. Then, I thought about Liz. She was ten years younger than he was and searching for ways to have fun. Between the long evenings in the nightclubs and her acting career, it was easy to slip on the wrong path and get tangled in relationships without a future. I told myself Denis was just trying to protect her, that they were only friends like he'd said, but I couldn't stop wondering what might have happened after he'd taken her home.

The diary, I thought. *That'll distract me*. I picked it up and settled in my mother's rocking chair by the window.

***

December 31st, 1970

For our anniversary, Anders took me to Paris—a city of romance, intoxicated with love. The two weeks we spent in there were the most passionate ones I have ever experienced. Paris looked lovely in the evening, with lamps burning at every corner and couples knitting their fingers as they walked on sidewalks lined with stylish boutiques and restaurants. The perfume of lilies and jasmine filled the air, and there were bushes of velvety roses separating the streets. Garlands of colorful clematis hung at the windowsills, and the sounds of happy people in restaurants and pubs filled the air.

Back at the hotel, Anders scattered red petals over the bed, wrapping my body in them. We topped everything with champagne, chocolates, and love. There was a sense of protection in his arms, and firmness in his gaze that made me think I would always be safe with him.

May 25th, 1971

Months after we returned to Vigo Bay, Anders came home from a business meeting in London, the smile on his face not reaching his eyes.

"What's wrong?" I asked. "Is it something with the business?"

"It's nothing; don't worry Clarisse," he said.

I wrapped my arms around him. "I went to Dr. Fernandez today."

Unveiled Secrets

"Is everything all right?"

"Our baby will come in February," I said.

His face lit up, and he hugged and kissed me fiercely. I knew he'd be as protective and loving with our child as he was with me.

One day I caught him looking at me strangely like he was worried or there was something serious on his mind, but when I asked, he said it was nothing. It happened again a few days later, and again a few days after that. Each time I'd ask him what was wrong, and each time he'd shrug or dismiss me with something vague like "It's been a long day."

I suspected he wanted to tell me, but he couldn't. Something was stopping him. His sleep became agitated, and nightmares tormented him. I wished I could chase them away, but what could I do if he wouldn't tell me the problem? I concentrated on preparing the baby's room, although I couldn't shake off a strange feeling. Had he found another woman? Was he not in love with me anymore? The nursery overlooked a garden with gardenia-lined pathways, where butterflies flitted among sheltered lilies and colorful irises. How I envied the butterflies for their freedom to choose where they wanted to go! They lived their lives without worrying about today or tomorrow.

Most days I sang to my baby and relished the little kicks in my belly, the swimming of the fetus a constant source of fascination. Anders would kiss the skin where a little elbow or a knee showed as if to let the baby know he was on the other side, waiting for his or her safe arrival, and I tried not to worry. The big day wasn't far off, just short of a few weeks after the New Year.

***

I closed the diary. Did all men keep secrets? My former fiancé George certainly had, and it appeared Anders did too. Did Denis? From what I had read, it was clear that Anders had loved his wife. But why wasn't he honest with her? The diary was supposed to help me find answers, but so far all it had helped me find was more questions. I shook my head. How I wished my mother was still alive and could help me sort through the events in my life! Obviously, Denis and I weren't just colleagues anymore. Our relationship had changed, and it was scary. Still, I convinced myself that Tessa's warning to stay away from Denis wasn't

45

Carmen Monica Oprea

necessary. Even if he took Liz home, he couldn't still be in love with her. He wouldn't hurt me. Would he?

The knock on my door startled me. I glanced at the clock on the wall—it was midnight. I rose from the chair and approached the door, looking through the peephole.

What is he doing here at this hour?

I was tempted to ignore him, hoping that he would go away, but the knocking intensified and I was afraid he'd wake up my neighbors. I jerked the door open.

"What are you doing here, Denis? Don't you know most people usually sleep at this time?"

"Now this is a vision I don't have every day," Denis said, leaning in the doorframe. "May I come in or shall I stay right here and make your neighbors curious?"

Denis didn't seem drunk, so I thought I could trust him to behave if I let him come inside the apartment. I could hear the alarms reverberating in my head when I searched his hypnotic gaze and listened to his deep voice. But despite all the warning signs, I invited him in. It wasn't until I saw my reflection on the large TV screen that I remembered what I looked like—legs sticking from under an old baggy t-shirt I'd had since college, hair chaotic from the shower because I'd forgotten to brush it, and eyes still red from the ocean's breeze.

"Why don't you fix yourself a drink? I'll be right back," I said.

"Do you want one?" he asked.

"Why not? Amaretto, please."

I ran back to my room and jumped into a pair of jeans. Then, I piled my hair on top of my head, secured it with a couple of bobby pins, and brushed my teeth for sixty seconds. When I returned to the living room, Denis was sitting on the couch with a glass of scotch over two cubes of ice in his hand.

Unveiled Secrets

"Your drink is there," Denis said, pointing to the bar where he had left it. I picked up the glass and joined him on the couch, bending a leg under me.

"Tasty," I said, savoring the liquor.

Denis said, "I wanted to ask you a few things, but we were interrupted. You disappeared before I had a chance to do it. I felt I had no choice but to come and get answers. I hope you don't mind."

A dimple formed on his cheek when he raised the corner of his lips to the right. Was there worry in his voice? Maybe the walk on the shore had affected him the way it had affected me?

I took a sip from my glass and said, "Not at all."

Now Denis's grin extended from ear to ear, mischief glimmering in his eyes. He had changed before coming over, and now, with his good looks, hair cut short, and a skin-tight shirt over a pair of worn blue jeans, he reminded me of one of those playboys from *Globe* magazine.

"You have a very well-stocked bar," Denis said.

"Is this the reason you came over in the middle of the night? To talk about my liquor?"

"Not really, but I thought I'd mention it."

"What brought you here, Denis? What is this really about?"

"My heart," he whispered, leaning toward me. "I don't expect you to understand. I just need you to trust me."

I knew Denis and trust didn't go together. I had vowed never to let a man hurt me the way George had, so why was I gazing into his eyes, hearing the pounding of my heart resonating in my ears? Even my skin burned being this near to him. There was a battle inside of me. Every molecule in my body wanted him to leave before I broke my vow and did something we would both regret in the morning, and at the same time, every molecule begged him silently to stay.

Carmen Monica Oprea

"I'm not sure I follow you," I said, sipping my liquor. The bittersweet almond taste excited every one of my taste buds, and Denis's proximity didn't help.

"This isn't easy for me to say because I've never expressed my feelings to a woman this way, but I didn't know what love was until I met you. I've tried to keep away from you until one morning, back in Paris, I finally decided I had to give us a chance, and if it was going to work, then I was lucky. If not..." Denis shrugged. "I couldn't stand the idea that some guy might come along and sweep you off your feet right under my nose."

I stared at Denis. He was just as blunt and aggressive as he was when he conducted a business meeting, and I wondered how I had survived working with him for the past months. His energy was like an ocean storm, wild and filled with dangerous undercurrents, too powerful to resist. Although I feared him, I was also drawn to him, my powers to resist diminishing with each passing moment.

"I'm not ready to start a relationship just yet," I said.

"I'm not rushing you. I just want you to get to know *me*."

I laughed. "It's a tempting proposition."

"What can you lose?"

Indeed, I had nothing to lose, except my head and my heart. I played with my earlobe. I wanted to know him, to give him a chance to know me, mainly because I was so attracted to him.

"Not all men are dangerous species," Denis said.

"I have my doubts about it."

"Let's meet tomorrow, in Central Park, around noon," he continued. "We're going to get a chance to hang out together. It's going to be fun."

"See you in the morning," I said, fiddling with the hem of my shirt.

"By the way, nice socks," he said, pointing at my pink, fluffy feet. I felt myself blush.

48

Unveiled Secrets

Denis rose from the sofa and placed his empty glass on the bar. I got up too and followed him to the door. He kissed me passionately, then walked to the elevator and got in. I stood in the doorframe, watching him go. Was I willing to open myself up to another relationship? I didn't know Denis, had never known him, and the thought terrified me—yet my limbs shook with a desire I had never felt before, not even with George. I felt so frozen between passion and fear that I couldn't move and stood on the threshold until the clock struck one in the morning and jarred me from my paralysis.

Four

Other couples had had the same idea we did—a stroll in Central Park, hand in hand. As I waited for Denis, I admired the rainbow of flowers in their perfectly arranged beds, thinking that capturing their perfection would be a challenge even for the most experienced painter. I snapped a few pictures on my phone, and then I checked the time.

Nearly twelve.

I was worried I had mistaken the time we had decided to meet when warm hands covered my eyes. I touched them and turned around to come face-to-face with Denis. He took my hand in his. It was warm and firm, but the skin was soft, the hand of a man who took care of his body. The shirt revealed his toned muscles, and the scent of his cologne enveloped us. His hair was still wet, his skin tanned, and again I thought how much he looked like a model. I didn't ask him where he was taking me or about what had happened with Liz Friday night. Of course, I was dying to know, but I decided I didn't want to ruin a beautiful Sunday with this man, whom I strongly suspected I was falling in love with.

"You look lovely. Let's go," Denis said, lacing his fingers with mine.

"Where?" I asked, pushing a lock of hair behind my ear.

"Let me do that," he said, rolling the same rebel curl around his finger. He let out a sigh when he caught my stare, and let the curl fall on my shoulder. We turned onto a hidden path, and, after a few steps, I spotted an old magnolia tree with white scented flowers in full bloom. It was cool under the magnolia's shade. A basket rested on a checkered blanket lying on the grass.

"Surprise!" Denis said.

My eyes widened. "I'm not fond of surprises," I said, not joking. "I find them terrifying."

"Really?"

Unveiled Secrets

Denis's eyes glimmered with a warm light. He chuckled and lowered himself to the blanket. I followed him, took my sandals off and sat on my knees. A few rays of sun peeked through the thick leaves when the wind blew, creating a pattern of ovals and circles on the ground.

"It's a fantastic spot, and it's quiet," I said.

"I knew you'd like it."

"Should I worry about your intentions?" I arched an eyebrow at him.

Denis shrugged his shoulders. "They are honorable, I swear."

As far as I knew, George had had honorable intentions when he'd asked me to marry him, but that hadn't stopped him from getting involved with another woman. I thought he had understood my reasons for not having children, that I was afraid of doing to my kid what had been done to me. Although Gabriela had been an exceptional mother, I couldn't stop wondering why my parents had given me away. I shivered just thinking about it. George and I had agreed that when we were ready, we would adopt a child, providing him or her with love and all the comforts at our disposal. There were many children for adoption in the orphanage where my mother volunteered that I felt was my duty to give my love to a child in a similar situation as I was. In the end, he wanted a child of his own, and the entire situation made me realize once again how fortunate I was to have had the unconditional love of a mother like Gabriela.

I turned my attention to Denis. He busied himself with the contents of the basket. Tessa had to be wrong about him. He said he wasn't used to expressing his feelings, which I didn't find hard to believe since he was always businesslike. He smiled at me and I back at as he took our lunch out of the basket: cheese, crackers, a fish salad, and fresh gooseberries. He finally pulled out two glasses and a bottle of Spanish red wine and poured a glass for each of us.

"To friendship," Denis said, raising his glass.

"To new horizons," I added.

Carmen Monica Oprea

As I sipped the wine, I couldn't help but wonder if the day would get any stranger than this. Denis with sparkles in his eyes and a goofy grin, the wine, the food—it was a dangerous combination. I nibbled a cracker and tried to shake off the alcohol that was threatening to impair my decision-making. I needed my head clear. I wasn't ready to fall in love, and certainly not with my boss. Then there was the whole issue with Liz.

What is the deal with that woman?

An affair with Denis was out of the question, and I intended to tell him so. Later. I wiped my fingers with a tissue paper. "What's the plan for today?" I asked.

"Other than trying to seduce you, I intend to take you for a ride. I hope you'll like it."

My heart threatened to break free from my ribcage. Denis looked cute with his imploring eyes and the grin of a teenager alone with his first crash, so I was tempted to play along. It was the first time after George's betrayal when I had decided to cast any doubts aside and let myself seduced by him.

Denis encircled my body, his mouth hungry for mine. Minutes had passed, and our tongues teased and played, as I tasted gooseberries on his lips. I was breathless, the air suddenly hot, and I pushed him away as I rose to my feet and leaned against the trunk of the magnolia tree. He ate the rest of the cheese, and then he leaned on his back, with his hands behind his head. The next thing I've heard was the sound of Denis's steady breathing as he dreamed who-knew-what since he smiled a lot in his sleep.

Denis appeared younger than his forty-three. He had never been married, not even engaged, but was never alone. He was what the world considered "a good catch," but I considered him to be way out of my league. He came from a wealthy family, with land somewhere in Connecticut, where his father tended to the family's apple orchards. No one knew much about his mother. Tessa said she had probably died when he was a young boy. I shouldn't be interested in his personal life. As soon as Denis woke up, I would tell him that our relationship was a mistake and it would be best to put a stop to whatever we were beginning to do.

52

Unveiled Secrets

I studied his oval face as I played with a loop of his hair where black mingled with silver, having the strange desire to touch the fine lines around his mouth.

"Enjoying the view?" he asked, startling me. Denis took off his sunglasses and looked straight into my eyes. I froze, my heart stopped beating, and even the wind stopped blowing. All was quiet. "Breath," he said. Then, he lifted his head, wrapping my lips in his kiss. It was sweet and intense, and I found myself kissing him back. The thought of his skin rubbing against mine reddened my cheeks. "You carry your feelings on your face," he said.

"I'm not sure what you mean."

"That's why I decided to hire you over the other candidates," Denis said. "You are honest."

"Excuse me?"

"You can't hide how you feel. You frown when you're in deep thought, just like you do now."

I chuckled, not entirely sure how to respond. Denis was the second person in this world who managed to understand me without needing words. I became anxious that I gave myself away so quickly.

"Denis, we should talk."

As if sensing the shift in my position, my indecision, my suspicion that our relationship would fail before it had time to blossom, Denis grabbed my hand and caressed my fingers with his lips.

"I think we should leave if we want to make it in time," he said.

I held the blanket, while Denis carried the basket. We passed couples with stars dancing in their eyes and broad smiles mirrored on their faces as we went to his car. He opened the door for me, and then the engine came to life with a roar. I couldn't pretend that I felt nothing for him, but I wasn't ready to strip off the layers of protection around myself. A shudder passed through me, and I rolled down the window, gazing at the fluorescent signs decorating the skyscrapers. A soft wind licked my skin, as rays of sun died with glory. Soon, all the honking and

53

Carmen Monica Oprea

the loud pedestrians remained behind us, and I closed my eyes, listening to the song on the radio.

Minutes later, we pulled up before the MMC. Just ninety minutes away from New York City, MMC or Monticello Motor Club was more than a racetrack. It was a country club with a luxury racetrack for those passionate about motorsports, who delighted in the driving experience and looked to fit among like-minded people. Denis Fraga seemed enamored of fast driving and was about to share that experience with me. He brought the car to a stop in front of the karting building and helped me out.

"You'll enjoy it," Denis said, trying to sound casual about something that looked scary and unsafe in my opinion. "Try to relax."

"I have my doubts," I whispered, convinced that I would faint if I made it out alive after the first driving test. From all the places in the vicinity, Denis decided to take me to the most frightening one. If he knew that I was one of the few New Yorkers who didn't possess a driver license at the respectable age of thirty-five, he would probably die laughing. I never learned how to drive since there were always enough cabs around.

I viewed the wooded acres of undulating terrain with curves reminiscent of the European tracks that had enough elevations of the ground to bring my heart into my mouth. There was a sense of anticipation, a tickling in my skin, just imagining myself sitting behind the wheel and dressed in one of those racing suits and a helmet.

"Martin, let me introduce you to Leila Isidro," Denis said when we came face-to-face with a skinny man with perfect white teeth. Denis turned toward me and said, "Martin is a regular at the club, and passionate about cars and races."

"Delighted to meet you, Miss Isidro," Martin said, winking at me.

Denis chuckled. "She's taken."

I could feel my cheeks catching fire, and I turned toward the first kart, asking, "So, Martin, do you think I can learn how to drive *this thing*?"

"It uses the same driving principles as a car," Martin said.

Unveiled Secrets

"Yes, but I never learned how to drive a car," I said, pretending to look guilty with a grin stretching from one side of my face to the other.

Martin raised an eyebrow, while Denis's mouth fell open. There, I had said it aloud. I acknowledged the fact that I didn't know how to drive. Perhaps, I was one of the few people not owning a car in the entire United States of America. Martin cleared his throat with a cough and invited me inside the club where men and women, dressed in white suits with purple straps were watching a training show about how to start the kart's engine and drive on the racetrack and still be in one piece at the end of the first round. He handed me a suit and directed me to a fitting room, while Denis whispered something in Martin's ear, something apparently very amusing since they burst into laughter. I wished for the day to end without further embarrassment on my side.

"I'm ready," I said after I came out of the fitting room, looking every bit like an astronaut and feeling as scared as a mouse in a live trap.

"Then, let's get you a kart," Denis said, taking my arm. "Are you shaking?"

I snorted and shook my head. "I think I'm scared. Can we just go back to our car, your car, I meant, and return to the city?"

Denis pointed to the front seat. I dragged myself in and secured the seat belt.

"You'll be just fine. Here, push the engine button," Martin said.

Pushing the motor's button was the last thing I wanted to do. I did as instructed, and the kart came to life with a roar. *Oh, boy, this will be an experience*, I thought, praying that I wouldn't faint.

"I'll be right behind you," Denis said, jumping in the backseat of the kart and taking the lead. "This one is specially built for the teacher and the student to practice together."

"Is this supposed to make me feel safe? Cause it isn't," I cried, my voice trembling.

"Take a breath, Leila, and then lift your foot gradually from the pedal. The kart speeds up when you take your foot off the pedal. All you

Carmen Monica Oprea

must remember is to hold the steering wheel and turn it slowly in the direction you want the kart to go."

I could do that, especially since Denis was there with me. I had to trust that he wouldn't let me die during a driving class on a racetrack. What would my headstone stone say? I could almost envision it—killed at thirty-five during a driving session in a kart. I chuckled.

Denis patted my shoulder, and I turned my head toward him.

"Keep your eyes on the road!" he yelled.

I had managed two laps inside the training room and had gone up and down the ramp. Then, the door of the training room lifted. I couldn't feel anything through the helmet I wore, although I longed for the wind brushing against my cheeks and playing with my hair as Tessa predicted would happen when driving in a convertible. Denis turned the wheel to the left, and I felt my hands going in the same direction. And then he turned his steering wheel to the right, and I did the same. We followed the track's route, and I could almost imagine how race car drivers felt with their adrenaline spiking when they raced.

"Take control of the kart," Denis commanded.

"I don't want to," I cried right back at him.

"You're in charge now. My life is in your hands."

Why would this man trust me with his life when I knew nothing about driving and didn't care to learn? But Denis did. I could see him in the mirror as he grabbed the sides of the kart and left me with no choice but to drive. I held the wheel tightly, my heart in my throat. Sweat covered my forehead, and the visor was blurry.

"Breathe," Denis suggested.

That was easy for him to say. I began counting until my heartbeats slowed down to a natural succession of thumps in my chest. I was driving for the first time, and it wasn't as difficult as it looked. We drove around the race track a couple of times and, with each new round, I became more confident in my newly acquired skills. I parked the kart inside the training

Unveiled Secrets

room. Pink and orange colored the horizon, and although my blood was still boiling, I couldn't stop smiling.

"Well? How was it?" Martin asked as he took off my helmet.

"It went surprisingly better than I expected," I managed to say.

"The first time is the most important. It will make you love driving, or hate it forever."

"Then, I am definitely in love with your kart," I said, laughing.

I went back and changed into my dress, while I left Denis and Martin chatting. Ten minutes later, when I joined them, Martin told me to return as many times as I wanted—to explore the courses and improve my skills. Then, we said our goodbyes and went to Denis's car. We were on our way toward the city when Denis suddenly stopped the car on the side of the road and said, "Look! Do you see Venus? It is right there, the most beautiful star in the sky."

"And the brightest," I added, following the trajectory of his finger.

"My mother used to point out the stars at night. It's all I remember about her."

"Do you want to talk about it?" I asked.

"No, not really."

Denis's teeth ground and he straightened his shoulders. I remembered Tessa mentioning that his mother had died, and I didn't push the issue further.

"We can't be together," I said in one breath.

Denis looked at me and laughed. "Eventually, you will learn to trust me."

"We work together. It is all wrong."

Denis lifted my chin and kissed me ever so gently. "You are special," he said, starting the engine and driving us away.

The car came to a stop in front of my building.

57

Carmen Monica Oprea

"I had a beautiful day," I said, leaning toward him. "Thank you for trusting me with your life."

"See you in the morning," Denis said as I got out.

***

Friday morning, I went over the arrangements for the party at the hotel. *Glamorous*, I thought as I inspected the ivory satin coverings we chose for the seats. The banquet servers had finished tying the last gilded ribbons just as I entered the ballroom. I gave them a thumbs-up for a job well done and walked between the tables. Tessa had been right to have golden sprinkles scattered over the crisp tablecloths. And yes, those roses added a romantic touch to the entire set.

"Is everything all right?" I asked the band leader, who was tuning his guitar for the evening. He nodded and hid his face among blond tresses while he played a few of Drew's favorite songs. The other men in the band were preoccupied with arranging their musical instruments on the podium we had improvised for them, so I thought best not to drag them into the conversation. As if sensing my need for reassurance, the band leader lifted his chin and flashed me a boyish grin.

"It will be an excellent night," he said.

"That was the intention," I stated.

I checked my watch. It was almost six.

"Hi, there," Denis said when he stepped through the door. My heart raced. He looked dashing in his black tuxedo as he scanned the ballroom. He waved from the threshold and turned back toward the door.

My feet got cold when I saw Liz. Her makeup was perfect, and she had whisked her hair into an elegant bun. Dressed in a red skintight halter dress with a slit that went all the way up her right leg, almost to her hip, Liz laughed at one of his jokes as she entered the ballroom. I pushed my back against one of the columns, trying to catch my breath.

How stupid of me to think that, maybe this one time, Denis was serious about a woman and that woman was me! Some things would never change. Liz clutched his arm, and the thought that I had been

58

Unveiled Secrets

played for a fool sent a shiver throughout my body. A rush of adrenaline flushed my cheeks, and I took a step back, not sure what to do next. After a while, I collected myself and was able to force a smile.

"It's good to see that you've regained your sobriety, Liz," I said.

Liz giggled. Denis frowned. I couldn't stop from staring at her big, blue eyes popping like stars from beneath golden eyebrows as all my expectations for a romantic night collapsed. She was every man's dream.

"Outstanding job with the decor," Liz said, looking around the ballroom. "Decorating is right up your alley."

"It was a team effort. Everything is better with teamwork," I said, visibly annoyed with Liz's air of superiority.

Liz pulled Denis close to her and narrowed her eyes as she scanned the ballroom. I tried to avoid looking at Denis, who, suddenly found the name tags on the nearby table fascinating. I straightened my posture and decided this was neither the time nor the place for a scene.

"Are you and Denis together?" I couldn't stop asking Liz.

"Only for tonight," Liz said, picking up a glass of champagne from a waiter passing by and looking at Denis, who was checking his cell phone, pretending not to hear our exchange.

Liz took a sip of champagne and played with the bubbles in her mouth before swallowing. "I love pink champagne," she said. "I think it's the world's best creation."

"I have to disagree with you," Denis said. "Women are the best creation and in men's best interests. They are like the salt and the pepper for a good meal."

Denis shut his cell phone and looked straight into my eyes.

"I'm not going to keep you any longer," I said, blinking fast. I needed air since the temperature in the room had suddenly increased by at least ten degrees. I opened the French doors leading to the balcony and took a deep breath as I stood in front of them. When I turned around, Denis locked his eyes on mine again before following Liz, who dragged

59

Carmen Monica Oprea

him to some newly arrived guests. Men seemed delighted to get her attention, while jealousy sprang from the women.

I joined Tessa at the bar, and the first sip of red wine went down fast.

"Are you having fun yet?" Tessa asked.

"Don't ask," I answered, rolling the rest of the wine around the glass.

Tessa sighed. "Can I say I told you so?"

I narrowed my eyes and pursed my lips. "Of course, you can."

I shot Tessa a look and turned around when I heard someone saying, "They are here." The lights went off, except for the spinning globe hanging from the ceiling and throwing rays of colorful light around the ballroom. The music and whispers died when Drew and Helen entered the room.

A collective "Happy birthday, Drew!" rang out from the crowd.

Confetti flew in every direction while experienced waiters uncorked the champagne. I hugged Drew and kissed the air around Helen's cheeks.

"All this is for me?" Drew asked, his face flushed, his eyes shining. "Gee, Leila, thank you. What a pleasant surprise!"

A big smile splashed across Drew's face.

"I'm glad you like it," I said.

"I owe you one."

"Don't mention it!"

Helen leaned toward me. "Great job, *Cherie*!"

"I'm glad you like it."

Couples flooded the dance floor as soon as the music started. Helen's jade-green eyes sparkled when she danced with Drew. I had never

Unveiled Secrets

seen Drew as happy as he looked tonight at his birthday party. I was standing by the band, watching Drew and Helen dance when Denis grabbed my hand. I didn't have much time to protest when he whirled with me around the ballroom, away from Liz and the other curious stares, until we reached the balcony.

Night fell over the sights of New York. From the twentieth floor of our hotel, the cars looked like fireflies, their honking fading as the darkness settled in. Denis closed the glass door with a shove of his foot, leaving the entire commotion behind us. He hummed in my ear as he danced with me between columns and stopped when he had reached an arch covered in purple lilac and white roses for the next day's wedding. Silver stars peeped down gleaming and glittering at us. Although they looked cheerful with their twinkling, I was far from being cheerful. My mood was floating somewhere between anger and stupor.

I've been played again.

"You look gorgeous in this dress. It matches your eyes," Denis said, trying to kiss me.

I pushed him away. "Stop it, Denis! How can you do this? Do you think Liz will approve of you being here with me, or don't you care about anything else other than what you want?"

"What is that supposed to mean?" Denis asked, trying to kiss me again, which, of course, I avoided. I walked past him, shuddering.

My hand was on the doorknob when Denis blocked my way with his body. He leaned on the door and forced me to look at him. I sighed, turned around, and sat on a chair with my elbows resting on an antique iron table. The exotic arrangement of Oriental lilies the bride had chosen for the wedding rehearsal was entrancing. I picked the bowl up and smelled the flowers as Denis left his spot by the door and took the seat next to me. He covered my hand with his own, playing with my fingers for a while. Then, he took his time lifting each one and touching them to his lips. There was something so infinitely sensual in his touch that every ounce of anger I previously held, had melted away.

"I didn't come here with Liz. She was in the elevator already. You've got the facts all wrong, but it was worth it just to see you jealous."

61

Carmen Monica Oprea

"I'm not jealous," I said, and the words dissipated when he circled his arms around me, pulling me closer to him, "but don't play with my—"

"I promise not to break your heart, Leila," Denis said, and the promise Anders had made to Myrna more than thirty years ago popped into my mind.

"I hope not," I whispered.

"It may be wise to return to the party before anyone notices our absence," Denis suggested. "I'll find you later."

I rose from the chair, and Denis did the same, holding the door open for me to enter the ballroom. As soon as we were inside, I went to the buffet table where a range of dishes from French pastries with cheeses to meats, bread in different shapes and flavors, and an abundance of fruits and vegetables were displayed attractively. Five candles burned on top of a chocolate cake, one for each decade of Drew's life, as Tessa had suggested. I forgot about Liz and her mischief as I surveyed the décor. Drew was beaming with a light I didn't know he possessed, chatting animatedly with Sam and Irene. He pointed at the screen where a slide show with events from his life had just begun to roll. There was Drew as a child playing soccer, and then it was Drew as a teenager driving an old Mustang. The next slide showed Drew in college with a group of his friends, another one showed Drew and Helen on their wedding day, and finally, the last slide showed Drew holding his daughter.

"You've done an outstanding job," Helen said, wiping a tear from the corner of her eyes. "The party is a success. Look at Drew! I haven't seen his face this radiant in a long time."

"It wasn't just me," I said, smiling back at Helen.

"I had a hard time convincing him to come with me out tonight," Hellen said. "I had to threaten him I would go alone if I had too. It always works."

Helen laughed and took a sip of pink champagne from her glass.

I surveyed the room, looking for Denis. People laughing, eating, and chatting filled the elegant ballroom. Then a hue of red caught my eye. *Liz!* Something about that woman made me uneasy. Hiccups shook my

Unveiled Secrets

chest when I saw Denis sitting in front of the piano. He leaned toward the keys and pressed them once. All eyes turned toward him, and the band stopped playing.

"I didn't know Denis played the piano," Helen whispered in my ear.

"Me neither," I said, catching his eye above all the people in the ballroom.

I remembered the stroke of Denis's fingers on my skin as he touched the keys so softly. I wanted to feel them again. Denis signaled me to approach, and I nodded. I turned toward the table, set my glass down, and lost the power to speak when I saw Liz already at his side, with a hand on Denis's shoulder. I took a deep breath and looked at Tessa instead. She was at the bar with a bottle of red wine keeping her company.

"I believe we nailed this party," Tessa said. "Did you see Drew's face? Isn't he the happiest man on the planet?" she asked when I sat on the chair next to hers.

Tessa giggled and hiccupped from the many cups of champagne she had consumed. When she lost her balance, I grabbed her elbow and led her to the refreshments' table.

"Eat something, Tessa, to sober you up," I suggested.

Tessa had just broken up with her boyfriend and was having problems coping with the loss. They had been together for two years. When he had said he wanted to talk to her, she hoped he would propose. Instead, he told her he had fallen in love with another woman, and he was moving out. It came as a shock to everyone, particularly to Tessa, a woman in love. How was it that the ones we love the most turned out to hurt us the most? First, it was George, and then Denis, and now, Tessa's ex-boyfriend. Although Denis had just denied he had anything to do with Liz, it was obvious that their relationship was strange. They still had unfinished business, and I felt caught in the middle. Tessa had been right all along. Men like Denis thought they could have everything at the mere snap of their fingers.

I turned toward Tessa. Rivers of black mascara ran down her cheeks. I grabbed a napkin and wiped her face while she picked up a

Carmen Monica Oprea

macaroon and bit into it. No man, regardless of how handsome or how much you loved him, was worth that kind of pain. Seeing Tessa heartbroken scared me to death.

"He left me for a skinny girl he met at work. He had gone out with that girl for four months before he decided to tell me. Can you believe that, Leila? Damn them all! We can live without men," Tessa said amid pitiful sobs.

"You're probably right, sweetheart. You'll sort it all out, but not tonight," I said.

The perspective of painful heartache left me wondering if I had entered a game whose rules were too hard to play. Life had a unique sense of humor. People caught with their guard down were the ones who suffered the most, and I didn't want to be one of them. If Denis stayed away from me, then I could protect my heart. I would tell him tomorrow morning that we must end it.

Tessa drowned her sorrows in glass after glass of champagne, chased with wine and scotch, and then a hint of liqueur. I had no intention of following in her footsteps. There had to be another way, a safer way to move forward, and I was determined to find it. I pulled my cell from my purse and called for a taxi. I looked for Denis and wanted to tell him I was taking Tessa home when I locked my eyes with Liz's, who became Denis's shadow. I could swear Liz threw me a hateful, victorious look, as an undying warning to stay away from them. After I had picked up my purse, I grabbed Tessa's arm and helped her into the elevator. As the party's sounds soon faded, the pain in my heart grew. I put Tessa into a taxi, sat next to her, and gave the taxi driver her home address.

We both needed a distraction, and I knew just the right one.

Five

Tessa's apartment was on the opposite side of the town. I decided to stay overnight with her instead of heading toward my flat. After tucking her into bed, I looked through her closet and picked out a pair of shorts and a T-shirt to change. I sneaked a look at her, crying in her sleep, and then sat on the rocking chair, lost in my thoughts. The grinding of the rocking chair back and forth on the floor merged with Tessa's sobs for a good share of the night.

Denis had hurt me all over again, and, ironically, I was offering comfort and advice when I barely dared to face my situation. In time, Tessa would find the power to heal and move forward—just as I had done when George had left me for my best friend and after my mother had passed away. Stinging tears ran free, and I did nothing to wipe them away. They lingered on my cheeks for a while before dropping onto my bended knees. I would come out of this situation with Denis. But just as Tessa would need time to heal, so did I.

Then, I thought of the diary waiting for me on my mother's bed. What if love hadn't been as strong as Myrna had hoped when she ventured, head on, into a marriage with a man she barely knew? And how do you even recognize the one you want to spend the rest of your life with? How do you know if you made the right choice? There must be certain signs of recognition, a revelation of sorts. I fell asleep pondering these questions, swaying between my love story and Myrna's.

The ring of the coffeemaker woke me up. I followed the caramel aroma to the kitchen and witnessed the slamming of pots, the breaking of cups, and the opening and closing of drawers at lightning speed. I stopped in the doorway and watched Tessa's manic gestures. She slammed two steaming cups of coffee along with freshly baked croissants, butter, and honey on the round cherry wood table.

"Breakfast is ready. Would you care to join me?" Tessa asked when she saw me. Her eyes were puffy and red, her voice hoarse, and I wondered if she was still dizzy from the drinks.

"Are you feeling better? You sobbed most of the night."

Carmen Monica Oprea

Tessa shot me a stare. "Do I look like I'm feeling better? Here, have a cup of coffee. Then go and take a shower. Your mascara ran all over your face. You look awful."

I barely recognized Tessa under all that sarcasm, and I just knew I had to come up with a solution, and fast, to get my old friend back. Time was running out. Tessa needed a diversion, a new purpose in life, at least until she was strong enough to see the sunny side of things as she once did. I took a sip of the coffee, its taste bittersweet inside my mouth. Tessa sat down on a chair across from me and cut a croissant in two, spreading butter and honey on one half and handing me the other half. I declined with a shake of my head. The first bite merged with the tears running down her cheeks. She chewed on it for a while and then she set the rest of the croissant on her plate, sighing. I stretched out my arm and wiped her tears. She picked a napkin and blew her nose.

"I love this song," I said when our favorite song played on the radio station.

"Enough of this madness," Tessa said and leaned back in her chair. "You need a shower, and I need to stop feeling sorry for myself."

"My thoughts exactly," I said, not entirely confident that I was the right person to offer her comfort at all.

My thoughts turned to Denis and Liz, and to their strange relationship. I wondered if he had left the party with her, and my heart ached at the thought of them together.

I must stop thinking of him. I must.

"I'll go and take a shower," I said, emptying the rest of the coffee in the sink and leaving the kitchen.

My stomach clenched with a sudden feeling of nausea, and I rubbed my skin with the remainder of the mint oil in a bottle on the bathtub.

"Why don't you come with me to meet the kids at St. Anne's? We could use a change of scenery, don't you agree?" I yelled at Tessa.

"I'm not good with kids," Tessa said.

Unveiled Secrets

Her excuse sounded lame to me. I shook my head and dried my hair before exiting the bathroom. Tessa had let me borrow a pair of jeans and a clean t-shirt. I brushed my hair for a few minutes and then returned to the kitchen.

"It's not a big deal," I said.

Tessa shrugged, then she sighed. "When do we leave?"

"Now, if you drive," I said.

"Still afraid?"

"I don't think I'll ever learn how to drive. Not after my mother's death."

Tessa and I found her car parked between a Toyota and a Volvo. I sat in the passenger's seat, put the seatbelt on, and held the handle above the window firmly. Tessa fixed her sunglasses and handed me a pair of oversized glasses while the engine came to life with a roar.

"How about you tell me why you are so attached to those orphans?"

"I was adopted when I turned five. My mother didn't change my last name. When I asked her about my biological parents, she said I would find out when the time was right."

I wiped the sweat from my forehead, pretending the sun was too bright and, with a weak attempt at a smile, I continued. "My mother always had a melancholic look when she thought of certain things from the past. She didn't tell me what she was thinking about, and I respected her privacy. But now I wish I would have insisted she told me, forced her to open up to me."

Tessa's face brightened as she looked out the window. The city remained behind, with all the noises and its hot asphalt, green rolling hills replacing them. The winding road followed the shape of the river, and since it was only six on a Saturday morning, we still had the highway to ourselves.

"It must have been hard for you to live without knowing the truth about your real parents," Tessa said.

67

Carmen Monica Oprea

"I always wondered who they were and what tragic affair influenced their decision to give me up. My mom knew their story, but with her gone, I'm left only with unanswered questions. Gabriela made sure that I went to the right schools, and that I befriended the right people, but she didn't give me the only thing I wanted—the truth."

"Your mother died a few months ago," Tessa said.

"Five. My mom was on her way back from the orphanage when a truck hit her. She died at the hospital. After her death, I continued her work, to heal," I said.

And all of the sudden, the sensation of being alone in the world brought a knot to my throat. It was a pain like the one I felt when my mother died. It caught in my throat, making it hard to breathe.

"I can't even imagine what you went through."

"These kids need love and understanding. They make my pain seem insignificant. You'll understand when you meet them," I added. ,

Tessa patted my hand when I fell silent, and then she concentrated on the road ahead.

"There is something else."

"What?" she asked.

"Before she died, Gabriela told me to find my real mother, and she invited me to read an old diary she kept in her room."

"A diary? It sounds mysterious. Maybe you are the result of a forbidden love affair, and your real parents had to put you up for adoption to protect you."

I looked at Tessa and shook my head, chuckling. "Your imagination never ceases to amaze me. It's a love story between a writer named Myrna and a businessman named Anders."

"Do you know them?"

"No, she never mentioned them."

68

Unveiled Secrets

"And?"

"They got married and seemed to have lived a happy life. Myrna marked the passage of time in her journal."

"Do you think they may be your parents?" Tessa asked.

"I don't know, Tessa. I wish I could tell you more."

Thoughts of Myrna and Anders invaded my mind, and I wondered if they were, in fact, my parents and Tessa had been right about her assumptions. My mother was like that, always thinking of the people she had left behind, at the ones who had touched her heart, more than she thought of herself. Gabriela continually tried to fix broken pieces, from the vases she rescued from the flea market to the children in dire need of love, who waited for her at St. Anne's.

"We should stop at the toy shop and buy gifts for the kids," I said.

"You're the boss," Tessa said and took a sharp left into the Toyland parking lot.

It seemed the whole world was shopping at Toyland. I grabbed a teddy bear and sweets for the children and a few water guns. The huge bear occupied the most space in the backseat of the car. It was a gift for Louisa, who turned five today. She reminded me a lot of myself when I was that same age—pigtails on each side of her round face and freckles. It was one of the few memories I had of myself at that age.

"We're almost there. I can see the rooftop of the orphanage," I said.

Old oak trees guarded the path, looking like watchful guardians with their branches lifted toward the sky. The winding road was shady and narrow, in total contrast to the highway's openness. Tessa parked the car in front of the rusty metal gates, and we waited for someone to acknowledge our presence. A tall nun dressed in dark clothes, as the habit required, emerged from behind the bushes hedging the dirt road that led from the gates all the way to the building. I recognized Sister Mary with a beatific smile on her lips and a chaplet in her hands.

Carmen Monica Oprea

"They are waiting for you in the garden," Sister Mary said. "The kids don't want to cut the cake without you. Hurry, hurry!"

We followed the nun. Sister Mary chatted about the weather, the heat, and the holes she had discovered in the convent's ceiling. Then, she reminded me of how the children missed my mother and how happy they were to see me coming to her place. Giggles and shouts came from the playground where the kids played. Their toys included two swings, a sandbox, a slide rusted by time, and a treehouse hanging from an ancient oak tree. Boys and girls from one to ten years old were running around, shouting, and teasing each other. A few kids were throwing sand at each other; others played with the toys used by many before them. They wore plain cotton garments of different colors, some mismatched, but in good condition. I made a note on my cell phone to buy new clothes for them as soon as I returned to the city, along with new toys for the playground.

Tessa walked behind us, carrying the chocolates and the water guns we had bought for a water fight later in the afternoon. I turned around and looked at her face. The sadness had left her eyes, and I could see that her qualms had faded when she stood in front of the children.

Tessa leaned toward me and whispered in my ear. "So many children! What brought them here?"

"Misfortune," I said.

"Unfit parents," Sister Mary said, turning around and coming to an abrupt stop. "Marcus, stop throwing sand at Anna."

"But she started it!" Marcus said, throwing another fist of sand into the girl's hair before he wiped his palms on his pants.

Tessa giggled, and I pretended not to notice as her features softened once more. She began looking like the woman I had come to know for the past months.

"Leila, you're here," a boy with curly red hair and blue eyes shouted while he ran toward me. "The birthday party can finally start."

"I lost a tooth yesterday," Michael, a seven-year-old boy with large freckles on his nose said, sticking his tooth in my face. "I wanted to show it to you before I put it under my pillow for the Tooth Fairy to get it.

Unveiled Secrets

Sister Mary says she collects them and gives them back to us when we get older. Is that right?"

I didn't have time to answer. Michael had lowered his voice before he continued, "Between you and me, I don't think so. Old people have no teeth left."

"If Sister Mary said it, then you must believe her. She wouldn't lie to you, would she?" I asked, tousling his hair. A smile spread across my face as I watched the little boy hiding the tooth in his pocket and patting the place as if he had just buried treasure.

"Now, children, you must behave. Leila has brought a friend, and we should use our best manners," Sister Mary said, hiding a smile in the few wrinkles around her pursed lips.

"Let them be, Sister Mary. I like making them happy," I said as I stroked Michael's hair. "Children, say hello to Tessa. She is a good friend of mine, and she has brought you presents. Why don't you go and help her unload the car?"

Tessa shrugged her shoulders, panic in her eyes as the children crowded around her. They touched her skin, the color of cappuccino, and played with her impossibly long caramel hair. Tessa was born in Hawaii and had arrived in the mainland with her first husband. After a marriage that lasted far too long, they had split up, and he had moved back to the island he loved more than he loved her. Tessa had quickly adapted to the chic lifestyle in New York, and she had just celebrated her twelfth year in the city.

"Let's go," Tessa said.

Shouting and shoving one another to reach for Tessa's hands, the children followed her to the car while I spotted Louisa all by herself at the swing. I approached her, holding the teddy bear in front of me.

"Hello, birthday girl. Come and play with me!"

Louisa turned around and burst out laughing when she came face-to-face with the fluffy pink animal with black eyes and a nose the size of a button. She hugged the toy, and I felt my heart melting like an ice cube under the sun at the sight of the girl kissing her new friend.

Carmen Monica Oprea

"He is handsome and soft," Louisa said about her new toy. "I've been waiting for you to cut the cake that Sister Mary baked for my birthday. Let's hurry."

Louisa jumped off the swing and took my hand.

In the meantime, Tessa returned to the playground with the rest of the packages, and we helped the children unwrap them. Then when Sister Mary whistled, all formed a line, Tessa and me at the end, and we entered the kitchen. The pale lemon color of the walls and the waxed floors shining in the light were the results of my mother's work over the last year. There were a few cabinets and a long rectangular table made of cherry wood. Everyone took a seat at the table, and Sister Mary cut the chocolate cake with blueberry filling and cream cheese, Louisa's favorite.

"Who's ready for a water fight?" I asked when the last remnants of the cake had disappeared into hungry mouths.

Nuns and children rushed outside into the playground while Tessa and I followed them closely. We filled the guns with water and split the kids into two teams. Tessa was captain of the boys' team, and I was designated the leader of the girls' team. It took us an entire afternoon to decide who the winners were. We finally agreed that it was a tie and gave everyone a lollipop, as a reward for a job well done.

Night had fallen by the time we had left the orphanage and reached the highway. The only sounds came from the radio. Tessa said nothing while she drove me home, and I could tell her heart was at peace.

"That was the most reviving experience I have had in years," Tessa said when we finally stopped in front of my building.

"I knew you would like it," I said.

"We should do it again."

"They are always in need of help around there."

I blew Tessa a kiss and entered the building. After the happy moments spent with the children, when worries about Liz and Denis and Tessa's experience with the cheating boyfriend had faded into the background, it wasn't quite comfortable returning to the reality of an

Unveiled Secrets

empty apartment. I took a quick shower, which was refreshing, and after I had wrapped myself in my favorite pajamas, pink and black cotton, I picked up the diary from the bed.

***

February 20th, 1972

The waiting has ended. She is here. A pink doll with sparkling eyes and the tiniest fingers I have ever seen in my life. She enjoys sleeping in her father's arms, knowing no wrong will touch her if he is around. When he rocks her at night, he hums, and then Anders gets lost in his private thoughts—the world he keeps away from me. I watch them both, father and daughter, immersed in the moon's silver light and the quietness of the winter's long nights. A thin white powder makes the garden look like an enchanted place where the glittering lights give the vision of a lost fairyland. This year we are blessed with a mild winter, and we can take the baby for short walks outdoors. Anders carries her tiny body in his arms, and it gives me great pleasure to watch them.

We are perfect together. Our friends envy us for what we have. But we fight with our fears, and we manage to stay afloat, to go forward, and to concentrate on daily matters. My life navigates between my books and motherhood. Anders attends more business meetings than usual, and he leaves the house for two or three days at a time. When he is back, he locks himself in the nursery, and he stays there for hours. I know Anders is troubled by reasons he doesn't want to share, and I'm scared. He acts differently from the man I married.

"Clarisse, I will be away next week for an unexpected meeting," Anders said one evening, and I nodded.

When I watch him leave, my heart sinks a little. I have never become accustomed to the way his life divides between the rest of the world and us. His trade carries him all over the world for months at a time. All I have left is to wait for his return. Anders inherited his family business ten years ago, and he has spent his time traveling and introducing his products to clients around the world. His factory designs the embroidery for a variety of merchandise, from furniture to covers for journals and books. He ordered this diary for my thirty-fifth birthday. The white lilies on a pale-blue silk seem to dance if you peer closely at them. Every page has

Carmen Monica Oprea

a flower with three buds inwrought, one for each of us. The sturdy stem holding the flowers suggests our family's unity.

July 31st, 1972

Some days I have the sensation that something terrible will happen. An evil eye will cast a spell on our home and destroy it. I shake my head to chase away the emotion and then return to the studio to work on a new book. It's my third one. The baby girl in the crib next to my writing desk is still asleep, sucking on her thumb. Her skin is as white as porcelain, and her eyes remind me of her father's. I brought her into this world five months ago, in February. It was a cold morning when she arrived.

How much time passed—two hours or three—before the doorbell rang, its echo reverberating throughout the hallways? The mail carrier handed me a small package and waited for me to sign the delivery slip before he left on his bicycle to carry on with his job for the rest of the day. The return address said one word: "Madrid."

I had traveled to Madrid a few times with Anders. Hotel Agumar on Paseo de la Reina Cristina was our choice since it was close to all the main businesses Anders wished to visit. But the hotel was not on the return address. The package contained some documents in a sealed envelope, a letter for me, and another one for my daughter. When I recognized Anders's writing, panic seized me. All of the sudden, the room became smaller and darker, and I had to sit in the first chair before I opened my letter.

***

I turned to the next page in the diary, where a sheet of paper with a silky texture, folded in two and glued to one side, grabbed my attention. The smell of time invaded my nostrils. The ink had faded a little, and I had to get closer to the desk lamp to read it.

***

My lovely Clarisse,

Believe me when I say you are my only true love. You came into my life like a storm on a hot summer day and saturated my thirst as the raindrops drench the earth's craving. I was always yearning, and nothing

Unveiled Secrets

seemed to satisfy my longing. You stepped into my life, laying balm over my derailed heart and filling the emptiness of the days and nights.

I've never regretted choosing you because you complete me. I am sorry for not growing old with you and watching our little girl blossom. You will do it for both of us. The work and the stress will be double, but your reward will be getting twice the hugs and love. Though delicate on the outside, like the lilies you treasured so much, you were always stronger on the inside than I was.

Don't ever change who you are to make others like you! Be yourself, and the right people will love you just as you are. You were the only one who saw the pain in my eyes when the others believed the smile on my face. And for that, I need to go away. I can't bear to have you witness my fall into a dark and distant world. You will make changes and find within you the power to adjust. Never give up because, with every moment and each day, you will have a chance to start anew. Have faith in yourself, and no stone will remain unturned!

Live life for both of us, filled with happiness, and keep writing. For the extent of my days, I promise to read your books. I couldn't bear to tell you I was dying and there is nothing to be done. The business trips were a cover for finding a cure for my disease. Unfortunate destiny! No treatment exists, just the slow waiting for the end. I didn't want to be a burden to you. You already have so much to deal with, with the baby, the book, and making it through these moments of darkness, and now you need all the power inside you to move forward.

The documents you'll receive in just a matter of days are the selling contract for the business and the trust funds I've opened for the two of you. The other letter is for our daughter, and I will let you decide the best time to give it to her.

Forever yours,

Anders

* * *

I reread the letter; my heart skipped a beat, and my hands became cold. Anders was dying, and he ran away. He couldn't face Myrna. I began crying. I clenched my fists, and my heart throbbed for Myrna and

Carmen Monica Oprea

Anders. He couldn't bear to let his wife see him die, so he decided to leave.

What did Myrna do?

Six

Three weeks had passed since Tessa, and I had gone to St. Anne's. I didn't see Denis before he left for Spain the Monday following Drew's party. There was no apology, no goodbye note, not even a text from him. Drew thanked me for the surprise birthday party, and Tessa recovered somewhat from breaking up with her boyfriend. Every night, I read a few more pages from the diary and thought of Myrna and her baby girl. Then I thought of Anders, imagining just how terrified he must have been to discover he was dying, and he would spend his last moments far from his family, and my heart ached for all of them.

This Friday morning Denis me an e-mail and asked me if I would like to have dinner with him. I replied that I already had plans. I didn't think he would like my answer or my refusal to meet him.

It was the usual third Saturday of the month, and I was getting ready to meet Tessa at the supermarket when a sharp knock on my door startled me. *Tessa's arrived*, I thought. Then I remembered telling her when we talked on the phone last night that I would take a taxi and just meet her there. I jerked the door open and came face-to-face with Denis. He was looking fit and tanned. Spain had been good for him.

"What are you doing here? I'm on my way out," I said.

"Then I'm coming with you," Denis said with the same seriousness with which he approached a crucial business matter, and I knew well enough not to argue with him.

"OK, let's go then. Tessa is waiting for me, and with this traffic, we'll be late."

Denis furrowed his eyebrows. "Late? Late for what?"

"Hurry," I said, grabbing my bag and locking the apartment door behind me. I pressed the elevator down button and stormed inside when the door opened, Denis following close behind. I turned around and saw him staring at me with piercing eyes and amusement on his face. The taxi I had requested the previous night was already waiting in the street, and the driver took off fast the moment we settled in.

Carmen Monica Oprea

"We should talk," Denis said.

"Not now," I said, avoiding his eyes. I wasn't going to let him drag me into a conversation regarding his relationship with Liz, which seemed more complicated than I initially suspected. I had decided to keep matters simple, business-like, and to keep my heart to myself.

The traffic was scarce at the early hour, and the taxi driver made a good time. Twenty minutes later Tessa waved from the store's entrance, where she stood surrounded by four overflowing carts.

"Wow, this is a lot of shopping," Denis said, as he jumped out of the taxi. "She has certainly been busy."

I paid the driver and got out of the car after Denis. Tessa used a complex combination of signs—raising her eyebrows, pointing her head into Denis's direction when he wasn't paying attention and shrugging her shoulders—as if asking what he was doing with us. I signaled back that it was a long story and that we didn't have time to go into it now.

"Denis? What a surprise!" Tessa said to him.

Tessa pushed the first cart to her rented van, and I grabbed the handles of the second one.

"Tessa," Denis said, "it's a surprise indeed."

"Are you here to help?" Tessa asked, looking at the carts on the sidewalk.

"Did you buy out the entire store?" Denis asked.

"I couldn't make up my mind what to buy and what to leave, so I bought it all," Tessa answered with a mischievous grin.

"That much is obvious." Denis chuckled. "Women."

"What is that supposed to mean?" I asked, stopping in front of Denis, with my hands full of shopping bags.

Denis frowned, turned around and then carried the rest of the bags to Tessa's van. Five minutes later we secured the doors and drove away from New York. The sky was tinged with pink, and golden sun rays

78

Unveiled Secrets

filtered through the few clouds hanging in the sky. Rolling green hills replaced the city views. I played with the radio's button for a while and settled for a jazz station.

"I didn't realize you and Tessa shared the same interests," Denis said, raising a brow.

"It's understandable. How would you know when you're barely in New York?" I asked, rolling down the window. A breeze laced with the fragrance of grass and wildflowers filled the inside of the car. I inhaled a couple of times, closing my eyes. The third Saturday of the month was ever so special. It reminded me of my mother's charitable work.

"I didn't know you two were a couple. You fooled everyone, acting like nothing was going on, Leila," Tessa said, giving me that look, the questioning look—brows lifted, lips pursed, and the tapping of her fingers on the steering wheel. "How long have you two been together, Denis?"

Tessa stared at Denis through the mirror and waited impatiently for his answer. A song played on the radio, and when she repeated her question, I growled.

"Tessa, this nonsense will stop immediately," I said.

"But I haven't done anything," Tessa said.

Visibly suffocated by the direction of our conversation, Denis giggled in the backseat. I turned toward him and stared. He shrugged his shoulders, pointing toward Tessa with his chin. I rolled my eyes, not entirely sure how to create a diversion. I remembered telling Tessa that nothing was going on between Denis and me and that whatever brief affair had started a month ago was now history.

I didn't like complicated love triangles where someone dated someone else who was someone else's love interest. The experience with George would always stand as the perfect reminder of love gone wrong for the rest of my days. Life had given me a lesson, and I had learned from it and moved on. I couldn't imagine how Denis would answer Tessa's question about the nature of our relationship, which had ended while still in the embryonic phase.

79

Carmen Monica Oprea

He said, "We started seeing each other around Drew's birthday party. I fell in love with her lavender eyes."

Denis blew me a kiss, and his face brightened. I felt my face get hot, and I looked into the mirror. A shade of magenta took over my otherwise-pale skin, and I began counting, eyes on the road. I hadn't expected him to answer the question that way.

"So where are we going?" Denis asked.

"To see the children from the St. Anne monastery," Tessa answered matter-of-factly.

Denis leaned forward on the back of my chair, his hands tightening on the backseat. He coughed, and a few minutes passed before he talked again, his tone sprinkled with shock.

"A monastery? I am going to spend my afternoon in a church filled with kids?"

"I can stop the car if you wish," Tessa said.

Denis moaned. "No, no, don't worry. I'll be all right."

I turned around and looked at him again. Denis's expression was precious—his eyes were as big as saucers, and hair stuck up like a little boy's. We hadn't spoken since he had left for Spain, other than exchanging the usual pleasantries and questions and answers about work. Denis supervised the opening of a new hotel in Vigo Bay, the city where Myrna and Anders had lived a long time ago, the same town where Clair had invited me to come after my mother had passed away. Although Denis didn't apologize for the time he had spent with Liz, the fact that he had shown up at my apartment the morning after his arrival, made my heart flutter with pride.

Sister Mary had called Friday morning to let me know that they had hired a handyman from the nearby village to repair the holes they had discovered in the roof not too long ago. Lightning had hit one of an old tree's branches. That broke enough shingles to cause an enormous crack in the already aged roof. The rain had cascaded inside the church, damaging the wood floors and the walls, and they were in dire need of help.

Unveiled Secrets

The two-hour drive ended, and the old nunnery appeared like a castle covered in ivy, its high towers reigning over the surrounding hills. Joyful screams were coming from the courtyard, just as I had expected, a sound I had come to love. Tessa stopped the car in front of the gates. I rang the bell and was waiting for a nun to acknowledge our presence when a movement caught my attention. One boy stuck his leg through the bars, hoping he would find a way to escape. Right behind him, a nun grabbed him by his T-shirt, blocking his escape.

"Marcus, where do you think you're going?" Sister Lucia asked, as she pulled the boy back and signaled us to approach. She took her keys out from a hidden pocket under her habit and unlocked the gates.

"What's going on, Sister Lucia? Is Marcus giving you a hard time again?" I asked.

"The same old stuff," Sister Lucia answered, stroking the boy's long hair.

Marcus, well-known for his rebellious attitude, had managed to sneak away from the monastery a few weeks ago. He had made it all the way to the highway before the highway patrol found him and delivered him back to the nuns. Although only seven, Marcus thought he was prepared to be on his own without those insistent nuns bossing him around as he had explained to me when we talked on the phone.

"Marcus, we can use your help, little man. The car is packed. Do you think you can help us unload it? Can you handle the task?" I asked him.

Marcus looked at me, suspicion in his eyes, deciding whether or not to take me seriously.

"What's in it for me if I help you?" Marcus asked.

"A treat," Tessa answered.

Marcus shrugged his shoulders and approached the car. He picked up the first bag and turned toward me expectantly.

Carmen Monica Oprea

"Where do you want me to put them?" Marcus asked. "The kitchen is filled with paint and brushes. There is barely any room on the floor."

"Come with me." Sister Lucia led the way to a classroom where the children studied during the week. "You can put them here. We'll sort through them later," she said. "Thank you for everything you do for us, Leila. St. Anne will protect you. Your mother would have been proud of you."

Sister Lucia turned toward me and kissed my forehead before her gaze fixed on Tessa. She said to Tessa, "The children can't wait for more of your cooking lessons. Even the boys are addicted to cooking now. At least it keeps them occupied during rainy days."

Sister Lucia turned toward Denis, who leaned on the door of the car, his arms packed with bags, and she asked, "And who are you, young man?"

I had never seen Denis flustered before, and it was quite a sight.

"Denis Fraga. Your place is quiet, peaceful. How long has this monastery been around?" he asked and walked alongside Sister Lucia, leaving Tessa and me to unload the car.

I grabbed a few bags and walked right behind them, listening to every word Sister Lucia said.

"St. Anne was founded one hundred years ago by the Anglican and Episcopal sisterhood as a place for prayer, study, silence, and service. God gave us a mission to help people in distress. These children are the ones who need protection and guidance," Sister Lucia said. "I must go now. Make yourselves at home."

After she had blessed us, Sister Lucia went to the chapel for her morning prayers. As soon as she disappeared, I eyed Sister Mary running toward us, an alarmed expression on her face. She examined Denis from head to toe before grabbing his arm.

"You must be the handyman. Thank you for coming." Sister Mary panted and drew mouths full of air before she continued, "Follow me, and I'll show you what you need to repair. You must do it today, since a storm

Unveiled Secrets

is in the air, and we just finished fixing the floors and the walls. Come, walk with me." Sister Mary pushed Denis toward the monastery.

I checked my cell phone. It was nine in the morning. Although the sky was clear, and the air was still, on the edge of the horizon, gray clouds were forming. They were still off in the distance, but the weather forecaster had predicted powerful storms coming in from the ocean. When Sister Mary encouraged Denis to follow, he didn't object. He turned around and winked. My mouth opened. Tessa had caught up with me, and we walked side by side.

"I didn't think there was anyone who could silence Denis. Did you see that? He followed Sister Mary without a word of complaint," I said. "I can't wait to see what he's up to."

"This is quite a sight, considering he likes to yap about everything," Tessa added, struggling with the weight of the box in her arms.

After I had dropped the bags I was carrying on the kitchen floor, I left Tessa alone with the kids and exited through the back door into the garden. The sound of shingles ripping from the roof and falling filled the air. I looked up to see Denis juggling a hammer and nails and the new shingles.

"Move the car out of the way!" he yelled from the roof.

"Got it!"

I couldn't believe Denis hadn't contradicted Sister Mary when she had mistaken him for the handyman. He began replacing broken shingles with new ones, the sound of the hammer hitting the nails breaking the silence of the morning. His muscles tensed when he lifted his arm and hit the nails, and I could see beads of sweat running down his back. My clothes were already soaked from the heat.

The nunnery's lands spread over three hills blanketed by oak trees. I could make out the hum of a spring passing close to the vegetable garden. Remembering my promise to help in the garden, I walked toward the back of the monastery after I moved the car. The dry soil and the plants needed a lot of rain, and the upcoming storm was heaven-sent. Tomatoes had ripened on the vine. I snapped one and ate it, the sweet

Carmen Monica Oprea

juice tickling my tongue and the inside of my cheeks. I began pulling weeds to give the plants room to breathe, and I lost track of time. A few hours passed. My hands were dirty, and I had broken two nails. Hearing a noise right behind me, I jumped and knocked over a basket filled with ripened bell peppers and cherry tomatoes that one of the sisters had left in the garden. Under a bush, not far from me, Louisa rocked the toy she got for her birthday. She signaled me to keep quiet, and I followed her play.

"What are you doing here, sweetheart?"

"Hush," Louisa whispered, touching a finger to her lips.

"Let's put him to bed," I suggested.

Louisa slipped her tiny hand into mine. In the vicinity, I heard the hammer hitting the shingles and smiled. Denis was busy. There were no numbers to crunch or problems to solve, other than the repairs in a place forgotten by time. I was still chuckling when I entered the bedroom. Twelve beds lined the room, six on each side, pressed against walls with peeling paint. Louisa's bed was the one closest to the window since she liked to gaze at the sky before drifting off to sleep. The toy had a crib near her bed. I had bought it one month ago so that she could put her toys to bed. I had grown fonder of Louisa more than of any other child because she reminded me of another child, about the same age, more than thirty years ago.

The image of a slender woman, whip-thin, with sunrise-gold hair shrouding her face, came back to me as if in a dream. I remembered her eyes, blue and sad. Apart from that memory, everything else had faded away. Who was the woman, and why did she never return?

After we had left the toy in the crib, we left the dormitory and joined a loud group outside. Several nuns closed the lids on the paint cans to shield the paint from being spoiled, while Tessa removed the dirty fabrics covering the floors to protect them from paint drips. Louisa joined a group of children in charge of cleaning the paint brushes, their laughter filling the air. I looked for Denis. He wasn't on the roof anymore. My heart skipped a beat as I shouted his name as loud as my lungs permitted.

"Why are you screaming?" Denis asked.

Unveiled Secrets

Hearing his voice close by made me jump. I turned around. Sweat dripped from his hair, trickling down his neck and following the pattern of his body.

"I was afraid that something bad had happened to you," I said.

"I haven't worked this hard in ages," Denis said, gazing from me to the new roof.

I patted his arm. "Thanks for tagging along."

"It reminded me of the life I used to have on my parents' farm. A life I left as soon as I was old enough," Denis whispered, a shadow crossing his eyes.

"I never knew you grew up on a farm."

Denis chuckled. "You don't know a lot of things about me. I sold the farm because I wasn't cut out to be a farmer. Manual labor wasn't exactly my favorite. I still remember the dust, the sweat, and the long hours under a dreadfully hot sun."

Sister Mary stopped in front of Denis with a shirt in her hand. "I thought you'd like a clean one," she said.

"Thank you, Sister," Denis replied. He pulled his dirty one over his head. My eyes lingered along the lines of his back, taking into view his strong muscles.

"Nice muscles," I said.

"Thanks," Denis said, turning around. His eyes flickered, a smile curling the corner of his mouth. He put on the clean shirt from Sister Mary and threw the dirty one in a laundry basket.

"Here, young man, this is all we can afford to give for your troubles," Sister Mary said, extending a check to Denis.

Denis blushed. He pushed the check back into the nun's hand and held her hand. His voice was soft when he spoke.

"I'm happy I could help, Sister Mary." His expression was kind.

Carmen Monica Oprea

"But your work," Sister Mary continued.

I smiled. "Denis is a friend, Sister. He is not the man you hired. We work together at the Golden Leaves Hotel. He wanted to tag along with Tessa and me today," I said.

"I see," Sister Mary said, tucking the check back in her pocket. "Thank you for all your help."

"It's been my pleasure," Denis said.

Just then the first raindrops began falling, pelting our bodies. It smelled like wet dirt, a mushy smell, earthy. I lifted my chin and caught the first drops, their touch soft on my lips. We walked back inside. The children returned to their rooms, resting after the day's hard chores. They had learned to comply with the sisters' requests without complaint. It was like a game. Life wasn't easy for them in the monastery, even if the nuns did their best to provide enough moral support until the children could be placed in foster care or adopted by families who desired a child. The sisters told me that many of the children they had raised over the years donated money or volunteered their time to the monastery. Some stayed out of trouble and got jobs in the city. Others ended up in jail.

"God has a mission for all," Sister Mary always said. "We are merely the means of completing his wish to look after the ones touched by misfortune."

I took Denis's hand, holding it tight. His palm was tense, his fingers tightening around mine. After we had said our farewells, Tessa and I got into the van with Denis as the designated driver. We waved to the sisters until they merged with the horizon. I rested my head against the cushion of the back seat and closed my eyes. I heard Tessa talking to Denis, but I couldn't make sense of their conversation. I was too tired to think about Elisabeth Thurber's name and the upcoming fashion show. I didn't remember the trip back to New York nor Denis carrying me in the apartment.

I leaned against Denis's body while he unlocked the door. "Are you going to make it?" Denis asked.

"Of course," I said, dragging my feet to the bathroom and hoping a hot shower would wake me up. Refreshed, I returned to the living room

86

Unveiled Secrets

and looked for Denis. He was sound asleep on the couch, still wearing his jeans and T-shirt. I didn't want to wake him up. After I had covered him with a blanket, I kissed him gently on the cheek. *Sweet dreams, my love!* I returned to my bedroom, leaving the door leading to the living room wide open. As I lay on the bed and thought of the strangeness of the day, I decided to read from the diary until I fell asleep.

***

August 30th, 1972

Weeks passed, and the sensation of betrayal and anger replaced the shock. Anders had left us because he was dying. My husband was sick, and he chose to live the last of his days alone, with no one to look after him and nothing to protect him from pain. What should I tell my daughter about her father? How would I survive in his absence when he had been my strength? I have no one to turn to and nobody to talk about my pain. I couldn't reach my brother, and my friend was in New York managing her pottery business. I picked up the phone a few times and dialed her number. And when she finally answered, I told her what had happened, and she assured me that she would be on the first flight to Spain. My sweet friend will be my strength in this dark hour of my life. I can't bring myself to look at the documents Anders left for me.

Gabriela arrived in Vigo Bay on a Friday morning. It was a gray summer day. Clouds gathered in the sky as if to cry for my pain. I told her the story, and she offered to stay for as long as I needed her. With Gabriela's assistance, I contacted Eric Franzone, a private detective from Vigo Bay, famous for finding missing people like Anders. He had forty years of experience in the field. Through Eric, I discovered that Anders suffered from Chondrosarcoma, a cancer of the bones starting in the cartilage and affecting joints and skeleton, especially in men.

Since he had found out about the illness, Anders had reached out to doctors from England and America in hopes they would find a cure. There is no cure for this cancer, but only the lonely waiting for the final breath. I finally understood the reason for his withdrawal into that foreign world that I was not allowed to follow. He wanted to protect me from this brutal truth, even at his own expense. The chances of survival were minimal, and in many cases, the patients lost arms or legs. Ashamed of

Carmen Monica Oprea

not being strong for me up until the very end, he wouldn't allow me to see him as an invalid.

***

October 7th, 1972

I can't stay in this house and continue my life as if he doesn't exist. He is somewhere waiting for me to come and rescue him from his darkness. His presence is in everything surrounding me. How I wish he had had faith in me! Why didn't he trust in my strength?

Eric's office, located close to the marina, had large windows overlooking the sea. Our first meeting took place in a day without a bit of sun, only the clouds hanging loose in a sky ready to cry. I gave him our financial records and Eric informed me that his search would start with Dr. Albert Gonzalez in Madrid. When I offered to accompany him, Eric stopped me, saying it would be quicker if he went alone. He would call with the details of the meeting, so I had nothing left to do but wait.

I asked Eric to find Anders at any cost. Even if it was just one day, I wanted him to live that day next to me and not alone in a cold world with people who didn't care about either of us. If life gave us just crumbs to enjoy, then we would feast on our crumbs, creating memories to last a lifetime. This way, in the final moments, we would be able to part with a smile on our faces, knowing that we had lived in a few years more than others did their entire lives together.

I am sure that one day I will find him. Why did he hide this terrible truth? Anders had always put my needs above his and didn't care if he spoiled me. As a proud man, he didn't want sympathy, not even mine. I asked myself what demon made him think I could live even one more day without knowing if he was well or haunted by a menacing pain. Was anyone around to hold his hand and tell him everything would be all right? I believe Eric will reach Anders if he is still alive. I've entrusted my fate into the detective's hands. He will help me bring Anders back where he belongs—home.

My friend tends to my child while I chase a ghost. She is more a mother to my baby than I am, but somehow, I can't stop the race of finding my husband. Rocking the baby in her arms, singing lullabies, all of these things are meant to be mine. I have become a shell of what I used to

Unveiled Secrets

be. I don't eat unless Gabby forces me. She is wonderful with both of us, and I am grateful to have her in my life.

Carmen Monica Oprea

Seven

Waves of light bathed the room. A soft breeze blew a mixture of fragrances inside the apartment—rain, asphalt, and exotic scents from the orchids I nursed in pots by the window. Gabriela said that orchids were the ancient gods' favorite flowers, and I agreed with her.

Thousands of nails pricked my muscles. My body was still sore from working in the garden the previous day. I lifted my head off the pillow and almost flew out of bed the moment I met Denis's eyes—honey sprinkled with gold—less than twenty inches away. I panicked. A knot caught in my throat, and I began coughing. My voice sounded hoarse when I finally managed to put a few words together.

"I thought you were asleep," I said, watching as Denis shook his head and pursed his lips.

"I woke up not too long ago, but I liked watching you sleep."

I traced the contour of Denis's face with the tip of my finger. Denis closed his eyes when my fingertip lingered on his lips. His breath felt hot. He leaned over, the weight of his body when he sat on the mattress pushing me straight into his arms. Our lips met in a kiss we both longed for, soft in the beginning, deepening as we explored each other, leaving us yearning and trembling for more. He rose from the bed and sat me on his lap, my legs encircling his half-naked body. I kissed the muscles on his chest as my hands caressed his back, following the line of his spine. He moaned in my ear and tightened his embrace.

"I want you," he whispered in a hoarse voice. "Now."

"Me, too," I whispered in his ear.

My body was burning, every ounce of resistance dissipating when Denis followed the line of my neck and stopped on my breast, playing with it, teasing, and biting slowly on the nipple. I played with his hair as our bodies joined. Waves of liquid heat filled the emptiness in my body. The sound of our hearts roaring against each other was all I could think about as he waited for me to recapture my senses, rocking me in his arms.

Unveiled Secrets

"I have something to say," Denis said, after a few minutes, looking deep into my eyes. "I like women, but I don't fall in love with them. Love is a toxin. Once you fall in love, you lose control of your life, because your heart and mind belong to someone else. You start to do everything to hold on to your loved one and lose all sense of danger. Love makes you as your lover wants you to be."

"Is this all you have to say?" I asked, holding back tears. I looked away as my mind tried to process what Denis had just said.

"Leila, I don't get attached," Denis said, a shadow crossing his eyes. "I thought you should know that what we have is pure, consensual sex and nothing more."

I waited. Denis lifted his chin and gazed into my eyes. "It has nothing to do with you. It's because of my mother."

"I don't understand," I said. "What our relationship has to do with your mom?"

Denis sighed, his forehead touching mine.

"She left when I was young. She ran away with a man she had fallen in love with. I hoped to find her one day, look her in the eye, and ask why she didn't come back."

"She might have had her reasons for running away," I said, thinking of my own story. Although Gabriella had made sure that I had all I desired, I couldn't understand the reason behind her refusal to talk about my parents. I wondered if this was the reason why I was afraid to have a child of my own. What if history repeated itself?

Denis continued, "My father turned bitter because of her. He loved my mother very, very much. He left his own country and his family to be with her. But his love wasn't enough. She talked about seeing the world, doing something more than tending to the family's orchards. When she had the opportunity to run away, she didn't look back. I heard she lives in Singapore with husband number two and their three daughters. She completely erased us from her memory. I worked on the farm until I was big enough to build my destiny. Then I left."

91

Carmen Monica Oprea

"And marriage or a stable relationship is not part of your big plan," I whispered.

"No," he said.

I trembled. There was a fire in his eyes that scared me a little. He hugged me. Our lips met, teasing, and playing again. We had only this moment, no past and no future. We were navigating between feelings stronger than us. I was afraid of myself, of falling in love, of being hurt once again.

"What's this?" he asked, pointing at the diary that lay open on the floor.

"My mother left it to me and wanted me to read it. She said I would find answers to all the questions I had regarding my real parents in this diary."

"That's good news, right?" Denis asked.

"Not sure if they're good or bad," I answered. "All I know is that the answers are on these pages. I can't understand my parents' decision to put me up for adoption."

"What are you waiting for? Go on, read while I take a nap," Denis said.

I leaned over and picked the diary up off the floor. Myrna, Anders, Gabby, and Eric were waiting for me to continue their story.

***

August 30th, 1973

A year passed with no news. It was as if Anders had disappeared from the face of the earth. There was no sign of him, and the uncertainty was worse than death itself. Eric called from Madrid after he had met with Dr. Gonzalez to tell me that Anders had gone from meeting with Dr. Gonzalez in Madrid to London, where he had met Dr. Robert Brown for a second opinion. Dr. Brown had explained to Eric that people who had bone cancer didn't show signs of sickness in the beginning stages of the illness. They would first notice a bony lump and then swelling, leading to limited movement caused by the lump. A pathologist would then analyze the

Unveiled Secrets

composition of the cells in the lump to come up with a diagnosis and to develop a treatment plan. Sadly, Anders's situation required a complete surgical removal of the tumor, limbs amputation being crucial for his survival.

According to Dr. Brown, the rate of survival ranged from five to ten years or even more for those with low-grade tumors. There were no guarantees, and the best avenue for the patient was to stay close to family for moral support and encouragement. Anders decided to deal with the sickness on his own. I missed him terribly, and every day meant living the previous day once again.

Leila learned to walk, and she called Gabby "Mommy." I didn't try to correct it. She hardly spent time with me. When I was at home, it seemed I wasn't there at all. I hid in my bedroom, immersing myself in the fading fragrance of his clothes to remember how Anders used to feel. My heart threatened to explode in my chest. There were days when I screamed as loud as I possibly could in the hopes that he would hear my anguish and return. But everything remained just the same, and all I did was just passing through another day. I never expected such madness to fall upon my family. I didn't plan to become a stranger to my daughter.

I had to accept this cruel reality and hope that one day, Leila would call me "Mother." I forgot how to live, and I followed Anders into the world he had chosen for himself, a world of darkness and suffering. Why did my life turn from a fairy tale into a nightmare?

Sometimes, I played with Leila in the gardens Anders, and I loved so much until a particular flower, or some other thing reminded me of him. Then, my tears would fall, my sobs turning unbearable. Gabby would put her arms around my shaking body, and even if she didn't say a word, I knew she would never leave me alone. She became a mother to both of us, pushing me to write to somehow ease the pain. I listened to her advice, and I wrote until I couldn't write another word. Money was not an issue because Anders had left us enough. Writing eased my suffering and gave me purpose in life.

February 20th, 1974

We celebrated Leila's second birthday in February. We baked her favorite chocolate cake with raspberry filling, and then we ate it together.

Carmen Monica Oprea

She resembled her father—the same lavender eyes and curve of the lips, the same way of sleeping on her right side with her hand under her head and her legs entangled in the sheets—and this acknowledgment made me miss him even more. When she laughed, two dimples formed in her chubby cheeks, and the image of her father reflected on her face. My friends said that time would heal my broken heart, but my heart wasn't healed yet.

Another winter went away, and another spring brought warm weather. I often took Leila to the rose garden, spending hours admiring the reds and the yellows in the rose bushes and listening to the birds. Gabby had returned to New York for the opening of her painted-pottery exposition. It was Leila and me and the torment of my unsettled heart. We talked about her dad when I tucked her in bed at night. I fabricated a story that he had gone on an extended trip to find a treatment for his illness. I assured her that he would be back as soon as his treatment ended. And every night I watched her as she prayed for his safe return. One day I saw her writing Anders's name, folding the paper, and hiding it in her crayon box. When she said her favorite prayer at night, she always asked for her daddy's return.

***

I sat the diary on the bed and paced through the room trying to connect the dots. Myrna and Anders were Gabriela's friends from Spain. And she had another friend in Spain. Gabriela called her Clair. My father had been sick. Probably he died a long time ago. I knew almost nothing about my mother, other than the fact that she had been a writer. I closed the diary and watched Denis, who was sound asleep, then I went to my laptop and typed her name, Myrna Clarisse Elmer.

Links popped up on the screen. I added the word "writer" after her name, and only one link came back. As soon as I clicked on it, a black-and-white picture popped up on the screen, showing a young woman. It was from the 1970s, and the short passage said that she lived in Vigo Bay with her husband, Anders Isidro. She became a widow when she turned forty. She never remarried after her husband's death and lived a secluded life, writing. My mother had curly, light-blonde hair and kind eyes. I couldn't tell their color. But she wore a dress with a floral pattern and pearls at her neck and in her ears. I closed my eyes and concentrated on

94

Unveiled Secrets

my breathing. It wasn't every day that you discovered a missing piece of your life. One parent was dead, and the other one was a total mystery.

I turned toward Denis. He snored softly. I leaned my head on his chest and followed the rhythmical beating of his heart until my own eyes became heavy with sleep.

It was past three in the afternoon when a noise coming from the kitchen woke me up. I peered through the half-open door and saw Denis wearing an apron, slicing red apples.

I giggled and said, "Hi, there."

Denis knitted his brows. "Hi, back. Hungry?"

"Starving."

"Give me five minutes, and I'll have dinner ready."

"Brussel sprouts with apples and sausage crumbles," I mumbled. "It looks amazing already."

Denis stirred the food in the pan, the sizzling of the sausage making my mouth water. I grabbed two plates and handed them to him.

"White or red?" I asked, pointing to the bottles of wine on the kitchen countertop.

"White," Denis said.

Denis filled both plates with generous servings. I poured wine into both glasses and handed Denis one of them.

"To us," I said, swirling the wine in the glass. It reminded me of the giant yellow citrons I passed on my trip through Tuscany last summer.

"To us," he said. "I hope you like it." Denis pointed to the hot food topped with aromatic herbs. I closed my eyes as the apples melted in my mouth.

"Delicious," I said, with my mouth full. "You're a much better cook than I am. I can only prepare the soup."

Carmen Monica Oprea

"Then you'd better stick to the basics," Denis said, and he chuckled. "We have a fashion show this week. Are we ready?"

"Denis, do you want to talk about work now? Do you think this is the best moment to ask me about it?"

"Why waste time?"

"I have something to say about my parents," I started to say just as Denis's cell phone rang and interrupted me.

"Just a second," he said. He rose from the chair and went to the next room, and when he returned five minutes later, he said, "I must run to the airport to pick up Liz. We'll talk later."

"Liz?"

He gave me an apologetic look as he ran out the door, and my fork fell onto the plate. So much for a cozy afternoon and a nice dinner together.

***

Every year at the beginning of fall, a variety of events from business meetings to seminars and fashion shows happened in our hotel. Helen Hyatt's spring collection was the major affair of this week. Her designs were a unique combination of silk, cotton, knit, linen, and wool. The hotel prepared to receive dozens of photographers and guests, and the engineering department put together a spectacle of lights for the end of the show.

Elisabeth Thurber was the star of the show. I couldn't stop the sudden feeling of envy that rose within me when my eyes rested on her lean, toned body. When she didn't perform, she modeled for well-known designers in New York, Paris, and London. Everyone in the hotel was under her spell because Liz had this fantastic gift for telling stories about the art galleries she had visited around the globe, about the remarkable people she had met, about the parties she had attended, and about all the gossip regarding her fellow actors.

Unveiled Secrets

"Isn't she gorgeous?" Irene, the front office assistant manager, asked one evening after the rehearsal had ended and Liz walked out of the bathroom in black leather underwear and no bra.

"She certainly is," I said with a hint of jealousy in my voice.

"I can't wait for the show to end. It's madness everywhere," Irene said, handing Liz a robe.

"Friday is the big day," I added. "Then we're back to normal."

"It is going to be glamorous," Liz added before she closed the door to her dressing room, leaving Irene and me staring at each other.

"I'm going to call it a night," I said and turned toward the front door.

Denis had been out of the town for the past few days and hadn't called even once since Sunday night when he had gone to the airport to pick up Liz. I knew better than to ask for an explanation I wasn't convinced he was prepared to give. I had no time for another excuse, especially not when I had finally discovered who my parents were. I understood that I was always going to be on my own to deal with whatever the future had in store for me. The past few days had been long and exhausting, and it seemed like the preparations for the show would never end. But tomorrow it would be the last rehearsal before the big night, and then it would finally be over. Denis was due to come back, and I decided that it was time to confront him.

I left the hotel and hailed a taxi, and before I knew it, we stopped in front of my apartment. I paid the cab driver. I was anxious for a hot shower and a good night's sleep, but I tossed and turned all night long, thinking that maybe Denis and I weren't meant to be together because we lacked the courage to discuss each other's expectations openly and that Liz had some weird hold on him. My heart ached, and I had an overwhelming need to slap Denis. If I were brave enough, I would have called Denis right then and there and asked him why he had to run to Liz every time she called him.

I poured myself a glass of wine and dropped into a chair, crossing my legs under me. Maybe if I had just trusted in my feelings for Denis and believed him when he had said that we shared something special, my

Carmen Monica Oprea

heart wouldn't be poisoned by insecurity. It was midnight when I finished moping in my disillusion about the fairy-tale love story I had created in my mind and went to bed.

**

Thursday morning brought pearls of light rain from the furrow of clouds above the city. They pinged off the hotel's roof—thin sheets, in the beginning, and getting heavier as the hours passed. The thrashing and echoing over the glass and concrete warned us to remain indoors. I hadn't seen Denis since the morning sales meeting, and it was already seven in the evening. As soon as I reached the first floor, the commotion in the ballroom designated for the fashion show grabbed my attention. Housekeepers, bellmen, and guests were all gathered. The sound of music filled the air. It was the last rehearsal before the next evening's show. Helen's team was going over the order in which the models would perform on stage and the dresses they would wear, their makeup and hairstyles, the intensity and the color of the lights, the flowers bordering the catwalk, and the gifts for the guests.

I peeked through the crowd and spotted Denis in the doorway, studying the ballroom. He was gesturing as he talked to the cameraman and the makeup artist. He wore a leather jacket over pastel shirt and black slacks. Determined to grab his attention, I waved at him. My heart started to drum roll in my ears when he didn't wave back. He always waved back at me, except now. I turned and sighed regretfully. Every cell in my body prickled with awareness. Finally, the music signaled the culminating moment of the show when Liz paraded along the catwalk in her coral pink organza dress, looking every bit like the movie star she was. As she walked down the catwalk, she blew kisses when she passed by Denis. My heart stopped. He caught one and took it to his chest. Millions of questions crossed my mind. Could it be that they were lovers? Had I been blind all this time?

I stepped until my back was plastered against the wall, and I gulped in a mouthful of air. A few tears threatened to break free, and I bit my lip. My mind drifted from the ballroom toward fragments of my unfortunate love story, the one where I was blinded by George and Becca's insensitive approach to life. Perhaps if I had developed a thick skin and acted just like Becca and Liz did, I could raise an invisible shield around my own heart, and thus I would protect myself from further

Unveiled Secrets

heartache. Gabriela would know what to tell me to do. She would guide me out of this darkness that seemed to grow thicker by the hour. Unable to concentrate, I returned to my office and seized my purse and umbrella. I was prepared to head to the only place I knew I would find comfort—my home. I looked around as if trying to register every detail from a life built on shattered dreams, on visions that would never come true, and I turned off the light. It was then that I bumped into Denis. He leaned forward to kiss me. I dodged and turned my back to him.

"I wanted to check on you. I haven't seen you all day," Denis said.

"Really?" I asked, narrowing my eyes. I sensed my cheeks catching fire. I froze.

"You know I worry about you, and I miss you every time you're not with me. Do you want to grab something to eat?" he asked.

"How about you take Liz instead?"

"What's wrong? Are you crying?" he asked, stroking my hair, and sending alert signals up my spine.

"No," I answered and swallowed the lump in my throat as my gaze ran over his face.

Denis seemed to understand my discomfort and took my hand in his and spun me toward him. I didn't know what to believe anymore. Half of my heart wanted to trust every word he had said to me. The other half remained uncertain. I was overwhelmed by the intensity of my own fears that I might lose the man I loved.

"Talk to me. Whatever it is, we will make it right," Denis said.

"Tell me, Denis, what's going on between Liz and you? I see the way she looks at you. Plus, you ran out in the middle of our dinner the other night the moment she called."

Denis's voice became soft while his arms embraced me. Attracted by his fragrance, by his lips, and by the mysteries hidden within his soul, and addicted to his touch, I didn't know how to cope with this feeling taking control over me: jealousy. Denis spun me around and took a good look at my tear-stained eyes. His face became somber when he talked.

Carmen Monica Oprea

"Nothing. She's just a friend. She had always been a friend and nothing more. Where did you get the idea that something was going on between us?"

"How could I not think that? I did my best to ignore her, the way she calls you, the way she smiles at you, the way you react to her."

I swallowed. There was a horrible moment of silence when Denis just looked at me. Then he straightened his spine.

He said, "I'm glad to have the opportunity to discuss this issue with you since it seems to affect your sound judgment."

I held his stare. "Don't lie to me. I can forgive anything else, but not lying."

Denis blinked, and then he closed the door behind us. He kissed me, his lips unusually full, sensual but also firm. My heart started to beat erratically when he touched my back.

"Let's go home. It's been a long day," he whispered.

A smile ghosted my lips. "Go get your briefcase from the office," I said.

"I'll meet you in the lobby," Denis said.

Denis entered his office, and I took the elevator to the first floor. I was talking with a new employee from the front office when I spotted Liz leaving the hotel with a man. My heart stopped, and for a fraction of a second, I thought that maybe I had imagined things. But even Irene had pointed out the fact that Denis had left with Liz. I had hitched my purse from the countertop and ran into the night.

As soon as I reached my home, I slammed the latch on my door as if I wanted to hold all the troubles out and threw myself on the bed, resting my forehead on my knees while I shook uncontrollably and felt light-headed.

Was he playing with me all this time?

I twisted this question over and over in my mind without reaching a satisfactory answer. Afraid to face the truth, I dismissed any

Unveiled Secrets

proper response, and I rocked back and forth in the center of a bed that seemed too big all of the sudden. One hour later I heard a knock on my door, but I remained silent. I had concluded that I deserved more than another pathetic excuse. Eventually, the person on the other side of the door grew tired and left. The rain continued to sizzle through the gray mist that had settled over the city. I fell asleep cradled by the rhythmic sound of the droplets drumming on the pavement. At about four in the morning, I woke with a terrible headache pressing at my temples. I dragged myself from the bed and popped two aspirins into my mouth. In spite of the early hour, I was fully awake.

I picked up the diary from the rocking chair and hugged it tightly. Myrna's story—my mother's story—was even more painful than mine.

Eight

May 15th, 1975

    Eric continued chasing the clues he had received from doctors, tracing Anders's steps and keeping me updated, but the avenues always ended in a dead end. From London, Anders had gone to America to meet with Dr. Lauren McCracken, a doctor who had dedicated twenty years of research to bone cancer in the hopes of finding an alternative cure based on the use of natural remedies and a complex of exercises to keep muscles toned and cells oxygenated. She remembered Anders, but she wasn't willing to disclose information because of the doctor-patient confidentiality.

    Hoping to find another path to solving this puzzle Eric decided to keep an eye on the doctor's office. He told me that he would respect the promise he had made years ago when we had first met in that shabby-looking office close to the harbor.

October 25th, 1976

    Finally, Eric's determination paid off. Eric saw Anders in a wheelchair, leaving the doctor's office. He had lost his legs and had only one arm left. A nurse pushed his wheelchair, and by the peaceful look on his face, Anders seemed reconciled to his fate. Eric followed the two of them in his car, and he reached a nursing home overlooking the Catskill Mountains. The name of the place was Sunrise Nursing Home, and judging by its size, only a few patients lived there. He called from a phone booth in the vicinity to give me the news, and I didn't know if I should laugh or cry if I should be happy or sad. Anders was alive, although an invalid pinned to a wheelchair.

    I booked the earliest flight available to New York. It was the first overseas trip for Leila, and despite my panic that she would be scared, Leila enjoyed the flight. She had been amazed by the grace of the clouds. For her, they looked like cotton balls thrown on the sky in different directions, as if they had been in a fight with some ferocious dragon. From her spot by the window, Leila spied every movement the flight attendants

Unveiled Secrets

made and, when they asked where she was going, her answer sounded like a whisper.

"I'm going to bring daddy home."

Leila had only met her dad in pictures, and I knew she carried one in her pocket. The picture where Anders held her close to his face had become her favorite. We traveled for eight hours. As we approached New York, she began fidgeting in her chair and continuously asked to know how many hours were left until she would meet the man in the picture.

Gabriela picked us up at the airport, and after a two and a half hour's drive, we reached Sunrise Nursing Home. A five-year quest was ready to be put to rest finally. Leila dozed on and off through the trip while I talked with my friend about my uneasiness to face Anders after such a long time. What if he would not speak to me? He had run away to hide from us. I was the one trying to find him all these years. He had never gotten in touch with us. He didn't write a single letter. Anders had just disappeared.

As we approached the end of our road, my heart thumped against my ribcage, and my ears rang. I tried to concentrate on the scenery to distract myself. Cities with strange names remained behind us with their mixtures of pedestrians, cars, and buildings, and their constant agitation. Finally, at sunset, after a long, exhausting trip, we arrived at our destination.

The area appeared quiet and isolated from the rest of the world, a hidden place where few people dared to venture. The road followed the snake shape of the river at the foot of the mountains and ended before two tall stone gates with the name of the compound. Gabriela stopped the car in front of the office, and I went inside alone to ask about Anders Isidro. The receptionist didn't divulge anything concerning the patient until I told her my name and the reason for my visit. She pitied me—I could see it from the look in her eyes—and showed me the garden, where a man in a wheelchair stared at the crumpled peak not far from the building. He was still the same man I had fallen in love with many years ago, even if his body was crippled.

I sat on the bench next to Anders without saying a single word. I tried covering his hand with mine, and I wasn't entirely surprised when he *pushed me away. I tried again and finally got hold of his thin fingers while we continued to stare past the horizon. The wind tousled his hair.*

"You've never been good at hiding your true feelings. You wear them in your eyes," Anders said.

"I'm predictable," I said. "Why did you run away?"

"For this view," he whispered.

I fanned my eyelashes and caught a few tears just in time. Only the stream that ran through the grounds disturbed the quietness of the place as it roared over stones protruding from the riverbed. Incapable of holding my tears back any longer, I let them roll down my cheeks. Some were tears of joy, some of pain. But neither joy nor pain could wipe the distance that had separated us for so long. I turned sideways to stare at Anders. The air burned my lungs when he stared at me with those lavender angel eyes. They were empty—two hollow seas where the dreams had died.

"You should have let go a long time ago. You should have lived your life, as I told you," Anders said, looking at me.

I felt trapped in his gaze and couldn't respond for a moment or two. His face and his jaw tensed as if he were suppressing himself from saying something bitter.

"Wasn't that an unusually selfish thing to do? To go on and live without you?" I asked. "You never told me how to do that."

I couldn't tell him that, in his absence, I had no purpose and no destination. That I got lost in a world, I didn't understand. And then, I traced his gaze as his eyes followed our daughter. Leila was holding Gabriela's hand, and the two of them were walking toward the garden. In an instant, Leila twitched from Gabriela's clasp and started to run toward us.

"Daddy, Daddy, I'm coming!" she shouted.

***

A sigh escaped my mouth as tears drenched my worn T-shirt. I closed the diary and my eyes, as I tried to recall that memory so

Unveiled Secrets

beautifully preserved in the diary's pages. I shook my head when nothing came back to me. It was as if someone had wiped out those memories. I couldn't remember the face of my mother or the image of my father. But both had lived and had loved and had got separated by miles of water and land, only to find each other again. Perhaps love could win if the hearts endured the tests. I embraced the diary and leaned against the pillow, for just a fraction of a second. Or so I thought.

It was the morning when I opened my eyes. I lurched toward the phone and dialed the hotel.

"Good morning, Leila, when are you getting here? Everyone is a madhouse."

"Sam, I'm not coming in today. I'm fighting an awful headache. Everything hurts. Let Denis handle the madness."

I could almost hear the resentment in Sam's voice. "All right, Leila, get some rest. We've got it covered."

"Thanks, Sam," I said, feeling sorry for lying. I shut the phone and returned to my bedroom.

I put on a pair of jeans and a silk blouse and headed toward the art gallery on Second Avenue North. It was about ten in the morning, and almost no one but the curator was there. I wandered through the winding hallways lined with canvases. The precision of the strokes brought to life images of the sea with boats and beautiful beaches, and the more I stared at the paintings, the more I realized that I had to leave New York and start fresh in a new place, far from bad memories.

As I looked at the dreamy blue waves drenching the sand, with seagulls lolling in the air and heaps of sun, goosebumps appeared on my arms. Those skilled painters had captured the best of the blue expanse of the ocean, and somehow, they had restored my hope, too. I had confined myself to a popular city for too long and had lost the courage to follow my heart. Perhaps God wanted me to go to a place where I could be happy, and this was the reason why I had decided to visit the gallery today instead of returning to the hotel. He was showing me something I'd been missing for years—the freedom to take control of my life. Like many others, I had followed a road blindly without allowing myself to think about what I wanted out of my life.

Carmen Monica Oprea

My feelings for Denis came to me in quick, powerful, mysterious waves. I had to get away from him and our twisted love story. I took a deep breath as I exited the gallery and as soon as I reached the street, the warm light of another fall day enveloped me. After I had bought a chocolate-mint ice cream cone, I walked back home and turned on the TV. The direct transmission of the fashion show from GLH came to life on the screen. Models floated on the catwalk in their stunning outfits—a perfect blend of style, color, and elegance. Helen Hyatt's collection seemed to be another success. Then right at the end of the show, Liz appeared wearing a gorgeous gown, the color of the sky at sunset.

My heart ached when I saw her. I called Denis but got his voicemail. It didn't leave a message, but I called the hotel instead, asking for him.

"He's gone to Europe, and he isn't coming back until the beginning of December," Sam said. "Are you feeling better?"

"I'll live," I said with a note of disappointment in my voice.

"Do you want to come over to Irene's? She's having a party."

"Thanks. But I'm not in the mood."

"Some fun won't hurt you," Sam continued.

"I'm not feeling cheerful, and I don't want to mess up the party, Sam. Have fun!"

Setting the phone on the table, I decided to take a shower before settling into bed for the night. Sleep didn't seem to come easy. I rolled and tossed. Finally, I turned on the lamp and noticed the text message on my phone:

"I'm not sure what got into you, but we'll talk about it when I get back."

It was from Denis.

When I went in Monday morning, I found out that Mr. Haden, the owner of GLH hospitality chain, asked Denis to handle the audit of the hotels in Europe and to arrange a thorough presentation for the board members. Before his departure, Denis had left a detailed agenda for the

Unveiled Secrets

next few weeks. He could be quite demanding when it came to the way he had managed the business. Focusing on the tasks regarding the hotel's operations helped me to forget about my issues. That worked well until I received a phone call from Liz.

"Will you meet me for lunch? I'll stop at the hotel on my way to the airport," Liz said.

"What time is best for you, Liz?" I asked her, checking my schedule on the computer screen.

"About twelve thirty this afternoon."

"I'll meet you downstairs in the restaurant."

Liz's invitation took me aback. I was still speechless as I stared at the phone, and although it was an opportunity to gather more information regarding her relationship with Denis, I couldn't shake off a bad feeling. Around noon, I was already waiting for her while sipping a glass of iced tea. I had chosen a booth overlooking the garden and was ignoring the drumroll in my ears.

I checked my watch nervously. Ten minutes to one and Liz hadn't arrived yet. As a diversion, I checked the messages on my phone, and soon enough I sensed a presence. I lifted my chin just as Liz prepared to sit at my table and stared straight into her blue eyes.

"Sorry for the delay, Leila. Traffic," Liz said, greeting me with one of those photogenic smiles I admired countless times in her movies. She took a seat across from me, threw her purse on a nearby chair, crossed her tanned legs, and pushed her back against the back seat.

"Good to see you, Liz," I said, my cheeks burning as soon as the lie flew out of my lips.

"The pleasure is all mine," she answered and signaled for a waiter. "Cappuccino, and hurry. My plane departs in two hours."

"I'll be right back with your order. What about you, Leila?" the waiter asked, waiting for me.

"A house salad, Leon," I said.

Carmen Monica Oprea

After he had left, I looked Liz in the eye and waited. She covered my hand with hers and sighed.

"I've come to advise you concerning Denis," she said.

Liz paused, studying my face. Then she continued. "I'm aware of the relationship you two share. But a man like Denis will never settle for a woman who can't keep him curious, playful, and interested. His partner needs to rise to his challenges. He worked hard to make it from the farm where he grew up to the man he is today. His ambitions will always come first on his list, and afterward, if time allows it, he'll turn toward romantic games. Because love is nothing but a game to him, Leila."

I coughed to clear my throat and then took a drink from a glass of water. My palm itched, and I pressed my nails into it. Not a muscle moved on Liz's face, and I found it impossible to take my eyes off her face. I wished that I possessed the same degree of self-assurance that she did so that I could mask the horrifying feeling that I would never understand this woman's motives. Before giving me time to react, Liz continued her rehearsed speech.

"For him, women are like cities: the moment he gets immersed in one, he moves on to the next one. He's afraid of commitment and, as soon as he thinks he is trapped, he steps away from everything and everyone without caring whom he hurts in the process. I understand Denis better than you. I'm sorry to be the bearer of bad news, dear. You should reconsider your expectations."

Liz crossed her hands over her chest and straightened her posture, looking every bit like a woman who understood men better than I. Although I thought she was inconsiderate and insensitive, I knew she was right. Denis himself had recognized that he didn't like attachments.

"And who has given you the right to meddle in my affairs?" I asked. "Do you think you understand me? You know nothing about me."

"Don't tell me I didn't warn you, sweetheart. You're not strong enough for Denis. He will devour you and move on when he's done," Liz said, finishing her drink as she rose from the chair. Her eyes sparkled, and her lips narrowed to a barely visible line. Then she turned around and left the restaurant, leaving me still shaking from her last remarks. The servers

Unveiled Secrets

hid their faces as I passed through the restaurant toward the exit door and ran out of the hotel.

I should have listened to Tessa and kept away from Denis. Back in the winter, after my mother's death, I had felt like my entire world had collapsed. Now—months later—when I had just begun to heal, the sky crumbled over my shoulders once more. I didn't understand men, nor did I have the desire to understand them. Perhaps Liz had been right to warn me. Her motives might not be entirely out of charity or the purity of her heart, but there was truth in everything she had told me. I could spend my entire life trying to understand Denis and Liz and their relationship, and I would still be puzzled. Once again, my heart was at crossroads, just as it had been with George.

"I need to talk to you," I told Tessa when I called her later that night.

"What's wrong?" she asked, sounding sleepy.

"Everything."

"Trouble in paradise?"

"Sharp observation. You are correct." I paused and caught a tear with my fingertip, and then I said, "I had an interesting discussion with Liz today."

"And?"

"She pretty much said the same things you told me a while ago. That Denis is not to be trusted. And that he lacks commitment to a woman and that all women are like cities for him. He just moves on from one to the next."

I sighed. "It is not as I envisioned it, Tess," I whispered.

"Stop feeling sorry for yourself," Tessa said. "No man is worthy of our tears. Have you already forgotten what George did to you?"

Of course, I hadn't. That was the reason I had been skeptical of Denis's intentions in the first place. I was convinced that Denis passionately loved me but that he just had trouble showing it. And that he had a problem expressing his feelings for me also.

109

Carmen Monica Oprea

"You will see everything clearer after a good night's sleep. See you in the morning," Tessa said, ending the call. I stared at my phone for a minute, and then I dragged my feet to the bedroom, where I picked up the diary, trying to find comfort inside the yellow pages once again.

***

"Would you like me to help you?" I asked Anders who had a hard time turning the wheelchair around.

"I got it," he said. He fixed the brake on the wheelchair. And then he faced Leila.

"Do you want to hold her?" I asked.

"That would be great," Anders said, sighing. "She grew up."

"She's almost five," I said, picking Leila up and setting her in Anders's lap.

Leila checked his face, and then she caressed his cheeks as he held her. He hugged her tight as if wanting to remove all the years spent without her.

Leila had inherited the same strong jaw and Anders's eye color, lavender, just like the flowers we saw growing in our garden back home in Vigo Bay.

"What happened to your other arm?" Leila asked.

"I had to let it go because it was making me sick," Anders answered. His entire body shook when he coughed. "I need water, please," he said.

"Let me help you." I held the bottle of water to his lips, and our eyes met above it. We rarely needed words to understand each other.

"Thank you. It tastes better because it came from you," Anders said, winking.

I chuckled. Anders's smile finally reached his eyes.

110

Unveiled Secrets

"You've got a lot bigger than when I saw you last," Anders said, looking back at Leila who was banging her legs against the edge of the wheelchair.

"Were your legs sick, too? That's why you had to let them go?"

"Yes, they were sick, too."

"But you're better now?"

"I am because you are here with me."

"Mommy missed you a lot." Leila played with his nose, and then she touched his ears. "Mommy says that I have big ears, like yours."

"Does she? From what I can see, I think they're beautiful."

Leila laughed, and I laughed, too.

"When are you coming home, Daddy?" Leila asked, touching Anders' s ears. "Mommy said that we would take you back with us."

"I wish it were that simple."

Anders closed his eyes and groaned. A knot seemed to have formed in his throat.

"Daddy needs to rest, sweetheart. Come here," I said, picking Leila up.

"One kiss for good night, Daddy," Leila said, standing on her tiptoes. Anders leaned toward her and let her kiss him. She beamed when she left us and ran toward Gabriela, who was waiting for her with her arms wide open.

Once we were alone, Anders told me that he had entered a bone-cancer study and that he had to stay in a nursing home under supervision. Alternative medicine had extended his life but couldn't save his legs or his arm. In this gamble with fate, some of the patients, the lucky ones, had made it up to ten years, while others had died shortly after they had started the program.

Carmen Monica Oprea

"I am not sure how long I have to live, but the prognosis isn't good. My condition represents one of the advanced cases. For this reason, I chose to fight the battle alone without dragging you into this mess," Anders said, holding my hand.

"Death, like birth, is part of life," I said. "How could you even imagine that I would go on living without you?"

"I only have one regret—the grief I brought you instead of the happily ever after I promised."

"Nothing matters as long as we are together," I said, pushing his wheelchair on the narrow path lined by pine trees.

"It reminds me of our home in Vigo Bay," he said, closing his eyes.

"You must rest."

"Yes, I have to. I get tired easily nowadays."

I caressed Anders's hair, now touched with gray, and then I kissed his forehead. We seldom needed words to understand each other. A few glances were always enough. Our eyes, our touch, spoke about all the sorrows. We were both content with the moment we had, happy to find ourselves once again. The past years seemed like a faraway dream, and I couldn't believe that I was touching Anders, that I was feeling his breath on the skin of my fingers when I followed the contour of his lips.

I was there to stay.

"I want you to come home with us, Anders," I said.

"It's not possible. I require a lot of medical attention. I can't be a nuisance to you and Leila. She'll get scared, seeing me like this," Anders said, pointing at his missing legs.

"I can't let you go now that I have found you. There is no sense in arguing. You're coming home."

"Clarisse, don't be a child. My days are almost over. It's just a matter of time," Anders said, contorting his face.

112

Unveiled Secrets

"Are you in pain? Should I call for someone?" I asked, signaling the nurse to come quickly.

The caregiver approached, carrying Anders's medicine in one hand and a bottle of water in the other one. She gave him two pills, and Anders swallowed them fast, thanking her for the attention. When she took control of the wheelchair, I walked next to him. Anders stretched his arm and touched my fingers, and I grabbed his hand, which felt weak in mine. I strengthened my grip as if to reassure him that I wasn't going anywhere anytime soon.

The nurse didn't allow me to follow him into his room, so I waited for her to return and tell me about his case. She must have been in her late fifties, and she had no wedding band on her finger. She had the face of a woman who had seen much during her life, a person who had witnessed death and cheered for life, and her understanding was overwhelming. I found out from her about an inn located next to the nursing home where other family members stayed when they visited relatives. I thanked her and left the nursing home behind, looking for the car, where Leila was asleep.

I told Gabby that the RN permitted me to remain with Anders overnight. She had assured me she would come back in the morning, and she would watch Leila over the night. I kissed my baby and embraced my friend, and then I stood to watch the car until the headlights disappeared into the night.

As I looked at the silver moon spilling its beams across the river, I wondered if there was still hope for lost souls, just like mine. A soft gust of wind caressed my face, bringing the sweet fragrance of jasmine back to me. Finally, I ventured into the nursing home to find Anders's room. As I closed the door, a new world emerged, one filled with the smell of medicine and sickness that wafted through the narrow hallways and into rooms and medical offices.

Anders's room was at the end of the hall. He lay on a bed facing a large window with silky blue curtains. I couldn't help but notice the pale blue color of the walls and the windows overlooking the mountains. The room didn't include much—a bed, one cabinet filled with a few bottles of pink liquid, clean bandages, and pills, and my books in an old rocking chair by the window.

I sensed Anders watching me and turned around.

His face was colorless in the dim light coming from the night lamp. I stopped by his bed and kissed his forehead and then his eyes before I brushed his lips with my own. Stinging tears found their way down my cheeks, stopping at my chest. He wiped them with the only hand he had left, and his touch felt cold, almost ghostly. Now that I was with Anders, everything else disappeared in the mists of time.

"Don't cry!" he said. "I don't like how you look with tears all over your lovely face. Give me a smile, that beautiful smile I've missed all these years we've been apart."

"It wasn't my decision to be apart, Anders. You never asked me what I wanted. You just took off without regard to what you'd left behind, hoping that I would pick up the pieces and move on. But you forgot one important thing."

"And what is it that I forgot?" Anders asked, the effort making him breathe hard.

"You forgot to tell me how to live without you."

Anders lifted his arm and touched my hair, and then he moved to my cheeks. He followed the contour of my lips as if to instill the shape of my lips in every cell of his body.

"Lie here with me," Anders whispered.

I nodded and lay down next to him. My head rested on his shoulder as I basked in the aroma of his skin, a combination of man and musk. We talked about my last book, the happy moments we had shared during the years we had spent together, and the uncertainty of our future. My fingers tangled with his, and just like in the times we had spent in the comfort of our home, I drifted into a dreamless sleep, surrounded by the murmur of a nearby river.

The hammering of the raindrops on the rooftop woke me up, their thump deafening. Lightning flashed across the sky every so often. It left behind the clapping and bellowing thunder to rip the delicate veil of silence surrounding the nursing home during the morning hours. I touched Anders to make sure he was all right, and, instead, I met the empty gaze of his eyes staring out the window. I checked for his pulse. My skin began itching. I opened a button from my blouse as panic crowded in my throat. I couldn't breathe. I put my ear on his chest and listened. There was no sound, no thumping against his ribcage. There was nothing, but a deafening silence. I sobbed as I shook his shoulders. His head fell to one side, and I embraced his body, holding him tightly. Then I lowered him slowly onto the bed. No sunrise would come for Anders. There would be no sorrows either, except for the pain he had left behind him all over again.

Anders had stepped into a place I could not follow.

Fate had granted us just enough time to say good-bye. I knew I had gotten more than I had ever expected, but I wasn't content. All thoughts drained from my mind, and my soul was empty, too.

I left the room and opened the front door. I stepped right in the middle of the falling rain and roared my pain. It was a tempest outside, but a bigger storm was rising inside me. Cold raindrops washed my body, but I couldn't even feel them. I felt nothing at all. I dropped to my knees in the muddy soil, my tears mixing with the millions of drops coming down from the skies. Nature itself was crying with me. There wasn't anything to soothe my heart.

Two nurses picked me up and took me inside the nursing home. I couldn't make out any of the words they said. One nurse gave me a shot to calm me down, and as soon as it started to take effect, I fell into a deep sleep. When I woke up, they were asking me what I wanted to do with Anders's body. I asked them who Anders was and why I should care about his body. They fed me more pills and told me to rest.

The same scene repeated itself for days. I couldn't distinguish day from night. I only recognized Gabriela's voice filtered to me from a faraway place. She told me that everything would be all right. She reminded me that I was a strong woman and that I needed to fight and snap back to reality. She mentioned how Leila missed her mother and needed me to return to her. But I didn't want to come back to anyone. I couldn't. I lacked the strength she seemed to think I had. My tormented soul just tried to hide inside my worn-out body. I was just like a butterfly whose wings had been crushed by a menacing tempest.

Carmen Monica Oprea

Sometimes my mind drifted to a comfortable spot. Then they would again ask me what to do with Anders's corpse, and I would sob uncontrollably. I hung on to Gabriela, and she decided to perform the burial in Spain. She knew that it was what I would want. In Spain, Anders would always be close to his home and close to me. I was grateful that she lifted that burden from me. Gabriela dealt with all details. And just like an abandoned child, I held his clothes in my arms, absorbing the last of his scent. I wasn't prepared to let go.

Very few people were fortunate enough to meet their true love during their lives, and I was one of the privileged ones. Anders had meant the world to me, and I wondered how I would be able to continue my quest through life after I had lost him. Where would I find the strength to put myself together and pretend life would smile on me once more?

Anders and I still had many things to say but not enough time to say them. We had rushed through our lives thinking that we still had tomorrow to handle whatever we hadn't accomplished today. But sometimes, tomorrow was just a distant day that would never come. I had no tomorrow but yesterday and the day before yesterday. There would be no tomorrow for Anders and me.

Unveiled Secrets

Nine

Denis finally returned from Europe. I hadn't gotten an explanation for what had happened before the fashion show when he had left with Liz or an apology. I wasn't even sure that any of his justifications would help alleviate the feeling of betrayal and abandonment. Once again, I was in love with the wrong man. He was handsome, wealthy, and single. And to him, I was just another girl.

It had been one of those Thursdays with never-ending meetings. One of our groups had decided to put a real fire truck on the terrace of the ballroom on the top floor for their upcoming convention. It looked like something from a movie. I went over the details with the engineering department for the next day's event when two hundred firefighters would be in the house.

Night had fallen by the time I walked back to my office. I hadn't heard from Denis all day and wondered if I should go to him. I opened the window and left the fresh air cool off my cheeks while my fingers clenched the windowsills. Summer was coming to an end, and the last days of August seemed to shrink. I grabbed my purse, left the hotel, and walked back to my building. As soon as I reached my apartment, I browsed through the mail the maid had left on the kitchen countertop. There were mostly bills and brochures advertising idyllic islands with white sandy beaches and turquoise-blue waters. One envelope from the stack had fallen to the floor. I picked it up and checked the address. It came from Spain. I tore open the peach envelope.

What on earth is that?

I blinked a few times, staring at the cashier's check with my name on, trying to control the pounding of my heart. I set the check on the countertop and poured a cup of black coffee, my mother's remedy for headaches, and then I looked at it again. I laughed.

With one million dollars, I can go in any part of the world and have no worries whatsoever.

117

Carmen Monica Oprea

Inside the envelope was a letter. The fragrance of lavender wafted through the kitchen. I dropped into the nearest chair and read the letter aloud.

My Dear Leila,

Use this gift wisely and make the right choice. Remember, true love comes once in a lifetime. People who find it are the privileged ones. Most of us live our lives just passing by and do not recognize love's worth. It is in your hands to unveil this secret.

With love,

MCE

After I had read the letter once more, I hummed to myself. Then I pushed my shoulders back against the chair and laughed at all the silly ideas filling my mind. I had everything I had dreamed about: money, freedom to go wherever I chose and do whatever I wanted, and a diary that held the answers to the questions about my past that had haunted me my entire life. My heart pounded fast. Maybe I should listen to MCE's advice. I had to tell Denis.

I walked back to the hotel to find Denis. He always worked late during budgeting time. It was dark on the streets, a gust of wind swirling the leaves on the streets. I ran a hand through my hair, and then I touched the purse where I had thrown the letter.

When I entered the hotel lobby, a tremor suddenly shook my body. A blast of cold air had replaced the outside heat. I looked around and saw Sam at the front desk computer checking in a family of four while one of the bellmen loaded their luggage on a cart. Irene waved to me, and then she dropped the cash she had collected from another guest for his parking tickets on the floor. Thinking of Denis, I took the stairs toward the second floor.

Not long ago, he had drawn the lines about the status of our relationship, and Liz had confirmed that he only slept with the women in his life. There was no emotional attachment, just pure, consensual sex. Love had no place in our relationship. I inhaled a few times when I reached the second floor. Then I turned left and walked down the hallway. Denis's office was the second room on the left, overlooking the

118

Unveiled Secrets

hotel's parking lot. Only a dim light coming from an old lamp and the reflections of the outside lights shining through the windows lit the room at this late hour. I checked my watch. It was almost nine thirty.

Loud voices and laughter came from inside the office. I waited in the doorstep, counted to five, and then entered the office. Denis was sitting in his chair, and Liz was on his desk, playing with his tie. Liz and I locked eyes, and in the heat of the moment, she leaned toward Denis and kissed him hard on the mouth. I bit my lower lip until I tasted my blood.

"I'm sorry to interrupt your little rendezvous," I said.

Upon hearing my voice, they both jumped, and Liz started to arrange folders on Denis's desk. Denis blushed, trying to wipe the pink lipstick from his mouth.

I chuckled. "Don't bother stopping on my account. It will only take me a minute. I'm leaving the hotel, Denis."

Denis rose from his chair and came out from behind the mahogany desk. As soon as he was next to me, he grabbed my shoulders, his face just inches away from mine. Liz stared at me. Shadows played on the walls when Liz shifted her position, got up from the desk, and walked to the window to look outside.

"We must talk," he said. "Don't judge before listening. I'm not the person you think I am. Please don't make decisions you will regret later."

"Why don't you want me to go?" I asked.

"I am not Denis," the man in front of me said.

"Oh," I managed to say. "Then you impersonate him pretty well."

"It's a long story…"

"I've no time for long stories. I just wanted to tell you in person. I only wanted to look you in the eye when I gave you the news. Now I've done it. It's as simple as that."

"Nothing is simple," Liz whispered.

I looked at her back and caught her reflection in the window.

119

Carmen Monica Oprea

"Don't tell me that I didn't warn you," Liz continued.

"You were always the person standing between us," I said, trying to keep my composure.

Denis, or the man who was his double or whoever he was, dropped his arms to his sides. His eyes were sad, and his lips tightly shut. Whatever I believed Denis and I shared, whatever I thought we had, it dropped dead the moment I stepped into his office and saw him with Liz once again. I walked back toward the door and left. I remembered the day when he had denied his involvement with Liz, telling me that she was only a close friend. I'd had a hard time believing him and accepting his explanation. But my love for him had clouded my judgment, pushing my doubts outside.

As I descended to the lobby, hot tears filled my eyes. I wiped them with the sleeve at my blouse, exited the hotel, and cast another glance at the hotel.

"A taxi, miss?" a man with dark skin asked from inside the yellow car parked just outside the hotel.

"No, thank you. I'll walk."

I went home, turned on the Internet, and checked the real estate in Florida. The money I had received from the mysterious MCE was more than enough for a down payment. And one evening, two days after I quit, I discovered Bluewater Boutique listed for $1 million. The quaint boutique in Rosemary Beach would be the perfect haven for me. I would get away from Denis Fraga, the man I was desperately in love with, the man who had broken my heart and whom I had to forget.

Ten

Endless love for the turquoise waters, the beach, and the soft breeze brought me to my new home one year ago. In "Paradise Found," how the locals described it, the white sandy shores stretched for miles, gleaming with the natural beauty of the Gulf of Mexico. Situated between Panama City and Destin, Rosemary Beach had gotten its name from the rosemary herbs hedging sandy pathways and filling gardens and parks. It was a safe, crime-free place with no thieves except the seagulls who stole crumbs in the evenings.

From the room above the boutique, I had a perfect view of the shore. Blue waters covered with white foam kissed the beach. The waters became dark, almost black, during the night. Some nights, it seemed that the moon rose straight from the sea. Ships crossed the horizon, and boats filled with fishermen dotted the sea. I looked around my bedroom: a bed covered with lace spread I had received as a gift and bookshelves that stretched from floor to ceiling, sagging under the many books collected. My favorite one—*Gone with the Wind*—rested on the old, squeaky rocking chair where I spent most of the evenings slipping into a world of dreams and desires.

Tonight, a soft breeze swept across the shore at that perfect moment when the day and the night played hide-and-seek with each other. After I had pulled my hair back in a loose ponytail at the nape of my neck, I closed the door behind me, descended the stairs toward the main floor where the store was and exited the boutique. As soon as I stepped on the white sand, I kicked off my sandals.

The sand tickled my feet while I walked along the coast, the warm waters touching them just like a frugal kiss. That mixture of sand and water brightened my face, made me forget about the life I had in New York. The white grains of sand slid between my toes, only to disappear with every wave that crashed against the shore. In those moments, I felt like I could disintegrate into tiny particles and scatter all over that vast expanse, becoming one with the sea. The cheerful tides had their way of telling me when the sea was happy. Today not a single undulation disturbed the tranquility of the sea. Seagulls sang their songs and hovered over the sea and the shores. I had witnessed days when the gulf was

Carmen Monica Oprea

angry and returned what it had stolen from unfortunate sailors back to the shore. It was a way of threatening and saying, "Stay away! Don't touch me!" The waters transformed from light blue to dark emerald, carrying little seashells along the coast like a rough blanket when the gulf turned angry.

I finished my morning walk and returned home, shaking the sand off my feet. A smile stretched across my face as I took into view the surroundings of my new life. And all of this had begun with a mysterious letter. That letter put a stamp on my heart and my mind, giving tomorrow a new meaning. I sat on the wooden steps in front of the store, the old diary in my hand. A picture fell at my feet in the sand. I picked it up, shook the sand off, and stared at it for a minute or two.

I recalled the moment when Denis and I had taken it. It was on our first date after he had taught me how to drive a kart. It had been my first and last lesson of driving. I still didn't own a driver's license, and it didn't bother me one bit. His hazel almond-shaped eyes smiled back at me from that picture. I followed the contour of his lips, recalling the way they curved at the corners when he laughed. When had I fallen in love with Denis? Maybe it happened the instant I had met him. Maybe it happened when he had touched my hand, and I had found it strange that he had held it a little too long.

I remembered the way his eyes pierced mine. Those entrancing, molten-brown eyes hugged me every time he looked at me. I had never found out if he had real feelings for me. I hadn't given him a chance to explain himself after I had caught him kissing Liz in his office. After I had quit my job, Denis had called me and had left messages, but I hadn't returned his phone calls. I had dismissed his attempts of reconciliation and sent him an e-mail asking him to stay away from me. He had stopped calling afterward. Only Tessa knew that I had moved to Florida, and she had promised not to breathe a word about my whereabouts.

I put the photo back in the diary, and a strange emotion ran through my veins. I could barely contain the tremors in my body. I pushed my back against the stairs and opened the diary once again.

***

March 8th, 1977

Unveiled Secrets

After Anders's funeral, I sunk into a deep depression and starved myself. Gabriela thought that it would be best for me to receive medical attention. I couldn't disagree—she had always been right. I appointed her Leila's legal guardian, and she took the girl to live with her in New York. I asked Eric to oversee the opening of an account in Leila's name in which my bank would transfer a monthly allowance from the trust fund her father had started on her behalf.

I was back at the house, where memories of Anders were still alive in everything that he had touched. I didn't recall much that had happened since his death, except that they had finally released me from the hospital after more than a year. They had decided that I was healthy enough to take care of myself and that I wasn't a suicide risk anymore. I found a reason to live—writing. In my novels, I could meet Anders in the form of a handsome man, and I could fall in love with him once again.

September 15th, 1977

Gabriela was busy with handling her own business and, the fact that she had become a mother unexpectedly, changed her priorities. Gabriela loved and nursed Leila just like a birth mother would do. Deep in my heart, I knew that I had made the right decision, although I would miss every precious moment of my daughter's childhood. But it was my duty to give Leila a mother with a strong will to live, and New York represented the perfect place for her to blossom. When she started kindergarten, I received a picture from her during the first day, and I was so proud of my daughter. Gabriela sent pictures from New York to Vigo Bay every season, showing Leila as a student, attending birthday parties, winning games of chess, and always smiling. And this was sufficient to give me peace of mind and confirmation that I had decided to leave her with Gabriela, who could provide her with a stable environment.

On my side of the world, I only lived through my books.

June 15th, 1978

I finally stared at my reflection. A woman with dark circles under her eyes and a pale face I hadn't recognized stared back from the mirror. I had thought someone else was in the same room with me. I had laughed at my reaction and had returned to my writing room, where I had buried myself in a note after note and page after page dedicated to another

123

Carmen Monica Oprea

unfinished love story. My editor had encouraged me to write to help with my grief. There were times when I had looked at the people in the garden and had hoped that Anders was in the crowd. His eyes were haunting me, and he seemed to follow me like a shadow wherever I went. Regardless of how much I tried to move forward, an invisible hand seemed to pull me back. I swung between feeling normal for a day or two, only to fall back into darkness.

April 12th, 1980

Gabriela called me almost every day and told me news about my girl. She asked me if I was ready to tell my daughter the truth. My answer was always the same: not yet. She just wouldn't understand yet. And she wouldn't have been happy here with me in a house filled with sadness. I had decided to watch her grow from afar and ensure that she had the care of a stable, happy, loving mother. This thought comforted me. Instead of bringing her to Spain and tearing her apart from the only mother she had known and loved, I attended her birthday parties in New York and basked in her joy whenever I could.

***

I set the diary aside, and my thoughts turned to the birthday parties my mother used to throw for me. I remembered the company of a tall, willowy woman with soft features. Gabriela had introduced her as her best friend from Europe, who had come for a visit in the States.

Somewhere stashed in a drawer, I had albums filled with pictures. I left the diary on the rocking chair outside and went into the house, climbing the stairs up to my room, two at the time. After a quick look around the bedroom, I opened the drawer where I kept the albums and pulled out the first one. I browsed through the pictures until I reached the one I was searching for.

It had been taken when I had turned seven, and my mother had planned a birthday party with lots of balloons and cupcakes dotted with white pearls made of sugar. She had invited all of my classmates. In the back of the room, as if hiding from the camera, was a woman with beautiful blue eyes. Her face wore a mask of sadness. I traced the contour of her face with my finger while trying to control my heartbeat. My mother had been present at all the crucial moments in my life. I had

Unveiled Secrets

always thought the woman had come to visit Gabriela. I remembered that my mom called her Clair, not Myrna or Clarisse, which was why I hadn't made the connection when I had searched the Internet for clues about my parents. One by one, I traced the outline of Clair's face in the pictures from the elementary school graduation ceremony, and from high school and college. I remembered chatting with her about literature and books and being amazed about our mutual attraction to the same authors and literary genres.

Clair's delicate figure was always intriguing to me, and Gabriela told me that she was a woman who had suffered a lot in her life and had had to give up a lot to survive. My mother said that Clair was a famous writer in her country, but somehow, I had overlooked making the association between the diary I had read and the woman I had known all my life. Clair attended my mother's funeral too. She sat next to me in the pew, holding my hand during the service. Clair told me everything would be all right while I sobbed in the comfort of her arms. I realized now that those were the same words Gabriela had told my mother when she had lost her husband. Life had completed a perfect circle and had brought us back to the same spot where it had all begun.

The day of the funeral was rainy, the raindrops drumming on the ground and making the service even more somber. Bouquets of calla lilies and red roses rested on Gabriela's coffin. Clair gave the eulogy, talking about how important real friends were and about what a wonderful person Gabriela had been over the years. She talked about how Gabriela had lived life on her terms, how she had never been afraid to try new avenues when the existing ones were blocked, and how she had touched and transformed the lives of the people around her, especially those of the children from St. Anne's Orphanage, to whom she had dedicated a significant part of her busy schedule.

Clair said that it wasn't easy to say goodbye to someone important to you. She mentioned that losing Gabriela was just another slap on her face. I had continued Gabriela's work after she passed away so that I could be surrounded by the people who loved her. I had needed to spend time away from a home filled with the memories of my mother. I knew she would approve of my decision. She was not a person who cried in the face of hardship. When she had assumed the responsibility of raising someone else's child or even when her studio had been destroyed

Carmen Monica Oprea

by a fire right after the grand opening, instead of feeling sorry for herself, she had looked for ways to be grateful for having the chance to find another way to accomplish her goal.

I was still holding my birth mother's picture when I returned to the rocking chair on the porch. It was the time when the day and the night mingled, and a smile crossed my face. I turned my attention to the last entry in Myrna's diary with the understanding of a young woman whose heart had been broken, too.

***

December 30th, 1990

In the beginning, I wrote all these passages for myself, to chronicle the events that had shaped my life. But later, after I had witnessed the struggle in your heart, I sent them to you, Leila, hoping that you would not follow in your father's footsteps and run away from the one you love. Anders wasted years we could have spent together, loving and carrying for each other. You are the only one who can decide the course of your life.

Love comes quickly to some people but takes a lifetime to reach others. You must listen to your heart. Remember, my child; true love comes once in our lives. The other flutters we feel in our stomachs are merely flings fading with the passage of time. Don't let your chance for happiness slip away from you. Gather your strength and fight for what you want. Your father wanted to teach you many things, but he had left you this letter instead. He would have been proud of the woman you have become. I hope that one day you will find compassion for a mother who didn't have the strength to stand by you and that you'll come back home, even if only for a day.

***

I wiped the tears from my eyes and turned the page. My father's letter was still in a sealed envelope, yellowed by time. When I opened the envelope, a single dried calla lily fell out. I picked it up slowly and held it in my hand for a few minutes. This was the first and only flower my father had given me, and it was still well preserved. I flinched, thinking that I would crush its frail body by mistake. I placed the flower next to me, on the chair, and read his words aloud.

126

Unveiled Secrets

***

Leila,

When you read this letter, I will be long gone from this world. I would have liked to be with you instead of sending this letter, to hold your hand and talk to you. But this is my only way of reaching you. How can I ever begin to tell you how much joy you brought into my life when you were born? Will you understand my love for you? Is this even going to mean anything to you?

You didn't get a chance to know me, as I will never get the opportunity to meet the woman you became. I am sure you inherited your mother's soft features and her grace. I wish we had time together, but as it was never up to us to decide the time we came in this world, we can't choose the moment we depart it. Listen to my advice: Give your heart to the one who can understand your inner desires, and not to the one smitten by your good looks. Looks will fade over time and what remains will decide who you are. Give yourself to the one who loves your kindness and your compassion, your laughter, and your tears.

He will be the one who stands by you in happiness and sorrow, for good and bad, until the last day of your life. In return, be truthful to the man who is prepared to sacrifice his own happiness just to make you happy, the one who will suffer just because he sees you crying. Our existences are nothing but a series of events, sweet and sometimes sour. Believe in love with all your being, but only trust the one who respects who you are, who accepts your downfalls, who is next to you to break your fall. This kind of love is rare and hard to find.

I may not be with you to tuck you in at night or rock you in my arms until your nightmares fade. I won't see your first steps and hear your first words, and I will miss your first day of school, your first kiss, and your first love. But I will always be a part of you because your eyes are my eyes, your smile is my smile; your success will be my success, and your downfall will be mine, too. I will be with you every step you take. I sense that you will grow as strong and beautiful as the wildflowers and that your beauty will shine from your passion for life.

So, live for me, too! Enjoy life with its small tokens of happiness, and love the sadness it brings, also, since every obstacle you overcome is *meant to make you stronger. Never take life too seriously—gamble a little. Learn something new each day and do not be afraid to share the news of your new skills with your friends for fear they might tease you. Do it anyway! Don't compromise! Life is too short to allow it just to happen, so move forward with each occasion you have. Don't panic if the storms seem stronger than you. Just wait patiently for them to pass. Someday you will laugh at yourself. Remember, light always follows dark, as good weather comes after a storm. Keep your faith firm, and you will conquer the world.*

And think of me as the first man who fell in love with you, before you were even born. The one who loved your perfect imperfections—a nose too small and tiny fingers a little too pink. I will watch over you and point you the way, just as the morning star shows the way to lost sailors.

With all my love,

Daddy

***

By the time I had reached the end of the letter, my throat was dry, and my hands were shaking. I read my father's message once again. This letter was my only connection with him. I didn't have one memory of my dad. I wasn't even sure that someone like the man my father described in his letter even existed. I had been waiting to meet that kind of man for so long. Months ago I had thought that I had finally found him. But it had been just a figment of my imagination, so I had left him. Anders had been an unusual man with an insight into matters of the heart that most men didn't possess. Now I realized why my mother had had such a hard time getting over him. She had been haunted the rest of her days by his memory and her love for him, so much that she even gave me away. In the terrible day of his death, they both had died in a sense since she never quite lived after that.

Rosemary Beach was falling asleep. The breeze had softened. I took a deep breath, inhaling the brackish fragrances of the seawater, a combination of kelp and salt. Still staring at the letter, I couldn't stop wondering what to do next. My eyes filled with tears as I reread the letter, hoping to uncover more hidden clues. My hands shook. I knew what I had to do. I had to go and meet my mother.

Unveiled Secrets

The waves crashed against the shore, and their sound was all I could concentrate at the moment. The willow tree branches swayed back and forth in the breeze. Goosebumps formed on my body as I thought of the diary in my hand. Gabriela had wanted me to learn about my parent's love story because she knew this was the only way I would understand them.

I jumped when I heard a voice saying close to my ear, "Good evening."

"Goodness gracious, John. You scared me," I said, chuckling as I covered my heart with my hand.

"Sorry. May I sit down?" John asked.

"Be my guest," I said, picking up the lily from the rocking chair and placing it back inside the envelope.

John flexed his muscles when he sat next to me, putting a plate filled with crepes in his lap and clearing his throat a couple of times. They smelled like raspberry and apricot jam, and I couldn't stop smiling.

"May I?" I asked and picked one up before waiting for his answer.

"Of course," he said. "They are fresh."

As I looked at him, his eyes sparkled. They were usually a light green, just like the waters of the gulf. His hair was tied at the nape of his neck, and he smelled of flour and sugar. We had met a year ago. Just like me, John had decided to embrace change and make a fresh start when he had moved from New York. He said he had the desire to get away from the city and from crunching numbers, and to find a sense of happiness and peace he couldn't quite get in the conglomerate of people and buildings in New York and Rosemary Beach provided him with the space to think about himself and his life. We made a habit of meeting at to my place in the evenings after dinner to savor the sweets he loved baking or just talking.

"What's going on? Did you have a good day sailing?" I asked him.

He shrugged his shoulders, and a sad smile settled on his lips. After I had finished three of his crepes, I stretched my legs to ease the

129

Carmen Monica Oprea

cramps from sitting for too long. An entire afternoon had disappeared, and until John showed up, I hadn't realized how late it was getting.

"The day was all right," John said. "The gulf was quiet, and I had plenty of time to sort through my thoughts. In fact, I stopped in the lagoon and swam. The crackling sound of constantly shifting life in the sea gets to me every time.

John finished the last of the crepes and lowered the plate to the sand.

"It never ceases to amaze me how," I said, "soothing the sounds of the ocean can be. Ever since you shared your hiding place with me, I consider it a refuge when times get hard."

"What are you reading?" John asked, pointing at the diary on my knees.

John grabbed the diary and flipped through the pages.

"It is my mother's diary. I discovered that MCE stands for Myrna Clarisse Elmer, a well-known writer from Spain."

"I've never heard of her," John said, shrugging his shoulders.

"You're not the only one," I said. I paused, giving John time to absorb my words, and when his eyes encouraged me to go on, I said, "She married Anders Isidro, a businessman who lived in Vigo Bay, and they lived happily for a while until something tragic happened. Dad got sick and left my mom and me to seek treatment. After she had searched for him for five years, just after she found him in a nursing home in America, he died, separating the three of us again."

And as I finished the last words, a chill traveled up my spine.

John paged through the diary, reading passages, jumping from the beginning to the end of the notebook, and then he looked at me and said, "So you are the daughter of a writer and a businessman from Spain."

"Yes, I am," I agreed.

"Is your mother still alive?"

130

Unveiled Secrets

I sighed. "Yes, she is, and I think she would like me to meet her."

"Home?"

I nodded. "Yes, to Vigo Bay."

"When are you leaving?" John asked as he stopped the swing.

The breeze stopped, and for a moment, the ocean looked like a frozen lake. I shrugged my shoulders as I looked sideways at John. "I haven't decided yet."

John had been my best friend for the past few months, and I could see in his eyes that his feelings for me were evolving into something I would never be able to return. He hadn't pressed the issue of us deepening our relationship. When I had told him about Denis, he had narrowed his eyes and listened. He didn't judge, and he didn't inquire further when I stopped talking; he just offered me his handkerchief to wipe away my tears. Then, John had told me the real reason he had retired to Rosemary Beach.

"You seem like you want to tell me something," I said. "I saw it in your eyes, and I've been waiting for you to tell me about it ever since."

"I've always admired you for your instincts. That's rare for women."

I raised my brows. "What is that supposed to mean? That we are not that intelligent?"

"Hold on a minute. Nobody said anything about women not being intelligent. They are more intelligent than most of the men I've known."

I chuckled when he began arguing his point of view about the usefulness of gut feelings when dealing with ambiguous situations. John didn't say anything about the black car parked in front of his house the other day and the man in a dark suit when we met last evening. I stared at him, waiting.

"OK, shoot," John said. "I know that stare."

Carmen Monica Oprea

"Who was the man who had stopped at your home yesterday? And does that have anything to do with the reason that brought you to Rosemary Breach?"

John coughed. "The FBI is investigating Dunes Corporation, and they want me to testify at the trial. It will be a dirty one, and to make matters worse, I would be a witness against a man who was not only my boss but my friend as well."

"I know you've been struggling with the decision to testify against him for years," I said, chewing on my nail.

"Regardless of how I look at the entire situation, there is no way out. I must do the right thing, Leila. I must. It's the only way I'll ever be able to live a decent, honest life again. It's time to end this insanity. Mark didn't change his ways, as I hoped he would do. He affected the lives of many people."

"Do you leave soon?"

"Tomorrow."

I sighed. "Let me know how it goes."

I remembered John telling me about the illegal transactions and the money transfers to offshore accounts one night after we had shared fish and drunk wine. Because of his friendship with his boss, he hadn't contacted the authorities and had just chosen to leave the city and the bad memories behind instead. His family liked New York, so they stayed. His wife remarried, and his daughter continued her studies for her business degree. His daughter spent her summers with her father in Rosemary Beach, sailing on *Ever Lucky*, John's boat, or getting a tan on the private beach in front of his home. John was looking forward to spending time with her again.

"Are you going to be all right?" I asked.

My voice trembled, and my hand tightened around his. I blinked rapidly to chase away the small tears forming in the corners of my eyes, unable to think of the penalties John might face because he had hidden the truth from the authorities. As if reading my mind, he turned around and smiled at me.

Unveiled Secrets

"Everything will be all right. Don't worry about me! You'd better make sure to go and talk to your mother," John said.

"Sure! I will work on that, John. When are you leaving?"

"I'll head to New York as soon as I've packed my things. It's time to get it over with."

He rose from the chair, leaving me alone with my thoughts, the moon, the stars, and the magical gulf. The waves crashed on the shore, as though they wanted to wash clean the present and the past and to make everything new. I stared into the night, thinking of John, and wondering about his future and mine, too. I missed Denis, also, and for a moment, the temptation to call him and hear his voice rose in intensity. He might have married Liz by now, and that thought brought me back to the cruel reality that I was still alone and still in love with a man I hadn't seen or talked with in over a year. Maybe John was right. It was time to let go of the past and to think of the future.

Holding the diary close to my heart, I went inside the house and locked the doors, as if to keep the sad memories away from me.

Eleven

Since I was a child, I had tried to ignore, block, and force my feelings away. I denied being angry when in fact I was furious with my parents for abandoning me. I kept telling myself that there was something wrong with me for feeling angry when I had Gabriela on my side. I told myself that the entire situation didn't hurt when the truth was that it hurt very much. Days had passed without having any idea how tomorrow would affect my existence or what changes time would bring. I only sensed that this day would be different from the previous one. Sometimes, things out of our control can shake our worlds—John's and mine's.

When the light first kissed the horizons, I heard the car's engine roaring outside and slicing the silence in Rosemary Beach. I went to the windows and pushed the curtains away, looking toward John's house. He left at the crack of dawn, just as he had said he would the night before.

I thought of Denis, and the temptation to call him send a tickling feeling down to my stomach. I wanted to tell him I had been terrified of my feelings, that I hadn't trusted his words, and that I had lacked the courage to stay. My feelings had frightened me, and the thought of losing him had made me run away. For the past months, I had concentrated on running my boutique, and I had forgotten about how I felt about Denis and Liz. Everything had been fine until I found his picture the other day and couldn't shake off the feelings of betrayal. Tessa had tried to make me change my mind about moving to Rosemary Beach. And even though she had come down here and helped me with the boutique's opening, Tessa found the idea of leaving New York ridiculous. Only after Bluewater opened its doors, she saw the potential.

As I jumped from one memory to another and sipped from a bottle of water, I heard the phone ringing.

"Hi, girl, how are you?" Tessa asked.

"I was just thinking of you. How weird!"

"Telepathy, little lady." Tessa laughed. "How's life on the beach?"

Unveiled Secrets

"Quiet," I said.

"You can always come back to New York. How long are you going to stay there? And what about Denis?"

I sighed. "What about Denis? We went over this subject before. Denis is in control of himself and his destiny, and I am in control of mine."

"Since you left, Denis had buried himself under mountains of work. He hired a man to replace you as business manager, and he uses every excuse to travel everywhere in the world. He spends very little time in New York," Tessa said.

"That's his choice. Denis has always worked too much and too hard, seeing everything as black and white. He has never had any concept of gray. If he were as passionate about me as he was about his job and Liz, maybe we would be together today."

"You're right," Tessa said.

"Sister Mary told me that Denis sends a check every month to help with the monastery's expenses," I said.

"Why don't you let me tell him where you are? You can ask him to come down to Florida and have a decent conversation."

"Tessa, I have to go. It was good to hear your voice."

"Do you need me to come down there?" Tessa asked.

"I'll let you know if I'll need you," I said, hanging up. Although Tessa's intentions were good, I didn't want to deal with her insistence for me to return to New York and talk to Denis. If the situation reversed, I was convinced he wouldn't have given me a second chance. His pride would never allow him to do so, along with the memory of his mother's betrayal.

I dressed in a white summer dress and descended the stairs into the store. Bluewater provided a steady income and kept me occupied. Pastel hues and whites created the peaceful atmosphere I was seeking when I left the big city. Scarves and locally handmade crafts, handbags, picture frames dotted with shells, whimsical wind chimes, ocean treasures, garden art creations, and lamps were spread over antique chairs and tables. When I reached the third step, the squeaky one I had

Carmen Monica Oprea

planned to replace ever since moving but never seemed to find the time to do so, I stepped over it and turned my attention to the storage room behind the store. I opened boxes I had received yesterday until it was past noon. I stopped for soup and French toast, and then I returned to the storage to finish the job.

When the last item was cataloged and stored on the shelves, I closed my laptop and entered the boutique to let the part-time girl go home at the end of her shift. And although it was a warm evening, a chill crawled up my spine, and my heart started to beat fast when I saw the couple entering the boutique. The woman picked up a seashell from a basket and raised it to her ear. She closed her eyes as she listened for a few seconds before she set the shell back next to the others. I ducked behind a mannequin and studied his profile. He hadn't changed much in the past year. He had the same natural good looks that made him stand out in the crowd.

Feeling someone's breath on my shoulder, I turned around, coming face-to-face with the woman responsible for my year of heartache.

"They are alike, aren't they?" Liz asked, staring at me, and with a snap of her fingers, she signaled her companion to approach.

I faked a pleasant surprise. "Liz? Denis?"

The man extended his arm. "I'm Lance, Denis's brother. Liz is my wife. We're here on our honeymoon. And you are Leila," he said.

"Lance?" I asked. "And how do you know my name?"

Lance checked me out, and I felt naked under his stare. And then his words hit me. I opened my lips and closed them again, as I studied Lance. Denis and Lance shared the same aquiline nose, hazel eyes shadowed by sickle-shaped eyebrows, and a square, firm jaw. Even their hair was the same color and texture. Only their voices had a different tone. While Lance's voice was sexy and mysterious, Denis's was masculine and deep. A thin, dark mustache grew above Lance's sensual upper lip, his seemingly bold personality was a perfect match for Liz.

"I can see that life suits you better here than in New York," Lance said.

Unveiled Secrets

I straightened my shoulders. "I never knew Denis had a brother, let alone a twin brother. He never talked about you," I said.

"We chose different paths in life, and we had our share of disagreements. I ran away when I turned eighteen. He decided to stay and help our father at the farm. Even today, he blames me for our father's death. I was young and restless, and I wanted to see the world. Show business called me, not farming with its endless hours of working the land." Lance stopped. I barely had had time to catch up my breath. "I guess I scared you in our last encounter. I hope you'll forgive me."

I closed my eyes for a fraction of a second when I heard a chuckle. I opened them quickly, and a sudden desire to wipe the smirk off that perfect face made me turn around and face her. Her eyes were like fire as she continued to smile. I closed my hands into a fist. Lance stepped between us, and I concentrated on him instead.

"Would you like coffee?" I asked.

"Why not? We will be outside, on the porch. It has a great view of the shore."

Liz and Lance exited the boutique. I looked after them, as my gaze traveled along the coast. The lights at a nearby restaurant turned on, and the breeze carried the sounds of music along with the aroma of fried fish.

"I'll be right back," I said. I went into the kitchen and poured three cups of coffee and put some dark chocolate macaroons on a plate. "Milk and sugar, anyone?"

"I like mine black," Lance said.

"Same here," Liz added.

I poured milk into my coffee and sat in the rocking chair next to Liz and Lance. As soon as the sun began to set, it cooled down. The sky was painted with purples and pinks, and the oceanic breeze brought the smell of kelp that tickled my nostrils. A few seagulls hovered above the waters, hunting for food. They looked like shooting arrows as they plunged into the waves for fish.

137

Carmen Monica Oprea

"Out of curiosity, it was you that day in the office with Liz, right?" I asked.

"Right," Lance said, lowering his gaze to the cup in his hand.

Liz giggled. "Denis would never get into a relationship with a movie star. He is far too boring for us, and we are far too shallow to capture his attention. He tried once or twice to go out with a model, and it didn't work out," she said, taking a sip of coffee.

Lance sat the coffee mug down on the iron table. "Denis loves you," he said.

I looked past him at the couples walking hand in hand on the beach. "He sure has a strange way of showing it," I said.

"He is not like me. Denis would have never made it as an actor. Actors must be ruthless because we live in a competitive world where physical appearance means everything, as well as talent and a whole lot of luck," Lance said.

Part of me wanted to jump from my seat and embrace Lance, and part of me wanted to ask questions and get the whole truth. Why had they all played this trick on me? Why was Lance pretending to be Denis and for how long? It was a lot to process.

I was glad I had been wrong about Denis betraying me with Liz, and that I had misjudged him. When and if we would meet again, I would make Denis understand that I had a trust issue thanks to my failed relationship with George and that he hadn't made it easy for me. Seeing him with Liz wasn't easy to accept, especially when I couldn't understand the nature of their relationship. And I had to find out who I had slept with while I was in New York.

I rubbed my temples trying to release the pressure.

"Have I slept with you or with him?" I asked.

Lance laughed. "Do you think Denis will allow anyone to come near you?"

"I don't know. I'm not sure I understand anything," I said.

138

Unveiled Secrets

"Denis cares about you. I've never seen him act this way before," Lance said.

Liz held Lance's hand and patted mine with tenderness. "I'm sure everything will work out," she said.

I cocked an eyebrow and coughed. Was it empathy I saw in her eyes?

"I'm sorry for the scene in Denis's office," Liz said. "I saw you coming and decided to play a prank on you—to make you jealous. We had stopped by the hotel to take him out to dinner and celebrate our engagement when you arrived. By the time we looked for you to apologize, you had moved from New York."

"So, there is still some goodness in you," I said, shaking my head.

Liz blushed and fidgeted in her chair. "Denis would never date an actress. He's a businessman, and, frankly, he's too cold to make a relationship work. How did you manage to capture his attention when no other woman could?"

Liz looked at me expectantly. Lance stopped breathing for a few seconds. I didn't know how to explain to her that I was only myself when Denis and I were together.

"I hope you'll forgive me. Denis is still upset because of the entire situation, and he needs you now more than ever," Liz continued.

As Liz spoke, my only thought was calling Denis and telling him that I now know the truth. I took a sip of my coffee.

"I should have told you right away that I was Lance instead of my brother," Lance said. "Liz and I hadn't even dared to say what we had done. I still remember the left hook Denis gave me when I told him we had tricked you."

Lance massaged his left cheek.

"This is why we stopped to see you today. We wanted to tell you the truth," Liz said.

139

Carmen Monica Oprea

I scrutinized their faces. "It's been nice meeting you, but I'm sure you have better things to do on your honeymoon than spend your time with me," I said, clearing my throat.

Liz raised her brows, her blue eyes sparkling in the dim light of the summer evening. Liz and Lance rose from their seats.

"Thanks for coffee and cookies," Liz said, waving goodbye as they walked hand in hand down to the beach.

"Good-bye," I said, as I watched them leave.

Lance kissed Liz, and she laughed, as they kicked their shoes off and walked barefoot together. Small waves embraced their ankles, and I saw them hugging each other, and then kissing again.

A dying sun, sinking into the ocean, seemed to spill fire over the gulf. Beachgoers with nut-brown tans and squealing children soaked up the fading last rays as they ended another day on the beach. Suddenly life seemed beautiful and worth living with me again. I left the patio where minutes before Lance and Liz had sat drinking coffee and joined the other people on the beach. The sand was cold under my feet, refreshing. After a few steps along the shore, my enthusiasm seemed to fade. What if Denis didn't want to talk to me or didn't want me in his life again? My breath caught in my throat.

I turned around and approached the house, shaking the last grains of sand from my toes. I had to call the hotel and ask for Denis. I knocked over a chair as I ran to my bedroom and dialed the hotel number. A gust of wind closed the door with a loud thump. I jumped and looked over my shoulder while I waited for Sam or Irene to pick up the phone.

"May I speak with Denis?" I asked when Sam answered.

"He's not here, Leila. He's traveling to a business meeting to Seattle," Sam said. "How's life at the beach? Are you not going to visit us anytime soon?"

"No plans to, Sam. I left New York for a reason. Talk to you later."

"We miss you around here, sweet face."

140

Unveiled Secrets

I hung up and sighed. Since it hadn't cooled down too much since the sunset, I grabbed a club soda before stepping onto the porch again. I leaned on the wall while sipping from my glass. The two palm trees, one on each side of my home, rustled in the breeze. My thoughts traveled to Spain. Myrna had never contacted me since she had sent me the check and the letter. I wanted to call her but had concentrated on running the store instead. The time had come to return home and to finally meet my mother. It was time to put the past to rest.

I looked to the right at my neighbor's house. John had left for New York to face his past and make those decisions he couldn't make when he had stumbled upon the fraud in his friend's company accounts. I hadn't heard from him yet and hoped he was all right and that he was still determined to make it right. I finished the last of the club soda, returned to the house, and locked the door behind me.

***

Rays of sunlight soaked the bedroom, warming my body. Wondering how long I had slept, I stretched and rolled on my belly to look at the clock. The old clock on the wall showed that it was only six in the morning, but somehow the mornings were always brighter at the beach. I threw the covers off and approached the window. As I looked out the window, I inhaled the salty fragrance of the gulf. The sun dotted the sea with golden beads while sleek yachts were sailing in and out in the harbor, surrounded by hungry seagulls.

The tranquility of my house by the beach was such a big change from the noises of the big city. I never missed New York with all its elegance and grandeur and madness. Life was unpretentious in Rosemary Beach, where all you needed was a pair of flip-flops, shorts, and a T-shirt.

As I looked out the window, a thought popped up in my mind. I turned around and opened the laptop and typed a name into Google— Mark Thurber—and several articles appeared. Mark Thurber was a successful entrepreneur and Liz's dad. I blinked rapidly. Then I clasped my hands in my lap, thinking. Mark was the reason why she behaved like a spoiled princess. He was the reason why John had left New York. One article emphasized that Mark Thurber was under investigation, his assets sequestered by the FBI.

Carmen Monica Oprea

I sighed, closed the laptop, and descended into the kitchen. The bell rang. I went to the door and opened it. The florist delivered a bucket with fresh irises, just as I ordered. I set the bucket on the countertop and started filling Gabriela's vases with the irises. She would have appreciated the free advertisement of her work in my own store.

Today was the part-time help's day off, and with no time for a real breakfast, I grabbed a power bar and a cup of coffee just before the first customer stepped inside the boutique. It was a young girl, with long, curly, blond hair, and a ring in her lower lip, probably here for summer vacation and in search of souvenirs. She was nut-brown, and her blue eyes seemed to occupy her entire face.

I threw away the power bar wrapper and smiled at her. "Would you like to see the items I received yesterday? They belong to an Italian collection. The combination of blues, pinks, and whites in these scarves would make a perfect gift," I said, pointing toward the back of the boutique, where I had spent the previous day arranging the new items.

"Great," the girl said. "Let me see them."

I showed her purses and sunglasses too. She chose two of each and asked me to wrap them. She left the store after I rang up her purchases. Shortly after, another girl in red shorts and a white tank top came in and asked for a bag with a floral design. After a brief inspection of the shelves, she settled for a handbag with white and red beads, and she attached a white scarf to her sunhat. Then she paid for her purchases and joined her friends on the beach. A tall man in the group, with a tattoo on his left arm, leaned toward her and kissed her. I smiled as I watched them. Life was less complicated and sophisticated in Rosemary Beach. It was just the way I liked it.

Flashes of memories return to life. I remembered the days when Denis and I had spent our lunchtime in the park, walking hand in hand and losing ourselves in each other's eyes. We had shared stories about our dreams, but somehow, we had never talked about our future. We had become comfortable with each other and grew closer. Denis—the man I hadn't understood. Maybe life had just decided to teach me a lesson of endurance and humility, that not all love stories have happy endings. I wondered if I had expected more of him than he was ready to give. Thinking about his involvement with Liz, I judged him harshly. And I had

Unveiled Secrets

been convinced of that right up until the meeting with Liz and Lance had proved me wrong.

Carmen Monica Oprea

Twelve

Denis and the diary were my two most pressing problems now. I walked outside the boutique and dropped into the rocking chair. The ocean breeze brushed my burning cheeks, cooling the fire in my body. My gaze wandered along the shore. A round moon hung in the center of the sky, its light guiding lost souls like mine. My fingers turned white from gripping the arms of the chair. After I had learned about my parents' heartbreaking story, I learned that pain didn't always ease with the passage of time. It remained an omnipresent feeling, accompanying you every step of the way. The diary left me with more questions than answers. I gasped for air just like a fish thrown on shore, and then I hugged my shoulders as I rocked back and forth, the cry of wood against wood somehow soothing to me.

The story unveiled through reading my mother's diary was my story as much as it was hers. But only after I had learned of their unfortunate destiny, did I begin to understand my own. I learned that true love existed, crossed miles of ocean, and waited thousands of minutes to be fulfilled. Contradictory feelings passed through my heart, and many questions still needed to be answered. Did people love with the same passion today as they loved forty years ago? Had I run away from my true love?

As I navigated between questions about the past and the future, the phone rang. I jumped from my chair, went inside the boutique, and answered. It was John.

"How are you? Is everything all right?" I asked.

"Nothing is all right," he said with a catch in his voice. "Something terrible has happened."

"What happened? Tell me."

"Mark Thurber committed suicide this afternoon at the airport. He was fleeing to Andorra when FBI surrounded him and told him to drop the gun. He turned the gun on himself."

"Oh, John, I'm sorry," I said. "Are you alright? Are you hurt?"

Unveiled Secrets

I had known John for a little over a year, and he wasn't the type of man to give up easily on a task. He stood by me when I faced a disastrous season with zero sales after I had just opened the store. John always told me the next day would be better than the previous one, and I believed him.

John paused, and after a break that seemed to last forever, he said, "I was there, right in front of him when he did it. He pointed the gun at his head and pulled the trigger. Blood spattered everywhere. "

"Oh my God," I said, putting my hand on my heart. I knew he didn't mean for this to happen. He wanted to set things right. This was the last thing I had expected to hear when I had picked up the phone. John's anguish seemed unbearable. His voice cracked after every word, and I felt helpless.

"It was my fault, Leila. I pushed him to do it. I should have stayed in Rosemary Beach instead of trying to set things right. Mark is dead because of me."

John's labored breathing made me cry. I remembered how terrified I was after I had lost my mother. Any words of comfort were useless now. I waited for John to continue, and when he didn't, I talked to him as gently as I could.

"You know this is not true, John. It was his choice to take his own life. His decision. You didn't push him. Mark realized he was out of options. Don't blame yourself for someone else's decision."

I could hear John's muffled sobs. Tears pooled in my eyes again, and I tightened my hold on the phone while I leaned on the wall, sliding down to the floor.

"I shouldn't have left the beach, Leila. How am I going to face his family now?"

"Tell me exactly what happened. Did you at least try to talk to Mark before he did it?"

John sighed. His friend had committed suicide, and John blamed himself for pushing Mark to the edge. John was ashamed of not having done the right thing for the employees working for Dunes Corporation

Carmen Monica Oprea

when he had the chance, and his anger was justified only by his wish to come clean before the trial.

John said, "Mark didn't want to hear about cooperation with FBI. I told him he could cut a deal if he provided proof of the offshore accounts where his millions had flown over the past years. His greed killed him in the end. He knew he was going to jail for a very long time, and he wanted out."

John paused as if giving me time to process the news. Then he cleared his throat with a cough.

"What about you, my dear? Are you okay? Have you decided yet?"

"What do you mean?"

"Have you bought the plane ticket yet?"

I ground my teeth. I wasn't ready to answer that question. "When are you coming back? New York doesn't have anything to offer you anymore. You paid your debts at a high price."

"You're avoiding my question," John said. "I miss Rosemary Beach, and I miss you."

My heart throbbed in my chest. I sighed before breaking the news to him, and for the first time since John's departure, I was happy that I didn't have to face him. The feeling that he was in love with me brought a knot to my throat. I couldn't return his feelings. It would be difficult for him to accept that I was still in love with Denis. I had to tell John about Denis's twin brother and his relationship with Liz.

"It turns out that Denis has a twin brother who married your friend's daughter, Liz."

"My God! Denis has a twin. Is he married to Mark's daughter? Does he know that you know yet?"

I sighed. "Denis is out of the country, so I haven't been able to talk to him."

146

Unveiled Secrets

"What about your mother?" he asked, changing the subject abruptly. As if reading my thoughts John said, "I'll look after your store if you decide to go to Spain."

"I'll think about your offer."

Tessa could come down to Florida and look after the store. They could look after it together. John could help her the way he had helped me when I opened the store. They were the only two people I trusted.

"My mother is waiting for me," I said.

John lowered his voice. "Do you know where she lives or how to trace her?"

"She lives in Vigo Bay, in Spain."

My voice broke as I thought that somewhere, on the other side of the ocean, I had a mother. She wouldn't have sent me the money the moment I needed it the most or left her diary for me if she didn't want to be found. Excitement, joy, and fear mixed in my heart, and suddenly, flying to Spain to meet the woman who had brought me into the world became as necessary as breathing.

John's voice brought me back to reality.

"I'll be back in a week, after the funeral. The memorial service is this Saturday."

"I understand," I said. "I might be gone by the time you return."

"I have to be with Mark's family in these moments. His wife asked me to come and stay with them. I'll return to Rosemary Beach after the memorial service."

"Take care of you, John."

"I'll try. Talk to you soon."

The phone went dead. John was right. I wasn't alone anymore. After reading my mother's diary, I wasn't angry with her because she had had her reasons to give me up. I learned her secret.

147

Carmen Monica Oprea

By unveiling her story, I understood my own. Myrna's story belonged to me as much as it belonged to my parents. They had shared a bond of profound sadness, loss, and pain. Then, I thought of the unique friendship between Gabriela and Myrna—beautiful and grand. My adoptive mother gave me the world. She taught me about life and the relationships between people. She stood by me when I had been ill and cooled my fever with devotion until all the sickness's demons ran away. Gabriela had been actively involved in my life, so accepting her unexpected death had been tough. I had to learn how to live without her, and St. Anne's children had given me a purpose. Gabriela had lived her life as an artist, and the things or the people she had touched changed. I changed, too.

I had closed her pottery business after her death but kept most of her vases. I couldn't give them away even when I had requests for her last pieces. I turned all the offers down and kept the vases instead. They were all I had left from my mother.

I stopped at the threshold and looked outside, bracing myself as a nervous tremor crossed my body. It was already dusk, and travelers were hitting the chic restaurants along the coast. The wind carried the music to me. Here and there, couples were immersed in the rhythms of salsa while the neon lights danced over the waves. A few strolled along the beach before taking a dip in the warm salty waters of the Gulf of Mexico or watching the sunset. I turned around and looked at the elegant interior of Bluewater Boutique, before turning the front light on and locking the doors.

I went to the kitchen and settled for a fruit salad of apples, oranges, and blueberries, and thought of John. He wasn't an ordinary man. John had moved from Germany when he was three and had never gone back. Nobody could guess his age, and the small wrinkles in the corners of his eyes were the ones betraying him. His honey hair was tied back in a ponytail most of the time.

One day, I had come across an article in *Fraud Magazine*. The photograph showed a man with short, military-style hair, glasses, and a thin mustache, the opposite of the person I met in Rosemary Beach. Only his green eyes still carried a metallic stare. Over the past months, I found out that he had worked as an internal auditor for Dunes Corporation in New York City for his longtime friend, Mark Thurber. John had met Mark

Unveiled Secrets

during college years, and their friendship grew over time into a family connection. Rebecca was John's daughter, and Mark was Rebecca's godfather. So, John found himself caught between two sides: family on one hand and honor on the other one.

John chose the easy way out. He left the company in the afternoon and the city by the end of the week. His wife couldn't understand John's decision to give up his position in the business. She stayed behind instead of supporting his decision, and months later they divorced. The only connection between John and his wife was their daughter, who divided her love and loyalty among her parents. When John left the city, he wanted to put all his association with Dunes Corporation to rest until the day the FBI agent had approached him and asked for cooperation.

***

One year ago

I met John at the end of fall. I saw him sitting on his porch admiring the beach almost every evening. My electricity went off one night because of the storm. I grabbed a lantern and was searching for the electrical panel when John startled me with his golf club. I turned around and kicked him in his groins. John screamed.

"Strong kick," he said between gasps.

"Go away from me, or I swear to God, I'm going to knock the hell out of you. I can't tolerate thieves," I said, punching him straight in the stomach.

John growled when I grabbed his arm and twisted it behind his back.

"Who is the burglar here, lady? I saw the light in the store, and I came down to catch the thief. If you let go now, maybe we can sort things out."

I grinned. John freed himself from my twist, and to my amazement, we found ourselves rolling on the cold surface. I had my back pressed to the wooden floor. John straddled me, immobilizing my legs with his weight and pinning my shoulders to the ground.

149

Carmen Monica Oprea

"Get off me, you rapist, before the police get here," I screamed, fighting my way out of his grip.

John didn't budge when I bit his arm. His eyes popped up in their sockets, and he snarled. He leaned toward me, his nose inches away from me. He smelled like the sea, his green eyes visibly amused by the entire situation. I studied his broad shoulders and the solid shape of his muscles. My mind raced, but everything came down to one thing. He was stronger than I, and I was at his mercy.

"I'll let you go, and we can wait patiently for the police to show up," John said while he released his grasp and jumped to his feet, watching me. He didn't offer to help me, but he stepped back, his eyes never leaving mine. "How can you choose such a disgraceful job when you look so cute? You can pass as a trustworthy person in any other circumstances."

John moved two steps farther away. I rose to my feet and massaged my arms. The traces of John's fingers on my skin were still visible. The spots turned a light purple, and I knew the bruises would remain for at least a couple of days. A movement to my right caught my eyes. John had found his golf club lying on the floor, and he grabbed it. I choked and coughed to clear my throat, hoping he wouldn't have a use for it later.

"Listen, I am a decent person. It is my store," I said.

"Are you the owner?" John asked me. "We hadn't been properly introduced."

"I'm Leila Isidro," I said, extending my hand in John's direction.

"John Gunter, neighbor," John said, shaking my hand. "I'm sorry for the rough introduction. I thought you were a thief trying to rob this store. I couldn't let this happen to my new neighbor."

"You are a great one." I laughed at the odd circumstance of our meeting. "With you around, my shop will always be safe."

I ducked and began cleaning up the mess I had created when I broke one of my mom's favorite vases.

150

Unveiled Secrets

"Sorry for scaring you," John said, holding the trash can.

The only light in the store came from the lantern lying on the floor next to the wall where it had landed when John and I fought.

"I should look for the electrical panel and fix your light," John said.

John went into the storage room where the electrical panel was located, and within minutes, the lights came on. We locked gazes on each other for a few moments before bursting into a boisterous laughter that sent us back to the floor.

"So, you wanted to hit me with the golf club?" I asked, pointing to the instrument lying on the floor between us.

"I was prepared to take a shot at you, but you were faster than me with your kick and punch routine. By the way, I think I'll have a bruise for a few days on my ankle. You are not as soft as you look."

"As a single woman, I have to know how to protect myself on the streets."

"You're quite good," John said. "Your grip was firm and unexpected, and the punch reached the right place. You took me by surprise."

"Not the inexperienced thief you thought you'd caught," I said. "Well, this date deserves a cold drink. I was on my way to the kitchen when you found me. I woke up thirsty. The storm had knocked the electricity out. That's why you noticed the light moving through the house."

John smiled. "The light moving through the shop made me curious."

"By the way, I'm sorry for the punches and the bites," I said, embarrassed for my earlier behavior.

A few hours passed before John decided to head home. He turned toward me.

"I'll be next door if you need me," John said, swinging his golf club in the air.

151

Carmen Monica Oprea

"Be careful not to ruin my store. I might need some help with the place if you have any to spare."

"It'll be my pleasure. I'm quite good with nails and a hammer."

John looked straight into my eyes, and the entire world disappeared. I wondered if that was the full effect of consuming a whole pack of beer.

"Time to go. Pleased to meet you, Leila! If you don't have any plans for tomorrow-I mean for today," he said, checking his wristwatch, "I'd like to invite you sailing."

"I'd like that very much. Thank you, John Gunter. It's been a pleasure sharing all of these beers with you. See you in a few hours."

John leaned a little toward me, and I was startled to meet his soft lips. They tasted like salt and beer. Then John climbed the stairs to the bedroom, and I got out the door and took a few steps down my porch. Where was I going? I halted and turned back to the house—my house. I entered just when John descended the stairs.

"Wrong direction," we both said.

"Well, good night, and I'll see you tomorrow," John said.

"Sleep tight," I said.

As I locked the door behind me, I hoped I wasn't dragging myself into something I wouldn't be able to handle later. And where had I come up with the idea that I would like to go sailing with a stranger? What an idiot!

I reached the bedroom and fell asleep. It was about ten in the morning when I woke up. My head spun. *Dear God*, I thought. I was supposed to meet John at the dock and sail with *Ever Lucky* as we had planned. I jumped from the bed and chose a dress with long sleeves and a strange logo "Your feelings are the fuel." Indeed, my feelings were the fuel for whatever the day would bring. I almost knocked down a few passing travelers in my jog toward the marina. I looked back, apologizing without stopping. A breath of relief escaped my mouth when I spotted John's yacht shining in the marina. One huge leap and I landed in the

Unveiled Secrets

center of the ship's platform. The ship was sparkling clean, and John was in deep concentration.

"Hello, John Gunter. It's a perfect day for sailing, don't you think?"

"Good morning, Leila Isidro. I'm glad you made it. I thought you were still suffering from the previous night's hangover. Tell me, do you have a habit of drinking beer with strange men at midnight?"

"This place has some magic. It made me think that I am in charge of my destiny," I said, grinning.

We avoided a conversation about the innocent kiss we had shared in the middle of the night. I decided to be on my best behavior and stick to water and coffee as much as possible. That way, I would be safe from transmitting mixed messages, especially after my awful experiences, first with my fiancé and then with Denis. I intended to stay out of trouble, and the man in front of me, with his robust shoulders and seductive smile, smelled like a hassle from miles away.

From his spot behind the wheel, John's gaze followed me as I walked toward him. His green eyes sparkled, and I pretended not to notice the way his lips parted with a seductive kiss. A gust of wind kissed his face, scattering his blond hair behind his head. He was a drop-dead gorgeous man, and I did my best to ignore the butterflies in my stomach. I blamed them on the alcohol I had consumed the previous night.

"What's the plan for today?" I asked matter-of-factly.

"I hope you like snorkeling. I discovered a beautiful place you'll enjoy for sure. Did you remember to bring a swimming suit? If not, there are extras in the cabin downstairs."

John waited. The wind also stopped, as if expecting my answer, too.

"Of course, I did. Sailing on a boat also asks for a swimming suit. Don't you agree?"

John busied himself with a rope he had left sitting on the vessel's deck. He rolled it around his arm and forearm and then tied it in a knot,

153

Carmen Monica Oprea

before shoving it into a wooden toolbox. His muscles tensed, and I found myself unable to take my eyes off him.

"See anything you like?" John asked, looking over his shoulder.

I averted my gaze and cleared my throat with a cough. "How can I help you? I trust you don't expect me to sit around and do nothing."

John chuckled. "You can start by preparing breakfast. You will find everything you need in the cabin."

"Aye, aye, captain," I said, following the direction he showed.

The truth was that I was hungry, too, so after I had descended into the cabin below the boat's deck, I decided to prepare eggs in a basket and toast. I opened the fridge and pulled out the butter and jam, and I exhaled when I rested my eyes on the bottle of orange juice. I filled a glass with ice, poured the cold orange juice, and drank it. Then I looked around the cabin, noting the immaculate walls decorated with pictures of John and a young girl at different ages. There were trophies perched on top of a wooden cabinet with John's name on—Best Fisherman of the Year. The sound of the toaster brought me back to the counter, and after I put the eggs, milk, coffee, toast, bread, and jam, along with plastic utensils and paper plates on a tray, I began my ascent. When he heard the squeaky sound of the door, John turned around. Our eyes met. It was a flash that lasted less than a second, but it made my heart skip a bit.

"Breakfast is ready, captain," I said, looking around.

John had taken the boat offshore, and we were sailing on the bluest waves I had ever seen.

"We'll reach the Laguna in no time. It's close," John whispered.

I nodded, speechless, as I stared at the foam forming around the boat. The pungent fragrance of the gulf enveloped us, and I giggled when I saw the dolphin jumping from the waters as it followed us. I turned toward John.

"Put sunscreen on your skin if you don't want to look like a boiled lobster," he said.

154

Unveiled Secrets

"Good advice." I opened the floral bag I carried and pulled the sunscreen spray out. "Do you need some?"

John refused my offer, swinging his head from left to right. "I'm good. I've already been toasted."

"Breakfast is ready," I said, sliding the sunscreen back in my bag. I set the plates on the round metal table and poured myself a cup of black coffee with one spoon of milk.

"Do you want some?" I asked John.

"Sounds good. One spoon of brown sugar and two spoons of milk, if you don't mind," John said, winking at me.

I poured coffee and milk into a mug and handed the cup to John.

"Tell me about the girl in the pictures. Who is she?" I asked John.

John took a sip of coffee and navigated the boat with the free hand. "She is Rebecca, my twenty-year-old girl. We had planned to spend this summer together. She just called the other day to tell me that she has decided to go to Europe with a group of her friends from college. Who can blame her?"

I stared at him, and the darkness of his eyes hit me in full. John had a story, just like me. I patted his shoulder and took the cup from his hand. John dropped the anchor as soon as we reached the shore where the waters were quiet. Here and there, the peaks were climbing above the waters. Not far from where John had anchored the boat, I saw an arched door made of stone, leading to a private white beach.

John sat on a chair, eating scrambled eggs. I was famished, too. I spread butter on a slice of toast and then added jam. Apricot jam—its spicy fragrance reminded me of my childhood.

"Why are you running away?" John asked, taking another bite of the delicious meal.

"Running?" I lifted my gaze from the plate and stared at John. "What makes you think I am running away?"

155

Carmen Monica Oprea

"You're on defense all the time. No man is around you, and you don't seem to relax."

John's eyes looked amused.

"I'm just preoccupied with the store. That's all," I said, blushing.

I rose from my chair and leaned on the ledge of the boat while my gaze wandered around. I followed the banks of fish swimming around the yacht, the seagulls hovering above, and the two dolphins swimming next to the boat. The waves crashed against the shore only to leave behind shells and seaweeds in their retreat.

"Do you like coming here a lot?" I asked.

"Only if I want to seduce a beautiful lady," John answered.

I laughed.

He was a handsome man, and I was single. John approached me. A sigh escaped my mouth when he turned toward me, leaning on one elbow. His dark sunglasses hid his eyes, but the twitching of his lips told me that he was as amused as I was by the entire situation.

"Are you ready to go snorkeling?" he asked.

"Give me a few minutes to change," I said.

"Have you done it before?"

"What?" I asked, not convinced he was talking about snorkeling.

"You know, the usual, going out with a man you just met."

I opened my mouth and closed it. I nodded. "Countless times," I said.

"You need more practice," John added.

"At what?"

John chuckled now. "At lying." He turned his back toward me and fixed his snorkels. "I'll wait for you in the water. Jump when you're ready."

156

Unveiled Secrets

I went back to the cabin and changed into a one-piece, red and gold swimming suit. Then I returned on deck and picked up my oxygen tank before jumping into the water. The waves felt cold against my skin. John submerged first, and I followed his lead, swimming between banks of red, yellow, and purple fish of different dimensions. We passed sponges, sea fans, and corals that clung to every surface of the underwater rocks while the turtles and mackerel were gliding by in search of a meal. Seagrass beds overwhelmed with crabs, scallops, and reef fish raising their young before migrating to the Gulf of Mexico surrounded us.

A couple of hours passed before we returned to the yacht. I dropped into a lounge chair to sunbathe. Other than the sound of the waves hitting against one another and the wind, it was quiet. The breeze was talking to the sea. Even the seagulls were resting on the rocks protruding from the gulf. I closed my eyes for just a few minutes and woke up with my skin burning and my stomach growling. The aroma of grilled steaks filled the air.

"You have everything you need here," I said, rising from the chair and grabbing a club soda from the cooler.

"Lunch is ready," John said, placing the plate with grilled steaks on the table.

"Thanks for sharing this fantastic realm with me. It makes you wonder how something so beautiful can live only a few steps away. I love the peace and this quiet world beneath the waves."

"I love being in the water." John removed the cork from a bottle of red wine and filled two glasses. "To us," he said, raising his glass.

"To a new beginning," I said. The liquid red was crisp and refreshing.

"Why did you move here, Leila?" John asked, filling his plate with salad, potatoes, and a generous steak.

"I am running away from someone," I said. "And you?"

"I'm hiding from responsibilities."

Carmen Monica Oprea

Then I told him about Denis and Liz and my mother's diary, and John talked about Mark, and how stumbling across Mark's Ponzi scheme. Three years ago, John's duty had consisted in searching for unreasonable items in the company's books. He was good with the numbers, and that's why one day he had come across wire transfers to offshore accounts that were not recorded in the company's registers. The lack of paper trail caught his attention. Vast sums of money were moved to Andorran bank accounts every month. John realized that if he wanted to find out more about the ins and outs of that suspicious activity, he had to follow the money. And this was what he did. Eventually, John arrived at a conclusion, and the truth was impressive, almost too hard to comprehend.

John confronted Mark with the evidence he had gathered, and the quick drop of his friend's shoulders was a blow in John's face. Instead of his longtime friend, John had met with the blank stare of a stranger. He couldn't believe that Mark could get his hands dirty. As the years passed, John learned that people change. Their needs altered with the passage of time until there was no way to control them. It was what had happened to Mark. Mark had swum in deep waters without thinking that one day someone would discover his deeds and ask him to pay.

Then John told me that Mark, a father of three children, became a seemingly wealthy community leader drowning in debt because of his terrible investments. His company created fictitious agricultural worker compensation policies with premiums as high as six figures. To keep up with the payments, Mark Thurber submitted finance loan applications under fake names and invested the proceeds in high-risk ventures. When he lost the money, he sent more loan applications to cover the ones he had already taken out.

His funding scheme went on for a few years without being discovered since Mark had used different addresses for the loans. He routed parts of the advances to his offshore accounts instead of using them to pay the old loans. His credit crumpled to the ground, and the banks saw Dunes Corporation as an insolvent business. When John confronted him with the proof, Mark said that he had made a mistake. He had seen an opportunity to become rich and seized it. Mark knew that what he had done was wrong. John and Mark argued over the entire situation, and John accused Mark of using him. Mark's family got involved

Unveiled Secrets

in an enormous scandal while the money sat in the offshore accounts to evade taxes.

After he had told me his story, John and I had become inseparable. Although I couldn't push Denis out of my mind, new feelings replaced the yearning I felt at night when I missed the warmth of Denis's arms around my body. Most of the time I just concentrated on organizing the store, and John helped me with renovations until one day we stood in the middle of the boutique and clinked our plastic glasses.

"It's finally done," John said, taking a sip of champagne.

"I couldn't have done without you," I said, kissing his cheek.

John laughed, and life seemed to smile down at me finally.

Carmen Monica Oprea

Thirteen

Present day

The phone call from John left me shaking. Meeting Denis's brother and Liz had been another unexpected turn of events. I grabbed a club soda from the refrigerator and went outside on the deck. I took a sip and leaned on the rail, thinking. I should talk to Denis before leaving the country. I should set the record straight and tie up all the loose ends. Regardless of the outcome, it was something I had to do. Only then could I start a fresh chapter in my life. Meeting Liz and Denis's brother, Lance, and discovering that I had misjudged Denis had been a huge shock but liberating at the same time. Gabriela had always said that time would heal all wounds. But I didn't have time at my disposal.

When the phone rang, I left the soda on the rail and went inside the boutique.

"Leila Isidro," I said.

"Hey, Leila, it's John. I just met Denis at Mark's funeral. He's a decent man, but his brother—that's another story." John's voice came alive on the speaker.

"John! It's so good to hear from you. Yes, that's right, Lance married your friend's daughter, Liz."

"Didn't you say that she was having an affair with Denis?"

"It turns out that Liz dated and married Lance. I had no idea Denis had a twin brother, so I'm afraid I got the facts wrong back then, and I didn't give Denis a chance to explain himself."

"He came to the funeral," John admitted. "I don't think he's got over losing you."

"Why would you say that?"

160

Unveiled Secrets

"I caught sight of your picture on his cell phone, and that's how I realized who he was. I told him you live in Rosemary Beach. Denis said he would find you."

Panic caught up with me. "But I'm leaving for Spain tomorrow. I won't be here when Denis comes."

"I'll tell him you had an emergency and you had to leave the country," John suggested.

"Thank you. Tell him I'll contact him when I get back. It's settled then," I said, my eyes wide with anticipation.

"Have a safe flight. Let me know when you land," John said. "And don't worry about your store. Bluewater will be safe with me."

"I know."

I ended the call and went back outside. A rainbow of colors from the lights of the nightclubs, bars, and the restaurants spread over the waves. Music, laughter, and loud noises from the people who were vacationing in Rosemary Beach filled the air. I thought about what John had said about Denis not being over me and a sense of excitement came over me. Our story was far from being over. My heart drummed in my chest, and a smile stretched across my entire face. Then I thought of the ironic twist in our story. I wouldn't be here when Denis came. John would explain to him that I had to leave. Denis would have to understand.

Just then the phone rang again. I shook my head to clear it.

"Did you forget to tell me that you missed me?" I asked.

"You're right. I missed you."

I became silent, my breath sounding loud in my ears.

"Denis?" I whimpered. "I didn't expect to hear from you."

"Your friend said that you're leaving the country soon."

"In the morning. Where are you?"

Carmen Monica Oprea

"I'm still in New York," Denis said. "I was getting ready to come down to Florida, but the first available flight doesn't leave until tomorrow morning."

"I won't be here."

Denis sighed. "I know. You're going to Spain."

"Denis... I'm sorry. I had no idea you were coming here."

"Isn't that the saddest story of all? I just found you and am losing you again."

"It's something I must do. I hope you understand."

"I'll find you again," Denis said, his voice moist with an emotion I didn't know he could feel.

"We must talk. Let's meet after I return," I suggested.

Denis chuckled. "Princess, now that I've found you again, nothing will stop me from seeing you. See you soon!"

Denis ended the call, and I held the receiver, trembling. My heart quivered with suppressed emotions. I sat on the floor, back against the wall, and closed my eyes. The trip to Vigo Bay was starting to sound like a complicated idea.

***

Thirty years had passed since I had seen the sights of Vigo Bay. I landed at the airport at around nine in the evening. A disharmony of voices on intercoms, flight attendants and pilots hurrying about, food fragrances with spices I didn't recognize, and an overwhelming avalanche of my native language, Spanish, made my head spin. I knew a little bit of Spanish, remembering enough to hail a cab and ask the driver to take me to the Golden Leaves Hotel, where Tessa had booked a room.

A short taxi driver with dark skin and glimmering eyes sped on narrow streets crowded with cars. Pedestrians hurried up and down on the sidewalks. Stores with beautifully decorated windows occupied the first floor of every building we passed on our way toward the hotel. People chatted animatedly while children ran around adults, pulling at

162

Unveiled Secrets

their clothes, crying loudly, or simply gazing at the forbidden wonders inside the stores. A different world unfolded before my eyes, one in total contrast to the one I had left in the States.

By the time the taxi stopped in front of the hotel, twilight had colored the sky with hues of violet and pink, the first stars glimmering between clouds like tiny diamonds. I stepped into the elegant lobby and checked in before heading to the elevator. My room was on the tenth floor, and as the elevator ascended, I looked at the scenery through the glass walls. I could almost make out the marina my mother had mentioned in her diary, and I searched through the canopy of buildings, hoping to find the detective's office. Eric Franzone had died a long time ago, but his detective agency might still be in the same location where Myrna had found him and hired him to find my father.

The room faced the center of a town teeming with life. Cars honked, teenagers shouted, and music blasted out of nightclubs when bodyguards opened the doors to push the attendees inside. Streets wound between modern and historical buildings. The older ones had an impressive architecture. I couldn't stop wondering how they would feel if I passed my hand over their surface. The streetlights were on, turning the city into a radiant sphere. I called for room service and had just enough time to soak in a bathtub before the food arrived.

After I tipped the server who delivered the food, I went outside on the balcony and gazed about the city's panoramic view while I nibbled on a cheese soufflé. I was finally home, just steps away from my mother.

Although it was close to midnight and Tessa would still be asleep, I called her.

"Bluewater Boutique, Tessa speaking! How may I help you?"

"Tessa, it's me. I landed in Spain in one piece," I said, taking a sip of my club soda.

"Good." Tessa yawned. "How was your flight?" she asked.

"Uneventful," I said.

"Oh, well, I can't say the same about things around here. I got to meet your neighbor."

163

Carmen Monica Oprea

I chuckled. John had said that he would keep an eye on the store and help my friend when she arrived at Rosemary Beach to tend to my boutique while I was gone.

"Isn't he the most delightful person you have ever met?" I asked.

"If you're referring to his physique, I can't deny that he's attractive. But our encounter didn't exactly go smoothly."

"What do you mean?" I asked, wondering how bad their first meeting would have been.

"Is he always in a bad mood?" Tessa asked.

"What?" Tessa's question took me aback. I couldn't imagine John with a bad disposition. He cheered me up every time I had one of my meltdowns. "He just lost his friend recently."

"This might explain his sullen temperament."

My eyes opened wide. "Tessa Wilmington, get a hold of yourself," I said.

"Just between us, I think he is in love with you," Tessa said. Then, I heard her humming.

"Nonsense," I said, although I had suspected as much for quite a while. John had acted hurt when he told me that he had met Denis at the funeral. *Men and their big egos!*

"You're like a magnet for troubles, little lady."

"John cares about me, like a friend, but that's all. He has a hard time trusting people."

I didn't want to divulge anything from John's past. It was his own business, and as far as I was concerned, he should be the one to decide how much of his life he wanted to share. If John had a problem with trusting people, it had to be his decision to start believing in them again.

"I assure you, John's quite charming when you get to know him," I said.

164

Unveiled Secrets

"The shop is safe," Tessa added. "I'll let you go, Leila. Take care of you!"

"All right, girl," I said. "By the way, ask him to take you sailing. It's the path to his heart."

"Thanks for the tip," Tessa said, hanging up the phone.

Then I called John. The phone rang a few times, and I was about to hang up when John's husky voice answered.

"John Gunter," he said.

"Hi, John, it's me," I said.

"How is Spain?"

"Different, from what I can tell. Did you meet Tessa?"

Silence.

"Are you there?" I asked.

"I met her. Very energetic. Laughs too much."

"Tessa is an incredible woman," I said. "When you get to know her, you'll agree with me."

"She's strange."

The sound of the waves humming and chanting filled me with longing for home. Not even a day had passed, and yet I already missed the quiet life on the beach, the smell of salty waters and wet sand, along with the combination of fragrances in the shop of homemade soaps imported from France and Italy. I closed my eyes, envisioning the leather belts and jackets that Tessa had suggested I should sell, along with the floral bags with handles made of beads, and blouses in pastel colors.

"Ask Tessa to go sailing with you."

"Maybe one day." John paused. He lowered his voice when he said, "Denis called."

"What did he say?"

Carmen Monica Oprea

"He asked if you left already."

"And?"

"He is coming to Spain."

"I'll be here," I said. "Keep an eye on my store—and on Tessa."

I ended the call, thinking of the friends I had left behind and of Denis. The thought of him coming to Spain filled me with hope. I was suddenly happy, although I didn't know how we would find each other. It was almost morning by the time fell into a dreamless sleep.

When I woke up, I was still sleepy and disoriented. I blinked a few times, wondering why my room was a different color until I remembered where I was. I thought of Denis. Then, of my mother. Later, I thought of Tessa and John. I tensed, then relaxed. It was almost ten, which wasn't entirely surprising considering the change in time zones and that I hadn't fallen asleep until nearly dawn. I heard sounds of people chatting in Spanish and remembered why I was in Vigo Bay. I sighed, pushing back the covers, and dragging myself out of bed. I looked down at my rumpled self, shrugged, and went to the bathroom.

As the sun made its way across the sky, all the excitement of exploring a culture that had once belonged to me once quickened my heart. I opened the suitcase and chose a knee-length violet dress and flats. Then I grabbed a sun hat and checked my purse for the envelope Myrna had sent me, before heading to the elevator.

"Good morning," I told the front desk clerk. "May I have a map of the city?"

"Certainly, miss," the clerk said.

I left the hotel and headed for the first narrow street overcrowded by tourists holding maps in their hands, just like I was. Those beautiful windows I had glimpsed at last night from the taxi were fashionably decorated with scarves, jewelry, miniature portraits of people I didn't know, vases like the ones Gabriela used to mold of clay, and beautiful faces of women with dark hair and bright smiles.

166

Unveiled Secrets

As soon as I turned left at the first junction, the aroma of fresh coffee made me stop cold. It was coming from a street café with tables covered by colorful umbrellas. I chose a table shaded by a blue one and spread the map out while waiting for a waitress.

"*Buenas tardes, senorita,*" a girl with a pad in her hand said.

"*Buenas tardes.* It is the most I can master in Spanish," I said, laughing.

The girl chuckled. "May I take your order, please?" The girl continued in English, writing on her pad as I asked her for a coffee. She entered the cafe and returned with a steaming mug of dark liquid with a hint of chocolate.

"Enjoy your coffee," the girl said. "We sell fresh pastries. Would you like to try one?" she asked while fixing her earbud.

"That would be great," I said.

The sweet aroma of baked goods filled my nostrils. Soon the same young girl returned, carrying a plate filled with sugar delicacies, a big smile on her lips. The scent of vanilla mixed with an aroma I didn't recognize. Just the smell of it made my mouth water.

"Those are my favorite," the waitress said.

"They smell delicious. Are they difficult to make?"

"We call them *Suspiros de Monja.* It's a traditional dessert. They are golden and crispy on the outside, rich and creamy on the inside."

I smiled and picked one from the plate. My eyes filled with tears as I bit into the first *Suspiros de Monja* I had ever tasted. As I debated in my mind whether or not to go for a second one, I listened to the girl explain how they were made.

"Is it complicated to prepare them?"

"The secret is to make the batter thick and to fry one spoonful at a time in boiling oil. After you remove them, it's best to sprinkle powdered sugar or to add candied fruit. It's up to you."

167

Carmen Monica Oprea

"They are delicious," I said as I bit into the second one.

"Where are you from?" the girl asked.

"I was born here in Vigo Bay, but grew up in the States," I said, wiping the sugar from the corner of my mouth. "I am half local and half tourist."

"I'm sure you'll find Vigo quite charming."

The girl left the bill on the table as she walked over to a table to tend to a couple with two small children and many shopping bags. I turned to the map still opened wide in front of me and looked at the names of the streets and prominent buildings. I located my first point of interest. I finished the pastries and the coffee and paid the bill. Armed with a plan, I had every intention of seeing it through.

First, I would stop at my father's grave. Then, I would walk toward the marina and try to find the detective agency where Eric had worked. Last, I would look for my mother. I gathered my belongings and flagged down the same server.

"Can you tell me where I can find a florist?"

The girl scratched her head. Her face brightened. "If you keep going straight, at the end of the street, you will find it. Impossible to miss."

"Thank you again for breakfast and the advice," I said.

The flower shop wasn't too far from the café. A couple of tourists stopped and turned around, handing me a camera.

"Can you take a picture of us?" one of the tourists asked.

"All right," I said. "One, two, and three." The camera captured their smiles. I handed the camera back to the man and waited while they checked the pictures I had shot.

Both smiled. "Thank you," the woman said.

"Where are you from?"

Unveiled Secrets

"San Francisco," the woman said. "We're here for our honeymoon."

"I hope that your entire marriage will be a honeymoon."

"Thank you," the man said, kissing his wife. "We've got the love part covered. The rest is a lot of compromise and understanding."

We all laughed, and then they disappeared between two old buildings.

The name of the shop was Emma's Flowers. The walls were painted pink, and it had enormous windows stretching from the street to the end of the first floor. When I opened the door, the bell suspended above it by an old, rusty chain, rang, its echo spreading throughout the store. Fresh bouquets of garden flowers, wildflowers, and evergreens overflowed the counters. The front door faced the main street, providing a decent view of the buildings across the street, the passing pedestrians and the hustle-bustle that animated the city. Other than the salesperson, I was the only one in the store. I passed my hand over roses in a variety of colors; then I turned toward the lilies.

"May I help you make a selection?" the salesperson, a woman in her late thirties, with hair as dark as night and hazel eyes, asked in English. "Do you know what you're looking for?"

"How did you know I don't speak Spanish?"

"I heard you talking to the couple outside."

I chuckled. "I know what I want," I answered, searching the flowers in wooden buckets. "I'm looking for irises."

"They are right here," the woman said, pointing to the back of the store. "What's the occasion?"

"I'm going to visit someone."

"Then may I suggest a bouquet of roses. They just arrived this morning."

"No, they won't be appropriate. But thanks for the suggestion."

169

Carmen Monica Oprea

When I found them, I paused. Irises reminded me of Denis and the flower he had left on my desk that rainy day so long ago.

"I'll take these," I said, pointing to an enormous bouquet.

"As you wish," the woman said.

The florist wrapped the flowers before ringing them up.

Fourteen

I unfolded the map. A few droplets of sweat dripped from my forehead, pooling on my hands. I shook my head and looked both ways before trying to decide whether or not to cross the street. The traffic was heavy, and the street noises seemed to grow louder with each passing second. Just then a taxi stopped near me, and the driver rolled down his window.

"Where are you heading to, senorita?" he asked me in a thick English accent.

I smiled politely and handed him the map. "Can you take me here, please?"

The taxi driver lifted his brows. "Are you certain?"

"Of course," I said.

"Fifteen minutes tops."

The minute the taxi driver opened the door, the air conditioning brushed against my skin. I leaned against the back seat and closed my eyes for a moment. The heat, the emotions, and just the thrill of adventure had caught up with me. My ears were popping, and I massaged my arms, all of the sudden chilled by the air conditioning. When I opened my eyes again, the taxi driver was studying me in the mirror.

"Are you going to visit someone close?" he asked loudly.

"Yes, my father," I answered.

His eyes widened. "I'm sorry for your loss."

I wished I could tell the cab driver how sorry I was for never meeting my father. "It happened many years ago."

The taxi driver grew quiet as he maneuvered the car through the crowded streets of Vigo. He stopped in front of Memorial Park, fifteen minutes later, just as he had predicted.

Carmen Monica Oprea

"Do you want me to wait for you?" the taxi driver asked. He looked grave and uncomfortable for being in that location. I was apprehensive, too.

"I'll rather walk back," I said.

"Let me give you my business card. Just call me anytime you need a car, senorita. Carlos will be at your disposal."

Carlos passed me the card, and I nodded. As he departed, I approached the stone walls surrounding the cemetery. Only the screeching of his tires against the asphalt disturbed the serenity of the place. The gates were wide open, so I followed the paved road lined with lilies and jasmine. It was peaceful inside. My heart beat fast as I circled graves and monuments, some older than others. The place was almost deserted at this afternoon hour. A chill went through my body. I looked back. A few birds chirped in a tree, and the sound of a bell resonated throughout the cemetery.

As soon as I spotted an older woman ahead, I increased my speed, wiping the sweat from my face. She carried flowers in her hand as she strolled, propping herself against a cane. Silver locks escaped from her bun, and she had glowing eyes, the color of the wet soil.

"I'm looking for the section of the cemetery where people who died forty years ago or more were buried. Can you help me?"

The woman searched me from top to bottom and nodded her head.

"*Usted no es de aqui. De donde es usted*?" she asked.

I shook my head. "*Ingles*?"

The woman nodded. "*Un poco.*"

"I arrived in Vigo yesterday," I said.

"Did you travel alone?" the woman asked with a heavy accent. I smiled, hearing a language with which I was familiar.

"I'm here to meet my family."

Unveiled Secrets

"Are they *enterrar aqui?*"

"Are you asking if they're buried here? Not all of them. Only my father. My mother is still alive," I answered, my impatience growing.

The woman pointed straight ahead.

"You will find what you're looking for," the old woman said.

"Thank you," I said.

We walked side by side for a while, in silence.

"*Mi esposo,*" the woman said when we stopped in front of a grave surrounded by rusty iron rails overtaken by ivy.

I nodded and thanked her again for helping me. She hugged me and then kissed me on both cheeks. I followed her directions. Stone and marble statues lined the alleys at various intervals. Grass and wildflowers covered the oldest graves. Old oak trees shadowed every path, their shade intensifying the somberness of this place forgotten by time. I read the inscriptions on the headstones and peeked at some of the pictures people had left. After I searched row after row, I jumped when I spotted a tomb with a stone bench in front of it.

Overlooking the crypt stood a guardian seraph with open wings that looked like he was protecting the person sleeping beneath the marble top. The angel was molded from white alabaster and had sad, delicate features that reminded me of the angels from St. Anne's Monastery. My gaze rested on the angel before lingering on a faded picture of the man buried there. My heart froze when I read the name: Anders Isidro.

A poem was carved on the memorial stone.

I should forget I have loved you,

Perhaps I would do it tomorrow.

I should forget your eyes, your breath,

Your smiling lips, your arms, your sorrow,

Carmen Monica Oprea

Everything I should forget about you.

And I will do it, maybe tomorrow.

I don't know why, but it seems

That tomorrow will be a sorrowful day.

And since you didn't want

My love to follow,

I would try to forget all about you.

I will do it, maybe, tomorrow.

But today let me love you a lot,

Like a flower loving the rain,

Like the moon wanting the night.

So, you see, there is no way

I can forget all about you,

Even if today is tomorrow.

I gasped and reread the poem. It was my mother's. No one had loved Anders more than she did. The beautiful verses brought sighs to my lips. I put the irises in the gray marble vase at the angel's leg, next to lilies that didn't seem older than a day or two. I bowed my head and talked to my father.

"I'm home Daddy. After many years, I finally got here. I read your letter, but I didn't meet the kind of man you wanted me to find yet. I wish I would have had a chance to know you. We would have been good friends. Gabriela was a beautiful person—the mother everyone should have. She told me to read my mother's diary and to find the answers I sought. I promised her that I'd meet my mother. If Mom hadn't been sick, our lives would have been different."

I sat there on the bench thinking that his blood ran through my body and that my eyes were his, as he had said in his letter. I rose from

Unveiled Secrets

the bench and was preparing to leave when I came face-to-face with a woman. Myrna Clarisse Elmer, my mother, was standing three feet away from me, staring. I swallowed hard, my heart in my throat. She had a penetrating gaze, and, for the first time, I felt as if I were a five-year-old girl who needed a hug.

"You came," Myrna whispered. "I thought you'd never forgive me. I thought you'd never come home."

The blue summer dress and the large, floppy hat she wore made her look frail. Her gaze pierced mine, and neither of us said a word for a few seconds. We just stared at each other. The only sound came from the wind blowing leaves and scattering particles of dust over the crosses and graves. Otherwise, it was quiet. I heard the pounding of my own heart in my ears. A knot rose in my throat as I stared at the woman holding a bouquet of calla lilies and red roses. She put the flowers in the same vase where I had put the irises, and then she set down on the stone bench next to me.

"I picked them from the garden this morning," she said. "Anders loved them. We planted the roses together after we bought the house. He spent hours tending to the flowers. I usually watched him as he worked. He never wanted me to help him. He said it was enough I was there," Myrna said.

I kneeled and busied myself with the flower arrangement.

"I wanted to come," I said, rising from the ground and facing my mother. I kissed her on each cheek. "I had to meet you."

"Do you see this tree? I planted it after I buried your father. I spent many weeks talking to him. I came and read to him, as if he stood nearby, unseen and unheard by anyone except me."

I dropped onto the bench next to my mother. She touched my hand. Her touch was soft, gentle, electrifying every hair on the surface of my skin. Her gnarled fingers showed the passage of time. Silence took control of us. I didn't know where to start, what questions to ask, or what to do. I hugged her, drinking in the scent of her skin—lemon.

"Come home with me." Myrna was the first to break the silence. "I'm not going to push you, but I'd love it if you came for the moment.

175

Carmen Monica Oprea

When I sent the diary and asked Gabriela to give it to you, my only hope was that one day I would be able to hold you in my arms. My baby, my beautiful daughter. I spent an entire life missing you."

Myrna cried softly, her head on my shoulder. I cupped her face in my palms and wiped away her tears. Then I shook my head, an unmistakable no. I didn't want to see her crying. Her eyes locked on mine, and I knew I had finally reached the place where I was meant to be.

"You remind me of your father," Myrna said with a sigh, her fingers tightening around mine. "His strength runs through your veins. Just like him, you were determined to make your destiny."

"You didn't remarry after Dad died, did you?" I asked the question, even though I already knew the answer. She was here, bringing flowers, shedding tears, holding onto memories in a place that brought her sadness and peace all at the same time.

"Anders may have died, but he never left my heart."

"But you were young when everything happened."

"I couldn't let go of him. He was the only man I ever loved. I went out and socialized and met interesting people throughout the years, but none made my heart beat the way he did."

Wisps of silver hair escaped from her hat. Myrna's face lit up when I tucked them back in, satisfaction mirrored in her eyes. The past became the present; the future was uncertain, but my mother's presence was the one constant. It was soothing. I was home, and she was there, next to me—the mother who couldn't be a mother.

I took in a deep breath and said, "Let's go home. You've been gone for too long from my life."

We walked toward the gate, where a car with a driver dressed in a black suit with a white shirt waited for my mother. He reminded me of Carlos, the taxi driver, and I wondered if he might be his twin brother. With eyes like pools of the darkness, Spanish men were seductive. I shook my head to chase away the wicked thoughts crossing my mind. Vigo Bay had a strange effect on me. The driver opened the door as soon as we stopped next to him.

Unveiled Secrets

"Are you going home, senora Isidro?"

"Yes, Miguel," Myrna said, "and this young lady is joining us. She is my daughter. Leila just came back from the States."

When we slipped into the car, the leather cover of the back seat was like ice against my heated body. Miguel was watching me in the mirror. I stared back at him and smiled. No doubt he was surprised to discover his employer had a living relative. When I lifted my brows, he coughed and started the engine.

"Welcome home, senorita Leila. I'm pleased to meet you," Miguel said.

"Same here, Miguel," I said.

I couldn't sit still in my seat as I took into view the crowded sidewalks and the beds of purple, white, and red petunias lining the streets. We passed the rose garden where Myrna wrote her novels while I ran around as a child. We left behind the center of the city where groups of teenagers played melancholic songs on their guitars, some sitting on stone steps. Girls wrote in notebooks on their knees while they sipped from cups of coffee, and artists painted the sunset, trying to capture the splendor of another summer evening when the sky turned from bright blue to soft grays and oranges.

The drive wasn't long, and before I knew it, we had arrived. I was still holding my mother's hand when the car turned onto the same path Myrna had traversed years and years ago on the snowy Christmas Day that had changed her life. I could picture a timid girl and a young man, madly in love, surrounded by snowflakes and warmed by the torrent of their emotions. Everything I had read in my mother's journal came alive.

"I'm glad you sent me the diary," I said as I admired the old house with its impressive oak door and large windows with white shutters. The fountain was still in excellent condition. Small birds quenched their thirst from its clear water, hiding between the stone edges.

"I'm happy you read it. I hoped it would help you understand what happened and how those events altered the course of our lives." Myrna turned toward me, tears in her warm eyes, her voice almost a whisper. "I wanted to bring you home when you were a teenager, but it

Carmen Monica Oprea

wouldn't have been fair for Gabriela. She was a good friend and an excellent mother, and you so fond of her. I didn't have the strength to pull you away from her, and I told her so. She loved you very much, and she loved you better than I could have. She never complained about the task I had entrusted to her. She couldn't bear a child of her own; that's why she didn't marry. She thought it wouldn't be fair to ruin a man's hope of having a family."

"You were always there. I didn't recognize your name at first. Gabriela used to call you Clair, and the journal talked about Myrna Clarisse. It took me some time to figure out that you were one and the same."

"Your father loved to call me Clarisse, but Gabriela always called me Clair. But there is only one name I longed to hear."

"Mother," I said.

"Yes, Mother," she said.

Myrna sobbed, bright tears rolling down her bony face. They looked like precious pearls before they disappeared into the creases of her summer dress.

"Please, Mother, don't cry," I said, wiping her tears and kissing her on both cheeks. I wrapped my arms around her body and held her close until Myrna her tears stopped, and she sniffled one last time. "Tell me, why did you ask Gabriela to give me the diary so late in life?"

"You weren't ready. When Gabriela realized she would never recover after the accident, she called me to tell me it was time you read the journal and got answers to your questions, and that it was time I took you under my wing."

"It still feels like someone else's story and not mine," I said.

"Let's go inside now. We have much to talk about. Come," Myrna said, and I followed. I looked back, just in time to see Miguel wipe a tear from the corner of his eyes. He stood by the car, watching us enter the brick mansion. Then he drove off, and everything grew quiet.

178

Unveiled Secrets

The grandfather clock in the corner of a large hallway marked the passage of time. Persian carpets covered honey floors, and over the fireplace, as if presiding over the room, was a canvas of my parents when they were young. I looked at my father—dashing and tall and incredibly sensual. His eyes dominated his face; his lips lightly parted, turned up in one corner. Next to him, Myrna looked like a schoolgirl. Waves of blond hair fell over her bare shoulders, and she had the rosy face of a woman in love. When I realized I was in my childhood home, looking at my parents, I couldn't breathe. Tracing my parents' steps wasn't as easy as I thought it would be. I was overcome with emotion. They had been young and in love once.

The sun's last golden rays slipped into the living room through the arched window above the front door. I looked at my mother, not sure what to do next. She took my hand in hers.

"Come and see your room," Myrna said. We climbed a flight of stairs to the second floor. The wood creaked under our feet. "This is where you stayed when you were little. I kept everything intact. Oh, how I lived for this day."

"It looks so...pink," I said.

"It's a color for a princess. Do you see this rocking chair? It was Anders's favorite..."

I let go of my mother's hand and slid into the chair, rocking back and forth. Goosebumps raised on my skin as I pictured my father sitting in that very chair and realized that I didn't remember anything from the time I had spent in that room. It happened a long time ago. I got up from the chair, and Myrna followed me through the room, tapping my shoulders every so often. A white wool spread covered the bed, and there was a dollhouse filled with figurines. An enormous bookcase filled with children's books covered a wall.

"Your father read to you every night," Myrna said, passing her hand over the books.

"I don't remember his voice. I don't remember anything from the time I spent here."

"It's understandable. You were only five when you left."

Carmen Monica Oprea

I looked away from my mother's stare and gazed out the window at the flower garden. The view was breathtaking—a rainbow of colors, their fragrances beckoning me to go out and explore. I inhaled their perfume through the open window.

"Your grandmother planted many of the calla lilies and the jasmine bushes. Anders planted the roses," Myrna said.

"I remember that from your diary."

"He used to spend hours under the jasmine bush. We talked about our plans for the future, enveloped in the scent of jasmine," Myrna said.

I turned around, closing the window. We left the room and exited into a narrow hallway with polished parquet floors and rooms on both sides. One was my mother's bedroom after she had returned from the hospital, and another one belonged to my parents as a couple. My mom had pictures displayed throughout the hallway. Many of them were of my parents on their wedding day. I studied my father for a while, his protective hold of his delicate wife bringing a smile to my lips. My gaze moved to the ones of a little girl playing in a crib, then to the same girl running through the paths in the garden. Some were taken with my mother, and many were with Gabriela, my other mother. I touched the walls, stopping here and there to admire paintings of my grandparents. It felt like home to me, even if I didn't remember any of the people I saw in the pictures.

Myrna stopped in front of an office with stylish mahogany furniture and a coffee-colored leather sofa.

"It was your father's office," Myrna said.

"It feels larger than life," I said.

A bookcase stretched from floor to ceiling, the shelves filled with business books. The room was neatly kept as if someone had just left for a few days. On the writing desk, faded documents lay in a pile. I browsed through them. The writing on them had lightened with the passage of years.

Unveiled Secrets

"I didn't change a thing," Myrna said, opening a window and looking at the garden. "Your father loved to come here and read or just work on matters related to the factory."

Then, she signaled me to approach. "Your grandfather planted that old willow tree after they moved here. Its long branches offer shade in the summer, and its flowers emit a sweet scent when they bloom."

"Did you spend a lot of time here after my father's death?" I asked.

"Every day... I needed to connect with him."

I turned around and looked at the stack of documents on my father's desk. Something was entrancing about them. I wanted to read them, to connect with my dad's way of thinking. I looked down at a page. The first few paragraphs talked about bank accounts he had opened at the Phenix Bank in Vigo Bay. I had to go back and study them.

"Aren't you curious about these?" I asked. "They might hold important things regarding the estate."

"I was never a businesswoman, and your father knew that. I'm sure he left everything in order. He understood my artistic personality."

"Do you know who he sold the business to?"

"He sold it to Mendoza family, and their son, Leonard, is the one in charge now. Not that he is half the businessman his father had been. I think he's in a lot of trouble; at least this is what the newspapers say. He may even face bankruptcy if he doesn't come up with a plan to pay off his loans. Albert Mendoza, God rest his soul, had an iron hand and a flair for trade. He came from a respectable family. His employees loved and respected him. I met him a few times at social gatherings."

"Mendoza family," I repeated to myself.

I searched through the papers as I listened to my mother.

"Albert changed the name of the company to Mendoza Embroidery Enterprise after he took over. But his son, Leonard, is nothing like his father. He wastes his time in casinos, gambling away the money

181

Carmen Monica Oprea

his father made. He is married, and his two daughters are delightful. But he keeps a mistress too."

"A what?" I asked, lifting my gaze from the manila folders.

"A lover, dear," my mother answered. "I'm sure that you know the meaning."

"How do you know this detail, too?"

"Everyone knows. Even his wife knows. But she won't do a thing. She enjoys her social position as his wife too much. She has money, power, and freedom, and she won't dream of divorcing him. Their arrangement is perfect."

I laughed at my mother's sense of humor. Myrna chuckled, too. Coming home wasn't nearly as terrifying as I had feared.

Fifteen

"Leonard Mendoza: One Step Away from Bankruptcy," I read aloud from the front-page headline of a newspaper Myrna had spread out on the desk.

"Exactly," Myrna said, shrugging her shoulders.

I sank into one of the comfortable leather chairs that matched the sofa and read the entire article describing the mountains of debt the Mendoza family had accrued and how the bank was threatening to take over its assets and sell them at auction.

"According to the news, they're in a lot of debt and the factory is falling apart. What are you planning to do?" Myrna asked, seeing the expression on my face.

There was a brief moment of silence. I leaned my elbows on the cherry wood desk and rested my head on closed fists.

"First, I'm going to visit Leonard Mendoza and test the waters. I think Father would want the company back in the family."

"Had he not gotten sick, Anders would have never sold the factory," Myrna said.

"We need to find out how much Mendoza owes to the bank. Do you know anyone who can help me? Do you have any connections?"

Myrna sat across from me and folded her hands in her lap. She leaned back in her chair and closed her eyes, thinking. I read the article once again and shook my head. Denis would know exactly what to do. During the time I worked with him, I witnessed him taking over hotels all over the world and reviving them to their former glory, just as he did with the boutique hotel in Paris. Thinking of Denis made me shift in the chair. I shouldn't think of him now. There was enough time tomorrow or the day after tomorrow, but not now. My mother needed me, and the thought of him brought a flutter in my stomach.

Carmen Monica Oprea

"Let me see what I can do." Myrna rose from the chair. "I'll go make a few phone calls. Are you going to be all right by yourself?"

"Mother, I'm home. I will always be safe here," I said, trying to sound more convincing than I felt. Everything was new, even my own mother. "And thank you for the check. It helped me buy Bluewater."

"I'm glad I could help," Myrna said, turning around and walking out of the room.

After the sound of her steps faded, I decided to shuffle through the pile of documents on my father's desk. I pulled out the sales contract of the business and browsed through the pages. Toward the end of the agreement, I noticed a clause that stipulated that Anders Isidro's family was entitled to receive five percent of the enterprise's profit. It was to be paid in any form Mendoza chose. I found that interesting and wondered if my mother had any idea about its existence.

"Did you ever receive money from the Mendoza family?" I asked Myrna when she returned to the room, holding a writing pad. "According to the contract, you were to receive dividends for the duration of your life. Your heir will inherit this right after your death."

Myrna stopped at the threshold, parted her lips as if to say something then shook her head as if she thought it was unimportant.

"I don't know anything about dividends, but I did manage to schedule a meeting with the bank's president for tomorrow morning."

"That's great news."

I rose from the chair, still holding the contract. "I may need this tomorrow. I will take it with me." I dropped the contract in the bag I carried, then looked at my mother. "Let's walk in the garden."

"Come this way," Myrna said, opening the French door leading to the stone patio.

We descended the few stairs to the garden. The evening sky looked painted with a rainbow. Fireflies began swarming around us, lightening up the entire garden. The fragrance of freshly mowed grass mixed with the jasmine perfume. At a junction of the garden paths, we

Unveiled Secrets

stopped, and I inhaled the aroma of calla lilies that my grandmother had planted and admired my father's favorite—the red roses. I turned toward Myrna.

"This house will know happiness again, I promise."

"Your presence here is cause for joy," Myrna said.

I switched my bag from one shoulder to the other as we walked toward the front of the house. I lowered my voice. "Tomorrow, I'll meet with Mendoza and ask about that clause in the contract they haven't honored. I'm curious to hear his answer. Then after the meeting with the bank's president, we'll decide if we need to hire an attorney."

We headed for the gate, where my mother's personal chauffeur was polishing the car. He opened the door as soon as he saw us.

"Aren't you going to stay here?" Myrna asked.

I wasn't sure if Myrna referred to my permanent move to Spain or just into her house for the duration of my stay. "I need to go to the hotel and get my things and settle my bill. I'll come home soon. I promise. Can Miguel take me to see Mendoza around eight in the morning? I hope he will see me without an appointment."

"Absolutely. Miguel, please drive Leila wherever she wants to go."

"Of course, senora Isidro, it will be my pleasure."

My mother kissed me on both cheeks, and then she waved from the doorway until I couldn't see her anymore.

"Where shall I drive you, senorita?" Miguel asked.

"Just drive around the city," I said.

Miguel fell silent as he drove. The streetlights painted the streets gold while the day's agitation seemed to fade away with the night. I thought of all the things I had experienced on my first day in Vigo—the visit to my father's grave, the meeting with my mother, and my early childhood home.

Carmen Monica Oprea

"What do you know about Leonard Mendoza?" I asked Miguel, breaking the silence.

"Handsome, devilish, a women's man with charm and money," Miguel answered.

"Great description. I guess I'll be the judge when I meet him tomorrow," I said, laughing. "Would you please drive to the harbor? I want to see it."

Miguel turned right at the first junction, leaving the center of the city behind. Shops with colorful flower boxes in the windows lined the streets. Girls in stylish and dangerously short skirts accompanied men twice their ages poured out of gentlemen's clubs.

"Ladies of the night," Miguel said, coughing. "Very expensive."

I opened my mouth and then closed it again, as I rolled down the window and tasted the salty sea air.

"The harbor starts from here," Miguel said, pointing to the marina.

"If you don't mind, I'd like to walk a bit."

Miguel pulled the car over. "This is a rough area. I'll follow behind you in the car if that's ok."

I opened the door and stepped out of the limo. Ships of all sizes were docked in the silent waters. People strolled by singing, drinking, and laughing loudly. They surrendered themselves to the sweet sounds of flamenco music. Gracious stars glimmered in the sky above, their shapes fuzzy in the waves. Buildings with iconic designs rose above the bay like concave pedestals. The offices were closed at the late hour, but I hoped to find the agency where Eric Franzone had worked. From what the diary had said, the windows of his office overlooked the marina, so the agency should be somewhere between the bars and shops lining the side of the street facing the harbor.

"Are you looking for something in particular, senorita?" a man passing me on the sidewalk asked. Still wearing his uniform with the name

186

Unveiled Secrets

of a restaurant where he worked sewn on the front, he seemed accustomed helping lost visitors.

"Do you know if the detective agency of Eric Franzone is still in this area?" I asked although I was sure there was very little chance that the office was still open after all these years.

"There used to be a detective agency at the end of this street, but it closed a long time ago. I was a kid back then. It's just an empty warehouse now."

A sigh of disappointment escaped from my mouth before I thanked the man. The man disappeared into the darkness and left me wandering the streets. Miguel was five feet behind me, per my mother's request to never let me out of his sight, so I decided to look at the boats and listen to the music for a while.

It was a different world here, from the people's customs and actions to their exuberant expression of emotion. They seemed to live every day passionately without worrying that someone might judge them for their behavior. People acted differently when the sea, the sand, and the moon were involved. Watching them on the beach made me miss my house and my simple life in Rosemary Beach even more.

I wondered if Tessa was doing all right, and if she had had a good time sailing with John. I would call her as soon as I returned to the hotel. The thought of my two friends made me smile. Both had been through heartbreaking experiences, and they deserved a second chance at happiness. Then my thoughts turned back to my present situation, and tension permeated every fiber of my body. So much to do with so few resources. I thought of Denis again, and of how much I missed him and how he would know exactly what to do.

Miguel followed slowly behind me, just far enough to keep a vigilant eye on the people of the night. When I had had enough of the marina, I signaled to him and got back into the car. I had a lot on my mind, and I needed time to prepare for the next day's meeting. I wondered if I would know what to say or how to approach the situation with Leonard Mendoza. I prayed silently he would be a reasonable man.

"Thank you, Miguel. See you in the morning, around eight," I said as we pulled up to the front of the hotel.

Carmen Monica Oprea

"It has been my pleasure to show you the city, senorita. I'll see you in the morning," Miguel said with a quick smile before driving away.

Back in my room, I filled the bathtub with hot water and poured aromatic oil into the tub before stripping my clothes off and letting the water take control of my body. I leaned my head on the edge of the tub and closed my eyes, breathing in the eucalyptus scent that seemed to work wonders for my tired body. Fifteen minutes later, I grabbed my pajamas and drifted off to sleep between clean sheets.

The front desk called my room at seven, and, after a light meal of toast, honey and a cup of black coffee, I was in the car with Miguel. He drove me straight to the factory, and it was eight thirty when I stepped through the glass doors of Mendoza Enterprises. I headed straight to the reception desk.

"Good morning. I'm Leila Isidro, and I would like to meet with Mr. Mendoza," I said.

"Good morning," the receptionist responded in English, peering out at me over her black designer glasses. "Do you have an appointment with Mr. Mendoza?" she asked.

The receptionist was already checking my name on the database to confirm an appointment. I nervously tapped my fingers on the desk while I waited.

"No, I don't. I just arrived yesterday, and I didn't have time to schedule one. But it's an urgent matter, and I'd appreciate if he could just take a few minutes from his busy agenda to talk to me. It's very important. This matter can't be delayed any longer."

The receptionist piercing gaze seemed to look right through me. She must have sensed my sincerity and the urgency of the matter; she clicked a few more keys on the keyboard and then rose from her leather chair.

"Let me see what I can do for you, Miss Isidro. Would you like a cup of coffee or a bottle of water while you wait?"

"No, thank you. I'm OK."

Unveiled Secrets

I dropped into one of the four leather chairs in the lobby and browsed through the stacks of magazines lying on a table. My hands started to shake, and I clenched them in my lap, looking around the room for something to calm my nerves. I knew I was about to face a prominent opponent, and I felt my confidence plummeting. The task wasn't going to be easy, but it was worth a try. I peered through the glass wall separating the lobby from the offices and wondered if they had preserved any of the things from when my father was here and if this was the view he saw every day when he showed up for work. After a few minutes that seemed like hours, the receptionist returned.

"Mr. Mendoza says he can't see you this morning, but he would be delighted to meet you in this afternoon. Would you like me to schedule an appointment, Miss Isidro?"

I rose from the chair and shuffled through my bag, pulling out the folder that contained the contract of the sale of the company. I handed it to the girl and said, "I would like for you to take this document to Mr. Mendoza. I'm sure he will squeeze in a short meeting after reading the page marked with a post-It on it."

Visibly irritated, the girl bit her lip, and her nostrils flared. She stepped out of the lobby again. After a few minutes, she returned, looking pale and shaken.

"Mr. Mendoza will see you now, Miss Isidro."

"Thank you, Isabella," I said. "I appreciate your efforts."

Isabella faked a polite smile as she led the way through a well-lit corridor. The walls were painted a pale lemon shade; the wooden floors polished to perfection. Other hallways branched out left and right from the main hallway. I counted my steps to relieve the tension that threatened to make my muscles explode. We passed offices where an army of employees concentrated on daily tasks. A quick glance in our direction was all we got before they returned to their work. We walked in silence toward the end of the hallway.

When we reached an office with massive double doors, we stopped. The receptionist opened the door, and I spotted Leonard Mendoza sitting behind a big desk and tapping his pencil furiously. A glass wall separated his office from the rest of the cubicles. I stopped in front of

Carmen Monica Oprea

his desk and waited for him to acknowledge my presence. Leonard lifted his chin and stared at me with the confidence of a man who knew nothing of the sorrows and pains of life.

"Miss Isidro, I'm Leonard Mendoza, the company's president. I'm convinced you already know all of this," he said, rising from his chair and coming around the desk, halting a foot away from me.

He was in his mid-forties, with dark hair neatly combed and soft hands with perfectly manicured fingers. Although I was standing in five-inch heels, I had to lean my head back to look at him. The purple shirt he wore emphasized his deeply tanned skin, along with his toned muscles. No wonder he had gotten involved in many highly publicized, thunderous love affairs.

"Thank you for meeting me on such short notice, Mr. Mendoza."

I shook Leonard's hand without losing eye contact. From what my mother had said, Leonard was a man who went for finer things in life. The art displayed on the walls stood as a testimony to his extravagant tastes, which had brought him to the verge of bankruptcy,

"Please, sit down," Leonard said. He went back to his desk, sat down, and leaned in his chair.

"Thank you," I said. My nerves were on the verge of cracking. I had to find a way to stop fidgeting in my chair.

Leonard started the conversation. "I didn't realize Anders Isidro had a daughter," he said, his voice sounding a little too sharp. His mesmerizing eyes bore into mine, and it took all my strength and willpower to focus on the conversation instead of his looks.

"I wasn't raised in Spain, Mr. Mendoza. I grew up in New York away from my parents. I returned to Spain just yesterday. An article about the company in the newspaper caught my attention. It said that the business is about to collapse. Since this is the company my grandfather built from the ground, I have decided to fix this," I replied.

"And how are you going to fix it?" he asked, his surprise showing in the way he lifted his brows and pursed his lips.

Unveiled Secrets

Leonard scanned the document the receptionist had given him. "From this report, I understand that your mother is a shareholder in the company and that she is entitled to receive five percent of the business's profit every year. When Anders sold the factory, his wife became the sole inheritor of the dividends. You are not mentioned in the contract at all."

"I'm here on behalf of my mother, Mr. Mendoza. We both know she hasn't received any proceeds for the past thirty years. She wasn't even aware that this clause existed. She is a writer, and I believe, along the way, someone took advantage of the fact that she didn't inquire about the money. We deserve an explanation, don't you think?" I paused, giving him time to grasp the importance of my accusations before I continued.

"I can tell you're a tough, unyielding woman. Of course, I'm liable for not knowing about the clause in the contract our parents drafted years ago. Also, they left a loophole when they signed the papers. It says right here," Leonard said, pointing at a paragraph in the middle of the page, "the payment will be made on Mendoza's fair judgment."

I sighed. When I went over the document the previous night, I had realized Mendoza had a loophole in the contract that could save the family from scandal. That loophole would give them leverage in any court of law. And I was oblivious to how the legal system worked in Spain, but from what Myrna had said, anyone could win if they knew the right person and paid the right amount of money. The difference between Leonard and me was that he had both of those advantages. I sat up straight in the chair.

"Indeed, but the company is facing collapse, and I want to make sure my mother receives what is rightfully hers before the imminent failure."

At this comment, Leonard's face turned from red to pale, and then back to red again. He fought to loosen up his tie and took a sip of water from the bottle he had on his desk.

"Water?" he asked politely, seeming to regain his composure.

I nodded. I cleared my throat. Leonard sat the bottle on the desk, closed the laptop, and leaned toward me.

Carmen Monica Oprea

"I have a business proposition," I said. "Interested?"

"I'm all ears, Miss Isidro."

"I offer to take over the company for the amount of money you owe my mother. This way, you get rid of the burden this company has apparently become to you. You're head over heels in debt. The bank will sell all the assets if you don't come up with a plan to pay back the loans. Think of it, Mr. Mendoza, and let me know your decision by the end of this week."

I picked up the bottle of water, unscrewed the lid, and took a drink, my eyes never leaving his. Leonard took his time before answering.

"You're sharp, Miss Isidro. I admire that quality in a woman. I'm sure we will come up with the best plan to benefit both of us."

Leonard rose from his chair. "I'm sorry. I have other meetings already scheduled. Please, leave your contact information with Isabella so we can reach you. Goodbye, Miss Isidro. It's been a pleasure meeting you," he said, and his voice sounded cold.

A chill crawled up my spine. I knew he was angry. But I was determined to take the business back and turn it around and make it the way it had been during my father's time. I walked down the same hallway I had walked with the receptionist, and this time I took my time admiring the setting. Men and women were talking animatedly at desks separated by plastic screens, pointing at sketches and drawings, and then making changes on their computers until the designs came out perfectly. Some bobbed their heads as they followed the rhythms of the songs they listened to in their earplugs, while others talked on headphones, their voices loud as they took orders and typed furiously on their keyboards.

I gave Isabella my phone number and exited the building into the hot summer air. Miguel opened the car door as soon as he saw me coming. I had been with the company for more than an hour.

"Everything all right?" he asked, closing the car door.

"I'm not entirely sure," I answered.

Miguel smiled. "He is an unusual man."

192

Unveiled Secrets

I nodded.

"Your mother asked me to take you to the Phenix Bank for your next meeting," Miguel said, looking in the rearview mirror.

"I hope it will go better than my previous one," I whispered, watching out the window at the people passing by.

Miguel was quiet as he drove toward the Phenix Bank for my appointment with the bank's president, an old friend of my parents. I sought confidential information about how deeply Mendoza was in debt. If the bank president would give this information, and if Leonard cooperated, I was confident that I could put together an excellent deal for both of us.

"We are here, senorita Isidro. They are waiting for you." Miguel held the door open as he helped me out of the car pointing to the front entrance.

"Thank you," I said, disappearing into the lobby where the chilliness of the air conditioning made me shiver. A man who looked to be in his late sixties rose from a chair.

"Senorita Isidro, I presume?" he asked politely. "We are expecting you. Please, follow me."

As I followed the short, hunch-backed man with a limp in his left leg, I wondered if I should care about his curious stare. The man stopped in front of the president's office, and I read: Luis Fraga. I flinched a little when I read his last name. He had the same last name as Denis. I wondered if it was just a coincidence to stumble over another Fraga. The man pushed open the door of an office at the end of a windowless corridor and invited me inside.

I looked around. The office had wooden floors the color of honey, and a carpet in a coffee color in front of a plush sofa. A laptop was open on the mahogany desk. Papers were neatly stacked on the edge of the desk, and a bookcase lined one of the walls. I went to the windows overlooking an interior garden with narrow paths dotted with evergreens. A fountain was in the middle spitting water, and a few doves nibbled bread crumbs a woman was throwing on the ground.

Carmen Monica Oprea

I found myself smiling. It seemed peaceful. When I heard a cough right behind me, I shifted my purse from one hand to the other and turned around so fast that I nearly knocked over a vase filled with daisies. I leaned forward and caught the vase just in time, blushing under that impossibly handsome man's intent stare.

He can't possibly be one of my father's friends. He is just too young.

Luis Fraga extended his hand for me to shake before I had time to continue my train of thoughts. His green eyes seemed to twinkle. He was more than six feet tall, and from the smile forming on his lips, it looked like he probably thought I was just another bimbo, all looks, and no brain. I shook his hand in return and tried to show a confidence that eluded me now.

"I've been expecting you, senorita Isidro. Any friend of my family is a friend of mine," Luis said, signaling the humped man to leave the room. "My father informed me of your arrival."

"Thank you for taking the time to meet me, Mr. Fraga." The name sounded strange on my lips.

"Please, sit down," Luis said, inviting me to take a sit on the comfortable looking sofa. "I've prepared a file with the information requested by your mother. I hope you realize everything I'm about to tell you can't leave this room."

"I appreciate what you're doing for my family, Mr. Fraga."

"Please, call me Luis. From our bank's records, it looks like Mr. Mendoza owes the bank around thirty-five million euro, approximately forty-seven million American dollars, and he's already in default. The last payment we received didn't even cover the monthly fee. We agreed to give him an extension to come up with a reimbursement plan that works for him. He has two months before we start the liquidation of assets to recover our money."

"He will be forced to sell at a public auction."

"Correct," Luis said, handing me the folder with all of the loans Leonard had taken out using the factory as collateral.

194

Unveiled Secrets

I shuffled through the documents, trying to ignore the soft musk perfume Luis wore and the way his eyes lingered on my face. His deep voice seemed perfectly suited to his muscular physique. I found it hard to breathe in his proximity, and his presence appeared to make everything shrink.

"I want to buy his loans from your bank. Is this something we can work out?" I asked, closing the folder, and setting it on the sofa between us.

Luis narrowed his eyes, probably wondering why he should assist me in buying a business as unprofitable as Mendoza Embroideries.

"It's something that can be arranged," he said.

"Your English is perfect," I said, probably sounding like an idiot.

"I studied in London." Luis paused and took my hands in his. "Do you know that the company needs capital to make it work and only a miracle could save it from collapse? It's suicide to take this on."

"For me, it is history. I hope you understand."

"We'll need to make Leonard agree to the terms of the contract. Paying off his debts gives you the same rights to the business as Mr. Mendoza. Practically, you become co-owner of the company alongside your mother."

"Can we make it happen?"

"He'll be indebted to you instead of to our bank. Are you sure this is something you want to do?"

I shrugged. "I will be frank with you, Luis. I'm planning to take the company from Mendoza and make it Isidro Embroideries once again, the remarkable venture my grandfather built a century ago."

"My father said that Anders Isidro was a sharp businessman before his illness. It was a shock to the entire community when he sold the company and disappeared, leaving your mother alone."

I gasped and pulled my hands out of his.

Carmen Monica Oprea

"I'm sorry. That was insensitive of me," Luis continued, looking apologetic.

I smiled. "It happened a long time ago, Luis. I don't remember my father. I was five when he died."

Surprisingly I felt comfortable in Luis's presence as if we were two old friends talking after a long time apart. I was hoping that Leonard Mendoza would agree to my offer and that I possessed the necessary capital to buy the company.

"Let's wait until next Monday to decide the course we're going to take," I said. "I gave him until the end of the week to think about my offer."

"Then let's have the paperwork ready, Leila." He rose from the sofa, and I followed him.

I asked, "Can I take the folder with me? I want to read the numbers tonight and make my own calculations."

Luis chuckled, revealing a string of perfect white teeth.

"You're new in town, right?" he asked.

I lifted a brow. "You're correct. I don't know a soul here other than my mother and you," I said, shoving the folder into my bag.

"We're having a party this weekend, and I wondered if you would like to come. We have this party every year. Relatives from all over the world are flying to Spain. This tradition has run in our family for generations. Just family members and close friends attend."

I knew from my mother that the Fraga family was a powerful one in Vigo. I had no excuse for not accepting the invitation.

"Thank you for the invitation. I'll be there," I said. "And thank you for your help, Luis. It's a risky venture, but it's important for me to rebuild the family business."

"I'd do the same if I were you."

Unveiled Secrets

Luis opened the door and accompanied me to the main lobby. The busy morning had left me feeling light-headed. I was suddenly tired and yearned for a warm bath and a nap. I was hungry too. Miguel closed the car door, and I leaned back on the comfortable leather of the backseat.

"Take me straight to the hotel," I said. "It's been a busy morning."

"My pleasure," Miguel said.

I closed my eyes for a few minutes, exhaustion taking over my body. I went over the events of the morning, my thoughts sliding toward Luis. I should have asked him if he knew Denis, but I pushed the thought away. I remembered that when we had talked over dinner, Denis had mentioned his Spanish heritage. But that was all. He hadn't mentioned relatives in Vigo Bay, and I had congratulated myself for not asking uncomfortable questions.

We drove in silence to the hotel. It was a relief, since I had developed a headache from a lack of hydration and food, and it threatened to become a migraine. As soon as the car stopped in front of the hotel, I dragged myself outside under the burning sun.

"Thank you, Miguel," I said.

"Call me anytime you need me, senorita," Miguel added. He rolled up the window and drove away while I entered the luxurious lobby of the hotel.

I went straight to my room and ordered lunch. I kicked my shoes off, and they flew, landing somewhere between the nightstand and the bed, while my dress fell to the floor. The warm shower felt refreshing after the busy morning, and I walked out of my bathroom just in time to hear a knock on the door.

"Room service," the server said.

"Leave it at the door. I'll be right out," I yelled, looking for something to wear.

I picked out a T-shirt barely long enough to cover my butt and added my favorite pink socks because the floors were cold. Still dabbing

197

Carmen Monica Oprea

the water from my hair with a towel, I pushed the door wide open. After I looked left and right, I stepped into the corridor. I was just getting hold of the cart's handle when the door across from mine opened too. My heart stopped beating when I found myself looking into those hazel eyes I had worked so hard to forget.

The last thing I remembered before passing out was my name on his lips.

"Leila."

Sixteen

I opened my eyes a few hours later. A sharp pain pressed against my temples. Then I sensed it—musk. Musk meant Denis. I jumped from the bed and looked around. Shadows fell across the floorboards of the room. I glimpsed at the balcony's door, now wide open, and gasped. Denis was gazing at the ships in the harbor. The beginning of a beard skirted his chin. His purple shirt hung loose and untucked over a pair of faded blue jeans. He had one hand resting on his right hip, and the other one was raking through his freshly cut hair. Just one look at him and all the suppressed desires resurfaced. I didn't want him to suspect that disturbing images popped into my mind—visions of Denis getting out of the shower, his naked body still gleaming with moisture, a thin towel draped on his lean hips. I stepped on the balcony after taking in long breaths.

"You're finally up," Denis said, turning around. "I wasn't sure if I should leave alone in your room and return to mine. I've decided to stay with you." His face and jaw tensed for a few seconds.

I felt my cheeks catching fire. "How did you know I was coming?"

His eyes glimmered. "By the sound of your feet on the floor," Denis said, pointing at my feet.

"I called you after I met Lance and Liz," I said. "You never mentioned a brother."

"You have never asked."

"I thought you like to keep things private, but don't you think this is the kind of thing a person should be told?" I shook my head.

A gust of wind swept the few leaves on the balcony, their rustling sounds in unison with my own bruised heart.

"Why didn't you call me back?" I asked.

Carmen Monica Oprea

"I wanted to talk to you in person." Denis leaned toward me, his nose inches apart from mine. I tilted my head. His tone had changed a little, but his voice was gentle. "You look charming."

"It is lovely to see you again, Denis," I said, taking a sip from the bottle of water I had left on the table on the balcony the previous night.

I blushed again. *Traitor*, I thought, touching my heart. I could feel it beating in my ears. I was convinced Denis could hear it, too.

Now and then, I noticed a twinkle in his eye when he looked at me, thinking I wasn't watching. "You've got me worried. You're thin. Are you trying to starve yourself to death?" Denis asked.

I rolled my hair around my finger. "I've been swamped during the past year."

I looked out at the park right across the street from our hotel. The weather was perfect, the air pregnant with oceanic freshness, and the company was excellent as well.

"So, I was told. Your friend John is an interesting man."

I suddenly felt like I was falling in love with Denis all over again, and I had to sit before my feet gave way. I had to force myself to stop the smile forming on my lips. He still cared. Denis pulled out one of the chairs for me and waited. I sat. His eyes shone as he studied me. I was lost in my feelings and still very much in love with him. I studied his full lips and the way he bit the lower one. It felt strange to be close to each other after all the time we had spent apart. I was yearning for him. I crossed my hands in my lap, averting my gaze from his.

"John is a caring man. He's helped me a lot with the boutique."

Denis looked at me directly, his hazel eyes honest and clear. "You're still as beautiful as the first day we met."

I wrapped my arms around my body. "Oh, are you thinking of the first day we met? The interview day when you held my hand into yours and didn't let it go?"

200

Unveiled Secrets

Denis blushed, but his voice was clear in the silence. "I don't remember the day. But I am acquainted with these fluffy socks," he said, pointing at my feet.

I giggled. "What a coincidence to be in the same hotel at the same time," I said.

Denis reached out, touching my hand. "I don't believe in coincidences. I believe in numbers and facts."

"I know," I said, turning my head to the side and ignoring the feel of his fingers against my skin. I slowly turned toward him and pushed his hand away.

He chuckled.

"At least, you can't run away and disappear as you did back in New York. This time you will have to listen to me," he said.

Denis pinned his gaze on me. I couldn't escape his scrutiny or breathe properly. It was as if he had sucked all of the air out of Vigo. I felt like a fish thrown on shore, gasping for breath and struggling to regain my composure and act like a mature adult.

"I can't go far in this outfit," I said weakly. My argument sounded lame even to me.

Denis, who was sitting across from me now, leaned back in the wrought-iron chair and crossed one leg over the other. The sparkles in his eyes betrayed his feelings.

"Denis—"

"Leila—"

"Just out of curiosity, did you ever pass your driver's test?"

I closed my eyes briefly. "Of course not. I'm still scared of cars and of driving."

"Why?" he asked, looking puzzled.

201

Carmen Monica Oprea

"I didn't have time," I said quickly, praying that he didn't notice the way I sidestepped the truth. I tried to shrug off my discomfort, not sure why I felt so uneasy with Denis about this topic. John and Tessa knew I didn't drive. Lots of people in cities across the globe didn't drive. Some didn't even own a car.

"We must correct this. I don't want you running around these streets by yourself."

"I'm perfectly capable of taking care of myself."

"How do you get around?"

"My feet... a taxi," I said, grinning. "After all this time, is this all you want to talk about?"

Denis shook his head once, briskly. "You were the one who ran away. I'm just trying to make you feel comfortable around me."

"Oh, I thought...maybe you had missed me a lot, and you were finally prepared to tell me the whole truth about you, Liz, and your brother."

Denis laughed. "I'd feel the same if I were in your shoes."

"Are you going to tell me why you had to go to Liz every time she called?"

"No, I'm not. You'll have to trust me when I tell you that nothing ever happened between Liz and me."

Denis wasn't inclined to make my life easy, and I wasn't prepared to let him take control of me or dictate what to believe.

"How can I trust you if you're hiding things from me, Denis? You have to tell me something, so I can understand what had happened in New York."

Denis sighed. "It's better if some things remain untold. Lance used to be a good man before he got involved with the wrong people. Liz introduced us to her friends, but Lance had made bad choices. I had to bail him out every time he got in trouble."

202

Unveiled Secrets

"So, Liz called you to get him out of jail?"

"Sometimes, I had to bail both of them out of jail and keep the entire affair out of the tabloids. As you see, it's not that simple to admit that your own family is involved with the underworld. But Lance is my brother, and I must watch over him."

"What about Liz?"

"All I can say is that they deserve each other." Denis put his arms around my shoulders and whispered in my ear. "I'll take you to the driving center tomorrow. You're a citizen of Spain. You shouldn't have any problems enrolling and studying for the exam. Then, I'll continue the driving lessons we started back in New York."

My grin faded. Anger rose in my throat. I coughed and adjusted the rhythm of my breathing.

"You must stop controlling the course of my life," I said, offended.

"It was never my intention to control you. I just think that a young woman like you should know how to drive and have control of her life. I'm returning to New York soon. You'll have all the space you need."

"And you think a driver's license will give me control over my life and make everything all right?"

"Yes," he replied so matter-of-factly that a surprised laugh popped out of my throat. I blinked rapidly, adjusting my sight to the dim light coming from the streetlamps. "Are you hungry?" I asked, trying to ease the awkwardness of the moment and to soften the realization that our first meeting after all this time wasn't going well at all.

"Famished," Denis said, smiling. He took in a sharp breath. "John told me you moved to Rosemary Beach after you left New York. I came down to Florida hoping to talk to you, but you had disappeared." His voice softened. "I'm glad you decided to stay at our hotel."

"I got here two days ago, Denis. It feels like ages," I said, the sound of his name sweet in my ear. "I'm happy you found me. You haven't changed much."

203

Carmen Monica Oprea

"Neither have you. Some people don't change with the passage of time. They only grow more beautiful."

I lowered my eyes. "You're right; they don't." My voice broke.

"And where do we go from here?" Denis asked.

"First, we should have dinner, and then we can try to pick up from where we left off, or we can pretend we never met. Any path we choose leaves our story incomplete," I said.

"You never gave me a chance to explain what happened that day," Denis said.

"You never tried to explain. I realized how wrong I was after I ran into your brother, Lance. He stood in the office that miserable day when I jumped to the wrong conclusion. But how could I have known?"

"Liz and Lance were waiting for me to come out of a meeting. They wanted to tell me they planned to marry. Lance has always been the black sheep of the family. That's why he and I went separate ways. He tried to apologize afterward, but you were long gone. Even when I persuaded and practically threatened Tessa to tell me where you went, she was tongue-tied. I figured you would cool down eventually and we'd sort it all out."

I smiled, as something lightened inside me. "Would you like to go for a walk before dinner?"

Denis looked at the park across the street. He remained silent, just looking at it.

"Very well. We can go under one condition," he said.

"What's that?"

"You have to tell me why you're here," Denis said.

"Let me change first."

Denis rose from his chair while I returned to my room. I settled on a white dress, added a drop of my favorite jasmine perfume, and brushed

204

Unveiled Secrets

my teeth. When I was ready, I grabbed my purse and poked my head through the balcony door.

"I'm ready," I said.

My senses sharpened when Denis whispered in my ear, "Me, too... I have always been ready for you, Leila. Let's go!"

Denis took my hand in his, and we left the room. We turned and walked toward the elevator. I had to stop myself from gasping as I looked at him. I felt a slight shudder pass through me. It was as if with one stroke, an invisible artist had made the past disappear and offered us a chance for a new beginning.

The day waltzed with the night, the people romancing each other as they strolled through the park, just like us. We walked side by side, acting a little wiser and more distant than months before. The snake-like alleys were almost deserted at the late hour, apart from other couples kissing and teasing. Denis tore off a red rose bud from a bush, and after he smelled it, he clipped it in my hair. My heart raced. But only the darkness hid my flustered face.

"I found my mother," I said.

"And?"

"It's complicated."

"I have time."

"She is not what I expected her to be. She is graceful but sad. And what's interesting is that she's always been a part of my life. Gabriela, my adoptive mother, always called her Clair, and she was her best friend. My father called her Clarisse. Her full name is Myrna Clarisse Elmer. And she is a well-known writer who helped me open Bluewater boutique in Rosemary Beach and told me always to follow my heart."

"Did you follow her advice?"

"About?"

"Following your heart."

Carmen Monica Oprea

"I did, or at least I was convinced I was following my heart at that time," I said, tightening my grip on Denis's hand.

As we walked side by side, I told Denis of my father's business and my decision to take back the factory. He listened quietly, and then he frowned.

"You'll find a way," Denis said. "You're a strong woman."

"I have someone's help, one of my mother's connections. He invited me to attend a party at the end of this week."

Denis turned toward me and looked me in the eyes. "Are you going?"

"I agreed to go," I said, lifting my brows.

"Why?"

Denis frowned. He pursed his lips, waiting for my answer. I looked around. The park was empty, apart from us, the leaves, and the torrent of our emotions. I trembled when he leaned toward me, slightly parting his lips. *Mint*, I thought.

"I'm new in town. I must make connections, and I need his help."

I wasn't exactly lying nor telling the truth. But Denis had a way of seeing right through me.

"Is this the only reason you accepted?"

I nodded. "I'm curious about one thing."

"What would that be?"

"The Fraga family here.... are you related to them?"

Denis whispered. "Maybe."

"Did you come here for the family reunion?"

"Partially," he said, watching me intently.

"Please don't stare."

Unveiled Secrets

"You used to like it," Denis said.

"It's late, and I'm hungry," I said, thinking that the excuse would work.

"We still have plenty of time."

Denis circled my shoulders and pulled me toward him. When he pressed his lips to mine, I thought I would melt. My brain seemed to have melted as well because I kissed him back. The long, wet, hot kiss controlled us in incredible ways. I could hear his heavy breathing and feel the tremors on his shoulders. My heart raced like that wild kart on the motorway, and I had only one wish—to take him back to my room and make love to him.

"Let's go back and have a proper dinner," Denis said, releasing me from his embrace. "I must rise early tomorrow."

"Yes," I whispered. I steadied myself and turned toward the hotel. I had plans for tomorrow too.

"When am I going to see you again?" I asked.

"Tomorrow. I'll take you to the testing center as promised. But only after I go over the hotel's financial statements."

"Really?" I shook my head. "As you wish, Denis."

We entered together into the lobby, the coolness of the interior hitting me like an ice storm.

"I'll be right back," Denis said, stopping at the front desk. "I have to talk with the front office manager. Why don't you go ahead in the restaurant and get something to drink?"

I nodded and turned toward the hotel restaurant when I heard someone calling my name. I glanced back, and my eyes widened when Luis Fraga walked toward me.

"Good evening, Leila, I was waiting for you."

"Luis? What a surprise!"

Carmen Monica Oprea

"Did you eat already? Please tell me you didn't."

"Is that an invitation?" I asked, amused by the turn of events.

Seeing nothing wrong with having dinner with Luis, I accompanied him to the hotel restaurant. The strangeness of being in close proximity of two male members of the same family was overwhelming. We entered the restaurant and waited to be seated. I glanced over my shoulder at Luis. He wore a white shirt, the gold of his watch glinting at his wrist. I stood there unmoving, feeling as if I were dreaming.

"How do you find your stay in Vigo?" he asked gallantly.

"I didn't have time to tour the town, except the marina. It appears impressive from my room and very different from the other cities I have visited. I enjoy being able to walk everywhere and the fact that the beach is close. In a way, it reminds me of my home in Rosemary Beach."

"Vigo is a fantastic city. It is home to the most romantic people in all of Spain. Lots of tourists come here every year, attracted by our beaches."

The waiter led us to a private table in the back. Even wearing heels, I was still a good three or four inches shorter than Luis. As he ran his fingers through his hair, his green-eyed stare flickered over me. I was overwhelmed by his presence, not to mention the extravagant artwork and luxurious setting.

"Have you ever traveled abroad?" I asked.

"Countless times. I love to go to a different place every year. I spent two weeks in Monaco last summer. This year I plan on going to the South of France. What plans do you have other than taking back the family business?"

Luis's gaze lingered on my face, his jaw looking tight.

"I'm not sure yet. I just arrived in Spain, and there are many things I want to learn about my heritage. And there is also my mother. She expects me to spend more time with her."

Unveiled Secrets

"Your story is incredible. You've been separated from your mother for thirty years." Luis reached up, his fingertips warm on my cheek. "Is there a boyfriend or a husband in the picture?"

The waiter uncorked a bottle of red wine and poured two glasses. Luis took a sip, waiting for my reply. A shudder passed through my body, and all the blood drained from my face. My eyes widened when Denis stopped at our table and stood right behind Luis.

"Yes, there is one, Luis," Denis muttered. "How are you doing, cousin?"

My heart drummed a primal beat against my breastbone. A strange, light-headed feeling came over me as I looked at the two men. There were things about Denis Fraga I just couldn't figure out.

"Denis, what a surprise," Luis said as he stared at Denis, who sat on the bench next to me and then poured himself a glass of wine. Electricity sparked through my veins.

"I see you still have the same old bad habit of stealing someone else's girlfriend," Denis said, taking a sip of wine. His eyes seemed to throw arrows at his cousin.

"Well, she's not exactly wearing a tag with your name on it, and you didn't appear to be taking her to dinner and were nowhere around," Luis said, grinning.

The hotel restaurant was the last place where I expected the cousins to run into each other. It was as if life loved playing tricks with everyone, and I realized that Denis wouldn't let his chance slip between his fingers. I remained silent. They looked like two boys fighting over their favorite toy, and I had the feeling that their war had begun a long time ago and it wasn't finished yet.

I glanced nervously from Denis to Luis and asked, "Should I leave you two alone to finish your conversation, or we can enjoy a pleasant meal together?"

My stomach growled. I signaled the waiter to approach and placed my order of seafood salad and black truffles. Both men ordered beef bourguignon and mashed potatoes with oxtails. The men knit their

Carmen Monica Oprea

eyes above the rim of their wine glasses. I blinked and looked at Luis. His green eyes were like gleaming crescents beneath hooded lids.

"Luis, do you think Mendoza will agree to my terms?" I asked.

"Who knows? Maybe he'll accept your proposal," Luis said. "He is a huge mess, and no bank will lend him more money to pour into his business. He has made quite a few wrong moves, and he will pay for his bad investments."

My heart leaped when Luis gave me one of his smiles. "I hope I'll hear from him soon," I said, ignoring the butterflies in my stomach. "I can't imagine he wants to go to court for not honoring his end of the contract. That would be imprudent, don't you think?"

"Leonard is not famous for being an unreasonable man, only for being foolish in his private affairs. His father carried the business before getting sick, and then he decided to transfer control to Leonard. I'm sure he'll reach out to you soon with a business proposal."

A swarm of questions buzzed in my head. Although Luis tried to reassure me as best as he could, only a miracle could save the company from an imminent collapse.

"Even as stubborn as you say Leonard is, he knows what's right for him. He should accept my offer."

"Anyone care to explain to me what's going on?" Denis asked, lifting his brows.

"It's interesting that you know so little of her affairs," said Luis.

"I don't have to explain myself to you," Denis said, his shapely, firm lips forming a small smile.

I looked into Denis's eyes and saw a sparkle of amusement there, along with something else... white-hot anger. A few seconds later, after I heaved a sigh of relief, I covered his hand with mine.

"Out of respect for his family," Luis said, "I assured Leonard that he could get money from the sale if he accepted the terms of your deal by the end of the week. The value of his business has grown over the years, and if he agrees to sell, he can even make a profit. It's a big decision, and

210

Unveiled Secrets

it's the only solution Leonard has to save himself from bankruptcy and litigation for not respecting his side of the bargain."

When Luis talked, I stared at him, stunned, the low, rough sound of his voice causing the skin at the back of my neck and along my arms to prickle in awareness. My worries melted when I realized what an important role Luis could play in making my dreams come true. From his spot across the table from his cousin, Denis studied Luis through narrowed eyes. His brows formed a bridge above his nose, and I knew the cousins shared a past. I could see that Denis felt threatened by his cousin's presence.

Denis put his arm around my shoulder, placed his hand on my jaw, lifted it, and swept down to cover my mouth with his. *God help me.* At first, I looked at Denis, startled because it wasn't like him to act on impulse. He always considered public displays of affection tacky. My day in Vigo had become a complicated occasion with events tumbling over each other. I had the desire to retire to the comfort of my room and meditate. For several seconds after the sudden and unexpected kiss, I just stared.

"Let's toast to Leila's success, and our reunion, Denis," Luis said, lifting his glass and breaking the awkward silence.

"Cheers," I said.

"Yes, cheers."

Denis stood up. Luis did too, and I followed the two men to the lobby. Before leaving, Denis turned toward Luis and said loud enough for me to hear. "You got the girl last time, Luis. She is mine, so you'd better stay away from her."

"Are you threatening me, Denis?" Luis asked.

I watched as fresh color rushed into Luis's cheeks.

"No, I'm only telling you that Leila is the woman I love. You got the girl years ago, and I stepped back because you loved each other. I expect you will do the same this time."

Carmen Monica Oprea

Luis leaned toward me and kissed me on both cheeks. Then, he turned around and left the hotel, a smile growing on his lips.

What happened between the cousins to make them hate each other so much?

Seventeen

After Luis left, I turned toward Denis.

"What was that all about? What happened between Luis and you?"

Denis coughed. "Dominique was eighteen when we met her. We both fell in love with her spontaneous personality, but she chose Luis that summer. She had come all the way from Paris to spend an entire year in Vigo with her grandparents. She was overflowing with wit, always laughing, constantly joking. I didn't know she had played me for a fool until I told Luis about my feelings for Dominique. He told me she was the girl he loved and asked me to back off, stay away from her. He wanted to marry her, but his family was against it. She wasn't of noble birth. In the end, she broke Luis's heart by leaving. Years later, Luis discovered that his parents had paid a generous sum for her disappearance from his life. The whole situation altered the course of his life. He didn't trust another woman, and neither did I. Dominique, and Luis were too young to fight for their romance, and his first love became the most painful memory."

"He could have tried to find her later. What stopped him?"

"Dominique was killed in a car accident in Paris, just days after she had left Vigo Bay. The news of her death was devastating."

I gasped, covering my lips with my hand. "Sometimes people get a second chance, even if it comes at a high cost, and sometimes they don't, as in Luis and Dominique's case," I said.

We turned to the elevator and pressed the up button. Another couple sneaked in just as the doors were closing. I stood in one corner, watching the lights over the marina while Denis studied his cell phone in the opposite corner. He was so close to me and yet so far away. Thinking of his touch and remembering the rhythmical breathing next to my face on the pillow made my blood simmer.

The elevator's bell dinged when we reached the tenth floor. We walked together toward our rooms, and all I could think about was the

Carmen Monica Oprea

warmth of his skin next to mine. I stopped in front of the door and turned toward Denis.

"Good night then," I said, trembling.

"I'll see you in the morning, princess. First, we'll have breakfast; then it's off to the driving center."

Denis kissed me on my cheek, then he slid his door's card in the slot.

"Sweet dreams," I whispered before entering my room.

I paced the length of the room like a caged animal. I didn't turn on the lights. I threw my sandals across the room, feeling the cold floor under my burning feet. Two things were clear: Denis was devastatingly attractive, and my thoughts about him had changed. I felt entirely different about him now.

Would he want me the same way he did in New York? Did he still love me after everything we had been through? I had to find out.

I approached my door and opened it, only to find myself gazing into his hazel eyes. Beams of lights came from the streets, fighting their way through the windows, bathing us in an eerie glow that only increased the tension between us.

"Do you want to come in?" I asked in a low voice.

Denis parted his lips in a smile. His cheeks were red, and his eyes were shiny.

"Why do you think I am in Vigo Bay?" Denis asked.

I wasn't sure what to say. "I don't know. Did you come for the view?"

Denis laughed. "Too much wine?"

"You better come in and not stand in the hallway if you don't want to become the talk of the hotel."

"I'm already used to it from New York. Don't you remember?"

214

Unveiled Secrets

I remembered that Tessa had warned me about Denis and his reputation many moons ago. But I knew I couldn't stay away from him and his love. He had been hurt, and he knew loss just as I did. First, he had felt his mother's betrayal, and then it had been Dominique. I had started to understand his hesitation regarding women.

He rolled his sleeves up, showing tanned, muscular arms. I remembered the way his skin felt when I touched it, soft, and hot. Denis entered the room and locked the door. He stopped in front of me. I took a step toward him, placing my hands on his shoulders and tilting my chin. Denis brushed his lips on mine. They were ever so soft, kissable, hot, knowing where to touch mine and how much to give or to take. I was dizzy, and the room spun. *It must be the wine*, I thought. Denis lifted me and sat in an armchair. My head fell on his left shoulder, my lips touched his sinewy neck, his pulse strong against my mouth.

I closed my eyes for just a second. Noises filled my ears when I opened my eyes. Morning sunlight filled the room. I was in my bed, wearing the dress from last evening. It took me a minute to recall the events of the previous night and gasped once I remembered. I had fallen asleep during my first night with Denis after all this time. I fell asleep in his arms, instead of making love to him.

"I don't think you should drink wine anymore. It doesn't seem to agree with you," Denis said as he stepped out of the shower. *My shower.* The room was filled with the fresh fragrance of soap and aftershave.

"Did we? Did I?"

"Embarrass yourself?" Denis grinned. "Not any more than you normally do."

"What did I do?"

"You snored all night and farted once," Denis said, chuckling.

I blushed. "No, I didn't."

Denis dried his hair, his chuckles growing into laughs that seemed to catch in his throat. "I ordered breakfast for both of us. I hope you don't mind," he said, trying to regain control.

Carmen Monica Oprea

"I'm not hungry." Just then my stomach growled with a thunderous sound. I lifted my brows.

Denis knitted his brows. "Your stomach seems to disagree. Come here!"

I pushed the covers away and approached the trolley. Eggs, crisp bacon, and croissants along with honey, butter, and slices of oranges were arranged in two plates.

"Give me five minutes to get ready," I said, heading for the shower.

"Take your time."

Ten minutes later, I emerged from the bathroom and took a seat at the iron table on the balcony. Denis was reading a local newspaper. He nodded while he read, and I smiled. I poured two cups of coffee and added milk into mine.

"Anything interesting?" I asked. The coffee was strong, just as I liked it. "Good coffee. Nice flavor. Rich."

"It's one of the perks of being an esteemed member of the GLH chain." Denis winked. "Are you ready for a test?"

"The driver's test? Not really. I haven't practiced since you took me on the racetrack."

Denis lifted his brows. "We must correct this immediately."

I choked on the last piece of toast and honey. Denis patted me on the back. "Better?"

I nodded.

"Leila, stop acting like a child. It's not as terrifying as you think. Come, get dressed. Time is wasting."

I poured more coffee.

Denis lifted my chin. "You have ten minutes to get ready. Then we're leaving."

216

Unveiled Secrets

I sighed. Ten minutes later we were in Denis's car and leaving the hotel's parking lot. As he maneuvered the car, a shiny black BMW sedan with tinted windows, I was still wondering why I had let him talk me into this. Denis seemed utterly in control as he drove through Vigo's traffic. I couldn't remove my gaze from his hands grasping the wheel, his touch light but sure, like a lover's. I shivered. Maybe he was right about driving and taking control over my own life.

"Is the air-conditioning too much?" he asked solicitously.

"No. Is this the way to the driving center?"

"No. We're going to the Museum Quinones de Leon," he murmured. "It's closed on Wednesdays. There's a large employee parking lot in the rear, where you can practice before your test."

Just at that moment, I had a vision of ramming the car directly into the elegant seventeenth-century manor's wall and couldn't decide if I was glad or uneasy that Denis was with me. I looked through the window at the clouds rolling in, hiding those beautiful golden rays. I was convinced of an impending disaster.

"You have good eyes and reflexes," Denis continued.

He glanced to the side and caught me staring at him. I blinked, my gaze bouncing off him. Half an hour later, I sat behind the wheel of the sedan while Denis sat beside me in the passenger seat. It felt extraordinary to be in the driver's seat.

"I think I covered the basics," Denis said after pointing out the relevant mechanisms and pedals to me. "Keep your foot on the brake and shift the car into drive."

"Is that all?" I squeaked nervously.

"Your goal is to make the car move, Leila. You can't do that while it's in Park," Denis said dryly.

Although I did what he said, my foot jammed against the brake.

"Ease up on the brake and then press on the accelerator...Easy, Leila," Denis said when I pushed too far, and the car jolted forward. I

Carmen Monica Oprea

slammed my foot on the brake even more aggressively, and we both flew forward against the seat belts.

Damn, I thought. I glanced nervously at Denis.

"The pedals are very sensitive. Keep practicing. It's the only way to learn," he said sternly.

I clenched my teeth together and pressed the accelerator. When the car began to respond to my urging, a thrill went through me.

"Excellent. Now turn to your right and circle around," Denis instructed.

I gave it too much gas on the curve.

"Brake," Denis said.

"I'm sorry," I said when we jolted again against the seat belts.

"When I say 'Brake,' I mean apply your foot gently to the brake to slow down. If I want you to stop, I'll say 'Stop.' You must slow down when on the turns, or you'll lose control. Try again," he said.

My jerky stops and accelerations smoothed quite a bit under Denis's tutelage, and I began to feel euphoric piloting the sleek, responsive vehicle.

"Park in that end spot there," Denis requested, pointing.

Rain began to spatter on the windshield as I did a nice turn into the parking spot and cried out in triumph.

"Very nice," Denis said, smiling at me when I turned to him. "We'll practice more. I'll forward the rules of the road to you so that you can study them, and you'll be ready to take the test in a week or so."

I was so excited that I didn't comment on his meticulous planning of every detail of my life. I gripped the steering wheel and stared out the front window, grinning. Learning to drive had been a liberating experience, more than I had imagined it to be.

Unveiled Secrets

"It's not so hard," Denis said as the rain began to fall hard on the windshields in fat drops. "Turn on your wipers and lights."

I did as Denis instructed.

"Now I want you to back out of the spot and turn the car to the left. Use your mirrors."

I began to reverse.

"Use your mirrors. No, no, the other way, Leila."

I fumbled, confused as to how to move the wheel while going in reverse to get the desired result. Meaning to brake, I hit the accelerator while I twisted the wheel in the other direction. When the car lurched, I slammed down the brake, and the car swung around on the wet pavement in a complete circle. Electricity sparked in my veins at the unexpected loss of control. The vehicle came to a halt. My hair flung onto the wheel. I snorted with laughter.

"Leila," Denis said sharply. He looked stunned and a little ruffled.

"Oops!"

"Put the car in park," he said.

I followed his instructions, feeling a little breathless and dizzy, not sure if my reaction came from the car whipping around in a tight circle or the glint in Denis's eyes just now.

"I told you I couldn't drive," I muttered, turning the key in the ignition so as not to cause any further unintentional havoc.

"You just need more practice," Denis said, his fingers furrowing into my hair, turning my face toward him. The next thing I knew, he was leaning over and capturing my mouth. The adrenaline rush that went through me when the car had spun around on the wet pavement was nothing compared to the surge of excitement at Denis's unexpected kiss. I melted against his chest, his taste inundating me, the hard thrusts of his tongue overpowering my senses.

"You're beautiful," he said roughly. "Move over to the passenger seat and let me take you back to the hotel."

219

Carmen Monica Oprea

My breathing still erratic, I unbuckled my seatbelt and did as Denis suggested. A steady rain pitter-pattered on the roof now, so I slammed the door shut. In the distance, thunder rumbled. Denis glanced over at me, wiping his hand over his slightly rain-dampened, dark hair.

"What do you want from me, Denis?"

"You know what I want," he continued. "I want you back in my life."

His deep voice echoed through my head. I whimpered when he placed his entire open mouth on my lips. It felt hot and unbearably exciting. I panted for air as he stroked one of my breasts.

"I'm taking you back to the hotel. You said that your mother is waiting for you."

I didn't say anything on the rainy drive back to the hotel. It was as if something had happened back there in the car that I couldn't understand. A sort of nameless, thick tension filled the air between us now. I would have thought it was the low pressure from the storm, but I knew it didn't exude from the rain clouds.

Denis was the source.

When we arrived at the hotel and pulled beneath the canopy, a young valet greeted Denis by name. Denis gave him directions about parking the car and handed him the keys along with a wad of cash.

"Thank you, Mr. Fraga," the valet gushed in heavily accented English.

"I told Mario I'd move him to the mail room if he learned English. He has an uncle in New York and a big American dream."

Denis led me to my room. I used the keycard to open the door. Denis remained in the hallway.

"Are you not coming in?" I asked, holding the door open.

He smiled as his hand ran over my face. He touched my jaw with gentle fingers. I shivered.

Unveiled Secrets

"Sorry. I have a meeting at two. I'll call you a taxi when you're ready to leave."

"I wish you'd come with me and meet my mother. She's an amazing woman. You'd like her. And I want you to see the house where I was born and lived before moving to the States."

Denis frowned. Something about what I had said encroached about meeting my mother seemed to make him uncomfortable.

"I'd be honored to meet her. What time are you leaving?"

"As soon as I finish packing my things. I could wait for your meeting to end."

"I'm expected in my uncle's home this evening, so it works out perfectly. Call me when you're ready, and I'll help you with your luggage," Denis said.

"Thank you for the driving lesson. It was interesting."

I leaned toward Denis to kiss him, but he had other plans in mind. He pushed me into the room, closing the door with his foot, and then he slipped his hands under my blouse, playing with my breasts and squeezing each nipple until it hardened under his touch. He sat me on the bed, kissing my mouth and parting my lips with his tongue.

"I want you," he said.

I moaned into his mouth, as he exposed my bare skin. His gaze ran over me. My breath stuck in my lungs when I saw the admiration in his face, mingling with a blazing lust. His nostrils flared slightly. Coming into full contact with him was like suddenly being thrown into a fire.

"I thought I could wait, but I can't," Denis muttered as he slid my jeans down my thighs. He looked into my face as his hands caressed my hips and things and moved toward a place of pleasure, touching me just the right way. I moaned as I got closer to ecstasy and my eyes sprang wide with anticipation, as I grasped his thick, crisp hair and whimpered when I felt myself go over the edge. He thrust his hips and plunged deep inside of me, making the air pop out of my lungs at the evidence of his full arousal.

Carmen Monica Oprea

In the hazy midst of my voluptuous ecstasy, I glimpsed the clouds through the window, watching us with supreme satisfaction.

Denis held me close to him until I calmed down. Then, he kissed me gently, rose from bed, pulled his pants on, and held his shirt in his hand.

"I'll be back at five."

"I'll be ready," I said, not taking my eyes off his handsome face.

Denis opened and closed the door, and I heard him open the door leading to his room and close it again. I lay naked in the middle of the bed, trying to regain my composure as I went over the details of the day. I felt my pulse began to drum at my throat when I got to the most recent events. I rolled to one side and rose from the bed, walking to the bathroom. I looked at myself in the bathroom mirror. My face looked pale next to my passion-stung, reddened lips. My eyes appeared unusually large above the shadowed circles beneath them. Feeling exhausted, I stepped into the shower. I applied moisturizer and ran a comb through my hair before I walked out of the bathroom and dressed. It took me one hour to finish getting ready and to gather my things. I decided to call my mother to tell her I was coming home.

She answered the phone on the first ring, sounding in good spirits.

"I'm going to send Miguel to pick you up. He will help you with your bags."

"Mom, I'm also bringing someone I want you to meet. His name is Denis Fraga."

"Fraga?" My mother let out a sigh. "Is he part of the Fraga family?"

Fraga was a famous family in Vigo, their good deeds bringing them the respect of Spanish society for hundreds of years. Denis didn't share his family's history when we were in New York.

Unveiled Secrets

I said, "Luis asked me to attend their upcoming family reunion. Relatives arrive from all corners of the globe to spend time at the beach every year."

Denis said that his family passed down this and many other traditions from generation to generation.

My mother said, "I attended many parties and met interesting people when Anders was alive," my mother said wistfully. "After his death, I continued to receive invitations. Sometimes I went out of curiosity; other times just to ease my boredom. But each of their parties created incredible memories."

"Denis and I reconnected yesterday after not seeing each other for a long time."

"Is he the man you ran away from?"

I paused, surprised at my mother's insight. Then I coughed to clear my throat. "Yes, he is. I didn't realize he was in Vigo Bay until I ran into him accidentally. Life is strange! It brings unexpected situations in the least expected places."

"Are you still in love with him?"

"I'd be crazy to say that I'm not," I said, choosing my words with care.

Suddenly I felt weak. And the room felt too warm. I took in a deep breath.

"What about him? Does he still love you?" Myrna asked, letting out a sigh.

I stared out the window. When the sun moved, it caused shadows to stretch across the floor. "I'll see you soon, Mom."

"I'll meet you both when you get home."

The line went dead, and I just stood still for a moment, trying to process everything. My cheeks were flushed when I answered the door. Denis stood there on the threshold, grinning from one ear to ear. His eyes sparkled as he looked at me.

223

Carmen Monica Oprea

"Ready?"

"I guess. As ready as I'll ever be."

I pointed to the two suitcases sitting in the middle of the room. Denis turned around and signaled a bellman to approach. He took hold of the bags and settled them on his cart.

"I'll be waiting for you in the lobby, Mr. Fraga," the bellman said.

I threw another look around the room and then followed Denis in the hallway. The bellman used the employee's elevator, while we waited in front of the guests' elevator.

"I took care of the bill for you," Denis said when the doors closed.

"You shouldn't have. I am perfectly capable of taking care of myself."

Denis laughed out loud. "You are so funny when you get angry," he said.

I surely didn't see it his way. As if it wasn't enough that he had forced me to drive when I had stated that I didn't have the slightest interest in driving, he had paid the hotel bill in my name. I wondered what would come next.

Unveiled Secrets

Eighteen

Miguel waited for us in front of the hotel. He put the luggage in the trunk, and after Denis and I had settled in the car, he left the hotel parking lot. He checked out Denis in the mirror and then, he winked at me. I looked at Denis too. He was buckling his seatbelt while Miguel drove the car down the winding streets of the city.

"Do you think she'll like me?" he asked, and then he shook his head. "I'm sure she will."

I giggled and cupped his hand inside of mine. His eyes shone, the right corner of his mouth lifting a little. Denis blushed when he gazed into my eyes.

"She'll love you, darling," I whispered.

"What if she doesn't accept me?" Denis asked.

"You'll win her over with your charm. Remember, I'm still adjusting myself to having a mother," I said, trying to sound more convincing than I felt. Not too long ago, I was in Rosemary Beach, without all of these confusing feelings. I shook my head too.

One step at a time. If only Luis can help me acquire the company, I thought. *If only Denis can learn to let me take my own decisions and stand by me.*

Fifteen minutes later, the car stopped in front of the main entrance of my mother's home. Denis helped me out of the car while Miguel carried the suitcases inside the house. Myrna was nowhere in sight.

"Charming views," Denis said, looking around at the garden as we approached the house.

I opened the front door, and we walked into the house. His eyes took in the elegant foyer, soaking in the details of my childhood home. I searched Denis's profile—the way he pursed his lips, the way he narrowed his eyes when he was in deep concentration.

225

Carmen Monica Oprea

I walked around the charming lobby, and I followed. The old pendulum clock struck seven, and Denis lifted his chin to see where the sound was coming from. When his gaze rested on my parents' portrait hanging above the arch connecting the lobby with the living room, a tiny gasp escaped his lips. His mouth opened and closed as he studied my parents' faces. The painter had captured the love in their eyes with precise strokes. My mother's hand rested in my father's open palm, her chin rested on his left shoulder as a smile cropped on her lips. It was impossible not to smile just from looking at them. They were young, and beautiful, and fueled by their dreams, just like Denis and I were.

Miguel lined up the suitcases against the wall.

"Mrs. Isidro will be right with you," he said.

"Thanks for your help," I said. "I'll let you know if I need you in the morning."

Miguel closed the door behind him, leaving me with Denis. When I heard the clack of heels coming from the top floor, I lifted my gaze. My mother appeared at the top of the stairs in a blue dress with a white belt. She was wearing pearl earrings, and her long blond hair hung over her shoulders. The click of heels on the wooden floor resonated throughout the house, disrupting the silence of the place.

"Welcome to my home, Mr. Fraga," Myrna said. She extended her hand when she stopped in front of us, and Denis kissed her delicate fingers. Pink spots appeared on her pale cheeks. "Mr. Fraga, you are too courteous. I thought this gesture was a thing of the past."

"Some men still hang on to chivalry and manners of the past. It gives them an advantage over ordinary men," Denis said with a hint of mischief in his voice.

I hid a smile as I glanced at Denis. His face reddened a little.

"I am honored to meet you, Mrs. Isidro. And, please, call me Denis. I'll feel more comfortable if you do so."

"All right then, Denis it shall be. Now follow me to the living room where we will get to know each other a little better."

226

Unveiled Secrets

I signaled him to follow my mother.

"Are you here for the family reunion?" Myrna asked as she led us to my father's studio.

"Yes," Denis answered. "It's an annual event that no one can miss."

Myrna turned around, stopping in the studio's threshold.

"So I've heard. I used to be invited to these parties, but I no longer went after my husband died."

"I am not too fond of them. But if I don't show up, my uncle would give me hell for an entire year. My father despised them, too. They were boring to him."

My mother laughed, and I looked at Denis.

"Sometimes relatives and friends can be a little too nosy. I like my privacy too," Myrna said.

"So do I," Denis said as we entered the room inside the studio.

Myrna sat on the sofa and Denis sat next to her. He let out an audible sigh of relief. I sat on a chair across from them, looked around the room and feigned a state of calm I didn't possess. My hands shook in my lap. I knit my fingers in a fist as a sudden sensation of nausea settled in my stomach.

Denis cleared his throat with a cough. "The gathering my uncle holds every year is an occasion for us all to come to Spain and spend two weeks together. With our complicated lives, we barely have time to talk to each other and to find out what's going on in our lives. It's a tradition my uncle likes to keep going."

"Are your parents coming to the reunion too?"

Myrna held his gaze, arranging her glasses on the bridge of her nose. I straightened my back, wondering if I looked as ravaged as I suddenly felt, and trying to convince myself that I had brushed my hair and flattened my shirt before leaving the hotel.

227

Carmen Monica Oprea

"They are no longer living, Mrs. Isidro, but I'm sure my brother, Lance, and his wife, Liz, will be present at the party."

Myrna rose from the sofa, and Denis stood up too.

"Please, sit. I'll be right back with some refreshments," Myrna said, leaving the room.

Denis sat back on the sofa, his hands resting on his knees. "She seems nice," he said.

I lifted my brows. "Are you nervous?"

"Not at all."

"Really?"

"Terrified," Denis admitted, laughing nervously.

"She is not that scary."

"You don't think so? Her eyes seem to pass right through my brains as if she's reading my mind."

I laughed. "I wish I could read your mind."

"Be careful what you wish for. You couldn't handle what's in there."

Denis winked at me. He bent forward as if trying to reach me when Myrna returned carrying a tray with a crystal carafe filled with ice and slices of lemons, three glasses, and a plate filled with pastries.

Denis rose from his seat and took the tray from her hands.

"You can set it on the table," Myrna said.

Denis did as she said, while Myrna filled the glasses. A citrus scent wafted through the room. Myrna took a sip of lemonade and encouraged us to do the same with a wave of her fingers. She sat her glass on the table and picked a pastry sprinkled with chocolate.

"I baked them this morning," Myrna continued.

228

Unveiled Secrets

Denis selected a pastry, too, and nodded as he ate it. They were filled with chocolate and covered in powdered sugar with almonds with a French shell. I picked one up from the plate and started nibbling.

"Delicious," Denis said, picking up another one from the plate.

Myrna giggled. "I am curious about something. Why do you live in the States, Denis? Wasn't your father a banker just like your uncle? Your grandfather is the founder of Phenix Bank, and of all his sons and daughters, only one followed in his footsteps."

"My father was never a banker and wasn't interested in finance. That world just never appealed to him. He always wanted to have a farm and live on his terms, free from the norms of society."

Myrna listened and nodded politely. "Do you intend to return to New York, Denis?" she asked.

I blinked quickly at this question while I stuffed the last piece of pastry into my mouth.

"I have to return to New York. I have a job to do." Denis finished his lemonade, glancing at the plate. "Your pastries are incredible."

"Thank you. It was one of my grandmother's recipes."

"I could eat this for breakfast every day," I said, as I nodded in agreement, taking a sip of my lemonade. Denis leaned back on the sofa, resting his hands on the couch, and stretched his feet out and gazed out the windows. Beyond the French doors, a variety of roses, jasmine, and lilac dotted the garden. A gust of wind lifted the silk curtains, bringing the scent of jasmine into the room.

"Why don't you accompany Leila and me to the party? I'd be honored if you come," Denis said, turning his gaze back to us.

"Thank you, Denis, but I have a previous engagement. Leila will be there though. And I hope I can count on you to keep my daughter entertained."

As I watched them talking, I remembered my father's letter and wondered if he would have liked Denis. I decided that he would have.

229

Carmen Monica Oprea

"You can count on me," Denis said, checking his watch. His eyebrows shot up. "It's time for me to go. I'm expected for dinner. I can't be late."

Myrna rose to her feet at the same time as Denis, and I did the same.

"It was a pleasure meeting you," Myrna said. "I hope you will come over one evening to have dinner with us."

"It would be my pleasure, Mrs. Isidro. Thank you for your warm hospitality and the delicious pastries."

Denis kissed Myrna's hand. He turned toward me, waiting.

"I'll walk with you," I said.

Denis nodded, and we walked toward the front door. He looked tired. He'd been working since the crack of the dawn; he had made love to me, and then he had accompanied me to my mother's house. Memories of the time when I used to work with him crept into my head. I was always making and changing schedules, prioritizing tasks, remembering special requests, and assisting everyone in the hotel.

"I never thought it would be so hard to let you go," I said.

Denis smiled. He leaned toward me and kissed me. I tasted the chocolate on his lips and a hint of lemon from the lemonade. I could feel his gaze resting on me. I opened the door, and we both stepped outside. Miguel was waiting next to the car and opened the car door when he saw us approaching.

"See you tomorrow, Leila, and I'll miss you until then."

"Miguel will drive you to your uncle's. I want you to promise me you'll be polite to Luis and your brother. Let go of the past. It's better this way."

As soon as I said the words, the air felt unbreathable, and I pushed my hands against my stomach, waiting for a response from Denis. But he just kissed me again and got into the car. I waved until the car made its way back onto the main street, encouraged by the thought that I

230

Unveiled Secrets

would see Denis again soon. Pausing on the stone steps next to a flowerpot, I let myself linger for a moment.

I was hovering between two decisions that had the power to change my life in profound ways. One decision involved taking over the factory and moving permanently to Vigo Bay, which meant giving up the Bluewater in Rosemary Beach. The other involved Denis, who had to return to New York, and my relationship with him. I had to choose between my heart and my duty toward my family, and I wanted both to work out. I didn't like having to put my relationship with Denis on hold soon after we just found each other again.

I returned to the studio where I had left my mother. She was staring out the window at the garden and turned around only when I stopped behind her. She grabbed my hand and urged me to follow her, without saying where we were going or for what. But whatever she had in mind, it seemed to be important.

"It's time to meet your family," Myrna said as she walked along the hallway. "I'm going to walk you through our history. This way you'll know your ancestors. Spanish people have a strong sense of family. They want to know everything about one's ancestors. You'll thank me later!"

"Mom, what do you think of Denis?"

Myrna smiled before answering my question. "*You* need to decide what *you* think of him, Leila. Follow your heart. Not all roads are easy, but you will find the strength to keep going if you believe in yourself and trust in your love for him. He is a determined young man, and I can see that he loves you. Only time will tell how your destinies will turn out."

I put my arms around her small shoulders and kissed her on both cheeks. Then we stepped together into my father's office, where pictures and albums lay on his desk and the floor. It looked like it was going to be a long evening, discovering and learning about a family I knew almost nothing about. We pointed, discussed, argued, and remembered relatives from both families. I learned of an uncle I had never met, my mother's brother who died in Africa, where he dedicated his life to the natives' education and preached the word of God.

Then we recalled the friendship between Gabriela and Myrna. My thoughts turned to Tessa and John. I missed them both and wondered

Carmen Monica Oprea

what they were doing in Rosemary Beach. I decided to call them in the morning. I always had this feeling of restlessness when my circumstances became challenging. It had happened when I had moved to Rosemary Beach, but luckily John had stepped in and had helped me with the store.

"Leila, pay attention! This is not the time for your mind to wander," Myrna said sternly.

"Yes, Mom, I'm sorry."

Our discussion slid to the business I planned to take over, my relationship with Denis, and then to my mother's books. We decided to go for a walk in the garden. The breeze brought sweet fragrances of jasmine and lilies. The leaves seemed to dance with each little breeze, their rustling reminding me of the ocean waves crashing against the shore in Rosemary Beach. It was peaceful and serene as if all my worries had disappeared to a faraway corner of the world.

"Are you ready for tomorrow?" Myrna's voice broke the hypnotic spell of the leaves in the breeze. She was worried about me meeting with Fraga family, and I wished I could find the right words to ease her fears. "They will put you through a test of fire before accepting you as one of their own. I have lived my entire life surrounded by powerful families. I know how they work. To be accepted as part of one of the prominent families in Vigo is a grand honor."

"I'll be just fine, Mother. With Denis around, nothing will go wrong."

"Just be yourself. You are smart, beautiful, and well-educated. And you are my daughter. The young in their family are a little spoiled, but don't let them get to you."

"Luis invited me to their reunion as a friend," I said. Then I told her about the odd exchange between Luis and Denis. "It seems the cause of their friction is an old, unsettled love story. Many years ago, there was a girl they both had loved."

Myrna looked at me and laughed. She caressed my hair and cupped my face in her hands, kissing my forehead.

232

Unveiled Secrets

"Spanish men are very passionate. They will do anything to get the woman they want. So, be aware of their tricks and don't fall for their games. Trust your instincts and stay out of trouble. I know Spanish men all too well. I have lived all my life in the heart of their love affairs. It is how I created many of my books. Spanish society was a great source of inspiration for me. You have the blood of your ancestors flowing through your veins. But you haven't been raised here so that you will be a foreigner to them."

"I'm not afraid of them, Mother. I will have a pleasant time. Denis will be there."

Myrna shook her head. "There is a light in his eyes when he looks at you. He reminds me of your father. Anders had sparkles in his eyes, too, when he looked at me."

"Do you still miss him, even after all these years?"

"My yearning for him only grew stronger with each passing year, but I learned to transfer my feelings into the pages I wrote. I know it sounds lame, but my words touched the hearts of many others in similar situations." Myrna looked exhausted. I checked my watch. It was past midnight.

"Let's go to bed, Mother. It is late."

"Let me show you to your room."

Myrna turned off the light and closed the door behind us. She stopped in front of her bedroom.

"I asked Miguel to put your suitcases in the room. See you in the morning."

"I love you, Mom," I said, hugging her.

"I love you too."

Myrna kissed my forehead and then entered her room while I walked toward mine at the end of the hallway. As soon as I entered my bedroom, I decided not to wait until morning to call Tessa. I dialed the Bluewater number and had a surprise when John answered the phone. He appeared to be in good spirits.

233

Carmen Monica Oprea

"What are you doing in the store this early? Is Tessa all right?" I asked.

"You've finally remembered your friends. I thought you had forgotten all about us. Yes, Tessa is OK. She is in the back, opening boxes. How's Spain?"

"Spain is different, John, sophisticated and unusual at the same time. Are you keeping an eye on my girl? I hope she's behaving."

Just then I realized that Tessa represented John's feminine version. They were like two halves of the same apple, but they hadn't figured it out yet. With their demons to fight, my two friends complemented each other and completed each other, but the most important thing was that they were my friends and I wanted them to be happy.

Then Tessa came on the line. "Hi, Leila, it's good to hear from you. I thought you'd forgotten about us. How are things with Denis going?"

"As well as can be expected."

"Meaning?"

"He taught me how to drive."

Tessa laughed. "He taught you how to drive. Is that all he taught you?"

"And we added a little bit of love in between."

"Love is good," Tessa said. "You have a second chance. Don't let it go to waste!"

I had always believed that good people deserved a second chance. John and Tessa had earned their right to be happy. Quickly I blinked away a few tears hovering at the corners of my eyes.

John's voice sounded like an echo through the phone line. "Leila, Denis loves you."

"I know he does. Denis is the best thing that's ever happened to me. Believe me! I will not lose him a second time. It's a promise."

234

Unveiled Secrets

"Am I hearing wedding bells?" John asked.

"That's too soon to say."

"At least he found you. You'll sort things out. How is your mother?" Tessa asked.

"My mom is a beautiful person. I moved home to be closer to her. It didn't make sense to live in a hotel."

"Take one step at the time, Leila, just like you did when you moved to Rosemary Beach. Give yourself space to understand their culture, although it's your culture too," John said.

John fell silent. I told him goodbye, and as I turned the phone off, I thought that sometimes fate offered a second chance to the ones willing to take the risk of being heartbroken again. It was all about having the courage to accept your destiny, to make the best out of the little things that life had thrown your way.

The night went by fast, and, in the morning, I knocked on my mother's door. After I waited for a few seconds, I pressed the handle down and entered her room. The walls were covered with a pale-green wallpaper. The bed was situated in the heart of the room, and a cherry desk was in the corner where stacks of books stood like silent witnesses to the love story that had taken place between those walls. A bouquet of jasmine was in a vase next to my father's picture. I picked up a book, and a piece of paper fell onto the carpet. It was in my mother's writing.

***

November 2nd, 1976

I will always remember the gray day and the rain hitting the ground when I buried Anders. My heart stopped beating. Only Gabriela's warm body and her hand embracing my shoulders gave me the strength to go on. How I wished they would have buried me with him! I was just a shell of a woman, who had forgotten how to live. Gabriela held the small hand of my little girl, who didn't understand what had happened to her daddy so soon after she had just found him. The tears in her eyes, her sobs, and the constant pain became agonizing. I didn't want to live, not

235

even for her sake. Death would help me cast out this unbearable ache. It was such a cruel life.

Had I reached Anders sooner, had we been granted more time, I would have found the power to move forward with my own life. But his death took my spirit past the threshold of sanity. My head got heavier by the day, and the only comforting thing was escaping into a deep sleep. In my dreams, I found peace, and I met Anders all over again. He talked to me and asked me to wake up and live my life for both of us.

But I didn't listen to him. I couldn't. There was no living without him. Joy and pleasure became foreign emotions. He urged me to look over Leila, and I didn't seem to recall who she was. She called me "Mother," and I didn't remember having a child. Another woman stayed with me, nursed me, and wiped my tears, and then she begged me to eat a few crumbs from an uninviting plate. In the beginning, I thought she was an angel, patient, and determined to make me live. She didn't understand that I had no will to survive.

November 30th, 1976

One day an ambulance stopped in front of my house. People in white uniforms carried me inside that uninviting place. Gabriela held my hand during the trip and said that everything would be all right. I didn't know where the people in white had taken me. I woke up one morning, and my home had just disappeared. In the new location, all the people dressed in white, and they called themselves doctors. They fed me pill after pill, forcing me to eat and to live.

The only comfort came from seeing the trees and the flowers behind the room's windowsills. Those awful bars in the window seemed to divide the outer world into sections. The jail was on my side and freedom on the other side. Part of me wanted to run toward the beauty outside, and the other wanted to just stay in the dark place with no escape. I tried to catch the sun passing through the window on warm days. I stood in front of the window bathed in the brilliance of the sunrays until the awful nurses forced me to bed. They said I must sleep and get better. Another glass of water and more pills.

Gabriela didn't visit until the first snow covered the ground. Then, she came every week, and sometimes she brought a girl who kept asking

Unveiled Secrets

me to return home. Home? I didn't remember having a home. I didn't even remember my name. The room with bars on the windows was the only home I remembered.

Carmen Monica Oprea

Nineteen

Goosebumps rose on my skin. The pages in my hand were the ones missing from the diary. In her anguish, my mother had torn them apart because she didn't want me to discover her struggle for life and sanity. Not that I would have loved her any less had I known. It wasn't my place to judge her.

I jumped when I felt a touch on my shoulder.

"I couldn't send those pages to you," Myrna said. "They were too sad to let you read them. All I wanted was for you to learn about our love story and its end. Now I'm just glad you found out that I didn't abandon you because I didn't love you."

"It is all right, Mom," I whispered. "It's been a long time."

Myrna's voice trembled. "I couldn't nurse myself back to health until years later, and you were just a baby then and in need of love. Gabriela was my gift to you, and you became the joy of her days. She gave you everything I wished for you—a normal life."

I hugged Myrna.

"I'm here now, and I'm not going away. We have all the time we need to learn about each other." I wiped the tears in my eyes and hugged my mother. "We will face many challenges together, but who cares about challenges anyhow, as long as we have each other?"

Myrna smiled tenderly and wiped a tear from her eye. "Yes, of course, as long as we are together, we will be fine. I almost forgot to tell you," Myrna said. "Luis called a few minutes ago. I told him you'd call him right back."

I frowned. "Luis?"

Myrna shrugged. "We can use the phone in here if you wish."

My mother left the room, and I picked up the phone and dialed Luis's number. He answered on the first ring.

238

Unveiled Secrets

"Good morning, Leila. I have news," Luis said.

"I'm eager to hear it," I said, leaning against the wall. I could almost envision him sitting in the black leather chair behind his impeccable desk tapping his fingers.

"Leonard Mendoza agreed to meet me late morning and look over the business proposal I drew up. I thought you'd like to know that the wheels are spinning as we speak."

My heart skipped a bit. "Did he say anything about me and my bizarre proposal?"

Luis paused for a few seconds. I could hear him breathing into the receiver.

"Only that you are an unusual woman."

I chuckled. No one had called me unusual before. I was quite an ordinary woman with extraordinary circumstances. I was a woman who had just discovered the mother she had never known and learned about the possibility of taking over her late father's business. I had to do something. I could not allow the business to rot. Luis seemed so focused on finding a way to help me, and I suspected that it was because of Denis, and not entirely because of me.

"See you later," I said.

"Yes, see you at the party," Luis whispered. I felt the hair on the back of my neck raising. Denis would be there too, and the cousins were still at war.

My mother returned to the room just as I finished the conversation. Her hair was secured in a neat chignon, and she wore a navy dress with a green scarf around her neck. I smiled. I had a mother, Denis was close by, and I was on the verge of taking back the family business.

"You should come with me this afternoon," I said, not wanting to let my mother see how terrified I was at the prospect of meeting Denis's relatives.

Carmen Monica Oprea

But she obviously saw right through me. "All you need is right here," she said, pressing her hand against my chest. "You'll do just fine."

"Denis will be there and Luis, too."

"All eyes will be on you," Myrna said. "Come with me. I'll help you get ready."

"I could use some help. That sounds like fun," I said, lifting my brows and following my mother.

Myrna stopped in front of a closet with French doors, and when she pulled them open, I covered my mouth. I took a deep breath before I spoke again.

"They are beautiful, Mom."

I touched silky gowns in pastel colors, picked a few of them and laid them on my bed. I returned to the closet and chose a pair of black sandals with small diamonds on each side.

"Let's find you a dress for the party," Myrna said, browsing through the dresses I had thrown on the bed.

A red dress with one strap on the right shoulder caught my eye. It was made of velvet.

"It's too hot for this one," I said after I tried it on.

"It does show off your tan though," Myrna added as she hung the dress back in the closet.

"What do you think of the short black dress?"

Myrna shook her head. "It doesn't look summery enough."

I chuckled. "You're right," I said, dropping the dress back onto the bed.

I went back to the closet and rummaged among dresses in violet and hues of pink until I discovered a peach silk one. The texture was flawless, the color was lovely, and the style sophisticated with one strap on one shoulder and a peach flower on the right hip.

240

Unveiled Secrets

"This one is perfect," I said, as I tried on the dress.

"Like a second skin," Myrna added, as she hugged me and nodded appreciatively.

I pulled my hair on top of my head, a few spirals falling from the bun I was trying to make.

"Just let it fall onto your shoulders. Here, put this pin in your hair," Myrna said as she handed me a diamond pin.

I brushed my hair, and then I pinned back one side with a diamond pin. Lastly, I clipped the diamond earrings I had received from Gabriella when I turned twenty-one. Then I checked my reflection in the mirror. Myrna, who sat in a chair near the bed, waited for me to finish dressing, and then clapped her hands. "You look beautiful," she said.

Myrna's eyes shone as she looked at me, and I saw something in them I had never seen before—regret.

I bent toward my mother, forcing her to rise from the chair.

"Let's get you ready. You're coming with me," I said.

"I'm too tired for parties. And I can't spend much time in the sun," Myrna added.

Myrna stopped in front of me. She arranged my hair behind the right ear, her touch soft on my skin. The excitement of meeting Denis's family sent a rush of adrenaline through my veins. The last time Denis and I had attended a party together was the one we had thrown for Drew. I also remembered how Liz had stolen my moments with Denis, and I admitted that I was a little scared of our forthcoming meeting.

"You must come. No excuses this time," I said, as I pushed my mother toward the door. "You look perfect in what you're wearing now."

"I guess I have no excuses," Myrna said, laughing.

We descended the staircase and exited through the front door. Before locking the door, I checked the grandfather clock in the foyer. It was after four. I sighed. Ready or not, there was no backing down now. I

Carmen Monica Oprea

lifted my gaze toward the sky and smiled. Small clouds seemed to dance in the sky.

Miguel drove the car to the Fraga estate, which opened to a private beach. Bright colors painted the sea where the sinking sun kissed the waves with the promise of a grand evening. The drive took half an hour, but the prospect of a fabulous party made the time fly by quickly. I admired the incredible properties lined along the shore, featuring beautiful architecture and remarkable gardens. It was the world of the wealthy and powerful, and I trembled with excitement. Denis would be waiting for me at the party, so there was no point in feeling scared, at least that was what I kept telling myself.

The Fraga estate was breathtaking. A mansion covered in red bricks with large white windows and pink roses crawling up a trellis emerged at the end of a long driveway lined by old pine trees. I closed my eyes while I breathed in the pleasant scent of pine. On each side of the main entrance, were two impressive marble lion statues. There were other cars in front of ours. Drivers held car doors open while men and women dressed in elegant suits and gowns emerged. I tried to swallow, and my throat felt dry. I took a sip from a bottle of sparkling water I had in my purse.

"Are you ready?" Myrna asked.

"As ready as I'll ever be," I answered.

I closed my eyes, counting until I sensed my heartbeats had slowed a bit. Myrna had already climbed the stairs and was talking animatedly with the hosts. I followed her while Miguel drove the car away. I looked around, hoping to spot Denis, as parts of my mother's conversation reached my ears.

"It's good to see you. Please, come in," Mrs. Fraga said as she kissed Myrna's cheeks. The lady of the house guided us into her magnificent home.

"Let me introduce you to my daughter, Leila," Myrna said, turning toward me when I stopped next to her.

"I didn't know you had a daughter. And such a charming and beautiful one like that. Where have you been hiding her?"

242

Unveiled Secrets

Mrs. Fraga kissed me on both cheeks, a European custom with which I wasn't yet accustomed.

"It's a long story, Maria, and your guests are coming," Myrna said. "I'll tell you later."

"Yes, yes, we'll talk about this later. Welcome to my home, Leila."

When I shook her hand, it felt like silk. She wore a short, blue summer dress and high heels. I couldn't tell for sure how old she was. Perhaps she was the same age as my mother or younger by just a few years.

"Thank you for the invitation, Mrs. Fraga," I said.

Mrs. Fraga led us to a room where brilliant chandeliers sparkled with a multitude of lights spread in every direction. The setting of the interior was as resplendent and glittering as the stone exterior was imposing and grand. Huge bouquets of calla lilies, jasmine, and pink roses decorated each corner of the ballroom. Silky curtains brushed against the floor as if waltzing in the evening breeze. The pungent fragrance of the sea sneaked into the house with each gracious movement while the band on the veranda played romantic songs on Spanish guitars. I went toward the bar and asked for a club soda, looking around while the waiter prepared my drink. Myrna joined me.

"This feels like a dream, Mother. I've never even imagined something like this. I'm glad I can share this experience with you."

"I'm glad too, dear. But I warned you about the people's curiosity, didn't I? And this is just the beginning," Myrna said as a group of people surrounded us.

"Mrs. Isidro, what a delight to have you here this afternoon," a lady in a pale green silk dress said. "I've read all your books. I can't even say which one I love the most."

"Well, thank you, my dear, this is the greatest compliment a writer can receive," Myrna said graciously.

"Do you have any new book coming out?" a man in a dark suit asked Myrna.

243

"Yes, I have a new one coming out this winter."

"I'll be around, Mother," I said, picking up my drink. "I'm going to mingle."

Myrna waved me off, and I disappeared into the crowd. After leaving my mother to enjoy her moment with her fans, I decided to explore that fabulous house to understand how the wealthy lived and what kind of art they bought and displayed all over their grand homes.

"You look beautiful this evening."

I turned to face Luis who stood across from me, looking handsome and somewhat dangerous in his tuxedo. He said, "Let me show you the rest of the house."

"Thank you. This home is beautiful, Luis," I said.

I looked around, hoping to see Denis. And just as I started to follow Luis, I noticed Denis talking to another man, completely absorbed in the conversation and too preoccupied to pay attention to me.

"This house is almost one hundred years old. My parents have done many upgrades, but they kept the architecture intact. They love art and beauty, especially my mother. She has collected many impressive pieces over the years," Luis said.

"It's an impressive home, Luis. I'm glad you invited me to the party," I said.

My gaze lingered on the paintings for a moment, but it was the garden that caught my attention. Narrow pathways wound among evergreens and jasmine bushes. How I longed to get lost between them!

I heard the soft hum of the waves nearby and felt the breeze on my cheeks. Not far from the mansion, I spotted the emerald sea. And suddenly, I wanted to rip off my sandals and dip my feet in those rolling waves.

"Luis, come here, please," Mr. Fraga called. "I want you to meet Mr. Smith from the Barkley Bank of London."

Unveiled Secrets

Luis nodded in agreement. "Enjoy the party, Leila. I'll find you later," he said.

I watched him as he went to his father, and then they both disappeared behind closed doors of what looked like an office. I turned around, almost knocking someone down. A smile spread across my face when I saw it was Denis. He took my hand and kissed my fingers.

"I was looking for you," Denis said, piercing me with his gaze.

"I was right here, waiting for you," I whispered.

Denis had always had the power to leave me speechless with his mere presence, and this evening was no exception. His salt-and-pepper hair smelled just like pine, and his black tuxedo fit his body to perfection.

"Let me introduce you to my family," Denis said, leading the way into the pathway and holding my hand possessively.

We moved toward a group of people who were laughing and talking. They all had one common feature: they were beautiful and well-built, physically perfect specimen of humans.

"Don't worry," Denis whispered in my ear. "They won't bite you."

I shrugged. "Sure, if you say so," I said.

The animated chatter ceased when we joined them. I recognized Liz and Lance in the group, Liz looking fabulous in a short, red dress with high stilettos, her blond hair cascading over her shoulders. She was leaning on Lance's arm and smiled when she saw us.

"Welcome to the party," Liz said.

"It's good to see you again, Leila," Lance said.

Lance bent toward me, kissing me on both cheeks. I tried to speak and felt a slight blackness clouding my mind. I grabbed Denis's arm for support. He knitted his brows as he leaned toward me.

"Are you OK?" he asked in a low voice.

"Never better," I answered. "I skipped lunch. Can't you tell?"

245

Carmen Monica Oprea

Denis chuckled, and then he turned toward the group. "Let me introduce you to my fiancée," he said.

I felt my knees go weak as I searched his face and wondered what had come over him to make him say something like that. He smiled and kissed me tenderly on the lips. He turned toward the crowd and embraced my shoulders. His statement had reduced everyone to silence. I cast another look at Denis, who seemed to be tearing up slightly.

"It's an honor to meet all of you," I said in a voice that sounded more confidently than I felt.

"Leila is Myrna Isidro's daughter," Denis added with a note of triumph in his voice.

"And your fiancée," Liz said slowly and carefully as if letting the words sink in.

"She is Anders Isidro's daughter too, the industrialist who used to own Mendoza Embroidery Enterprises," Denis added.

I couldn't help but smile when Denis stared back at Liz.

"Please excuse us. I need to introduce you to a friend of mine," Lance said to Liz, pulling her away from the group.

At that moment, I realized that people didn't change, they simply adapted to circumstances as best as they could. Although she was an actress, Liz hadn't managed to play the role of the happy sister-in-law convincingly enough and had let her dislike for me, and her distaste for the situation showed on her face.

As Lance and Liz departed, Denis held my hand tighter. He leaned toward me again, his breath warm on my cheek.

"Don't pay attention to Liz. She'll accept the situation one day," Denis whispered.

"I'm glad to meet you," said a man in a dark costume. "I'm Lorenzo Fraga, Denis's cousin. She is my wife, Ana."

Lorenzo extended his hand, and I shook it firmly, finding a strength I didn't know I had after the previous encounter had left me

246

Unveiled Secrets

feeling weak and a little dizzy. Lorenzo resembled Denis. They shared the same dark, slightly curled hair, and warm dark eyes. His wife, perhaps ten years younger than he was, and pregnant, looked very uncomfortable in the summer heat.

"When is the baby due?" I asked her.

"In two weeks. It's a girl," Ana answered. She turned toward her husband, looking flushed. "Let's get inside. This heat is not doing me any good."

Lorenzo patted his wife's hand, and then he said, "If you'll excuse us, the baby can't handle the summer heat. Thank God, it will be over soon, and my wife will return to normal."

Ana chuckled. "He accuses me of being a monster sent from another planet to torment him."

"It's nice to meet you," I said with a sympathetic smile.

Lorenzo and Ana went into the house, and Denis pulled me aside, guiding me to a canopy of oak trees lining a narrow path. Jasmine bushes dotted the trail, their fragrance intoxicating. I stopped, turned around, and put my hands on Denis's chest.

"What was that all about back there, Denis?" I asked.

Denis sighed. "What part are you talking about?"

"The one where you introduced me to everyone as your fiancée."

"It was easier than coming with a long explanation I had no desire to provide."

I parted my lips, prepared to protest when we heard someone calling.

"Denis, Leila, wait up," Luis said. "Dad wants to meet Leila, and I have a surprise for her."

Denis shook his head. The same light I had noticed when all three of us had dinner flashed in his eyes. "All right, Luis, lead the way," Denis said.

247

Carmen Monica Oprea

Denis and Luis flanked me on each side, and I could have sworn the temperature rose by several degrees. In the vicinity, a nightingale sang a lonely tune. No one said a word as we walked, consumed with our thoughts.

Inside the house, a few couples were dancing. Luis led the way straight to the center of the grand hall. When we passed by the buffet, I picked up a slice of orange covered in white chocolate, the sweet taste of citrus splashing inside my mouth.

"What do you think this is all about?" I asked Denis.

Denis shrugged his shoulders. "I guess we'll find out soon enough."

We entered the same office where Luis had met the banker a little while ago when his father had called him, and I looked first at my mother and then at Leonard Mendoza. I hadn't seen Leonard since the day I asked him to consider my business proposal. That was five days ago. He hadn't contacted me either, although Luis had assured me that he had everything under control when we spoke on the phone. Luis mentioned that he had a surprise for me and I could only hope it was a good one.

"Everyone, please welcome Leila Isidro, the future owner of Mendoza Embroideries," Luis said. Then he turned toward me and said, "Don't forget to breathe, Leila."

"I'm not sure I understood what you just said," I mumbled.

"Leonard Mendoza agreed to our terms. The company is yours as of September first," Luis added.

"What are you saying?" I cried out.

Luis pointed to the agreement my mother held. She smiled at me and nodded.

"Luis is telling you the truth, Leila," Myrna said. "This is the sales contract for the company. Mr. Fraga's lawyers went over the terms and ensured their legitimacy. All you need to do is sign it. Your father would be proud of you."

Unveiled Secrets

"I'm proud of you, too," Denis whispered in my ear before he retired to a corner of the office close to a door leading to a small private terrace.

Leonard Mendoza stepped in front of me, extending his hand. I was shocked by the change of circumstances, and I wondered how everything had happened so fast. My dreams seemed to materialize right before my eyes one by one, and I felt my luck was finally beginning to change.

"Miss Isidro, I'm sure you'll take care of the factory better than I did. You have your heart in it. To my family's disappointment, management was never my passion and running the company was not my strong suit. I believe congratulations are in order," Leonard said.

His handshake was firm, and for a split second, I sensed the room spinning. I couldn't believe how my life had changed in just a matter of days. Denis and I were together again, I was with my mother who was finally happy, and the business my grandfather had built from the ground up had returned to the family where it belonged.

My mother approached me and embraced me. Mr. Fraga, Luis's father, handed me a glass of champagne. I took the glass from his hand and the contract from my mother. I noticed the opening and closing of the office door, and all I saw was the back of Leonard Mendoza's head when he left the room. I was still speechless, and when I took a sip of champagne the room started spinning. I looked at Luis, who could see I was incapable of articulating words, and he gave me a thumbs-up.

"This is an extraordinary moment. It requires more champagne," Luis said, signaling a waiter for another bottle of champagne.

As we toasted, I looked around for Denis. Luis stopped next to me.

"It's your moment, Leila. Savor it," he said, obstructing the view of the door leading to the terrace.

"Thank you for all your help, Luis. I couldn't have done it without you."

Carmen Monica Oprea

Luis looked into my eyes, and then he said, "Denis is the one who made it all possible."

I searched the room for Denis once again.

"Denis? How?"

"He paid for everything," Luis said. "Go to him."

Luis pointed out the door and beyond the terrace to a man walking on the beach with his shoes in one hand and a bottle in the other.

"Thank you, Luis," I whispered, setting my glass on a table and putting the contract in his hand.

Luis nodded. "I'll keep your contract safe. I promise."

I smiled at Luis and left the room through the door to the terrace. Once I reached the beach, I took my sandals off. The sand was cold under my bare feet, the silver grains sliding between my toes. I glanced at the house where the party was in full swing, the music inviting everyone to the dance floor. Bodies swayed to the sultry rhythms while laughter filled the air along with the delicious aroma of various delicacies and gourmet dishes. Servers in impeccable uniforms carried trays with appetizers as they walked among the guests.

"Do you mind if I join you?" I asked Denis.

Denis nodded. He had rolled his pants above his knees while his jacket rested somewhere in the sand.

"Do you want a sip?" he asked, pointing at the bottle in his hand.

"I'm thirsty," I said, taking a sip from the bottle, the pungent taste of the pink bubbly liquid warming my entire body.

We held hands and shared the bottle of champagne he took from the party as we walked along the beach.

"Luis said you did a lot to help me. Thank you for your help," I said, looking Denis in the eye.

"I'd do almost anything just to see you happy."

250

Unveiled Secrets

I leaned toward him and kissed him. He put his arms around me, and I rested my head on his shoulder. He held me for a while in his arms and then pushed me away. "And where do we go from here, Leila?"

I hit the water with my feet. "You see, I'm not like these tiny droplets floating in the air and landing where the wind carries them. I need an anchor, Denis. I need stability in my life. I don't want to float away without direction or purpose."

"You know, in the moonlight, you look like a Greek goddess. I've always pictured you as Aphrodite." Denis paused and took another sip of champagne, and then he handed the bottle to me. "Theodor Haden wants me to go to Brazil for a few months, to supervise the opening of a new hotel. I'm leaving on Monday," he whispered. "And with your new business, you'll be busy, too."

"What's wrong, Denis? I can sense that something else is on your mind. What's bothering you? Why don't you open up to me?"

I stopped in front of him, blocking his path. His eyes were shiny as he gazed at me. I pressed my hand over his heart and felt its swift beating. He put his arms around my waist.

"Would you like to dance?" Denis asked.

"I'd be honored to dance with you."

"Would you dance with me for the rest of your life, Leila?"

"Yes, until my last day."

Denis let go of my waist and pulled a ring from his pocket. Then he got down on one knee in the sand.

"Will you do me the honor of wearing this ring on your finger?"

"I'll never take it off."

"Will you be my wife?"

"Yes, "I said, smiling through my tears. "I will be yours until my last breath."

Carmen Monica Oprea

The breeze carried our promises and scattered them to the winds, carrying our message of love to the world. The stars, the moon, and the sea were the only witnesses to our pledge of love, and we didn't need more. Happiness was right there at this moment, in the center of our hearts, like an unveiled secret.

Unveiled Secrets

ABOUT

Forever Rose

Forever Rose transcends all the possible boxes it could fit into, and is, ultimately, a wonderfully romantic, sometimes funny – sometimes poignant, strangely compelling story that takes you from the contemporary world of medicine and laser technology to eighteenth-century Florence, and makes you look up at the full moon and wonder what magic it might bring to your life.

http://www.bibliotica.com/2017/07/review-forever-rose-by-carmen-m-oprea/

ACKNOWLEDGEMENTS

Writing my books has been a labor of love. It all started in the summer of 2013 when I got a crazy idea to just start writing. I've always loved to read, something that has been lost on the younger generation these days, who prefers to sit in front of a game. I wonder where the adventure is in that.

Growing up, I remember going to the library twice a week to pick out new books to read. So, the first people to thank are my parents, for instilling a love of reading at an early age. There is something magical about reading. It's like directing your movie in your mind. I can't leave out the support I've received from my family because they didn't look at me like it was the craziest thing in the world. They've been nothing but supportive through all of this.

When I was editing my manuscript, so I can get it published on my schedule, my husband made breakfast and lunch while I toiled over my manuscript. I'm so happy that he believes in these books as much as I do. His support is overwhelming. I want to thank the editors from CreateSpace, the Editorial Department and to my advisor, S. M. Smith, for your thoughts on what worked and what didn't. I have to admit that I was so nervous to send my manuscript out to you all. I was so worried that I just wasted years of my life on something that totally sucked. So, thank you for telling me that it doesn't suck.

Carmen Monica Oprea

December 2017

Unveiled Secrets

Made in the USA
Middletown, DE
29 August 2025

12680881R00146